Studies in Jungian Thought

James Hillman, General Editor

Number and Time

Reflections Leading toward
a Unification of
Depth Psychology and Physics

Marie-Louise von Franz

Translated by Andrea Dykes

Northwestern University Press
Evanston   1974

Northwestern University Press
www.nupress.northwestern.edu

Number and Time originally appeared in German under the title *Zahl und Zeit: Psychologische Überlegungen zu einer Annäherung von Tiefenpsychologie und Physik,* © Ernst Klett Verlag, Stuttgart 1970.

Publication was assisted by a grant from the late Mr. Fowler McCormick.

Marie-Louise von Franz is a lecturer at the C. G. Jung Institute, Zurich.

Printed in the United States of America

10 9 8 7 6 5

ISBN-13: 978-0-8101-0532-4
ISBN-10: 0-8101-0532-2

CONTENTS

vii   *Contents*

PREFACE

Aᴼ Fᴛᴇʀ C. G. Jᴜɴɢ had completed his work on synchronicity in "Synchronicity: An Acausal Connecting Principle," he hazarded the conjecture, already briefly suggested
in his paper, that it might be possible to take a further step
into the realization of the unity of psyche and matter
through research into the archetypes of the natural numbers.
He even began to note down some of the mathematical
characteristics of the first five integers on a slip of paper.
But, about two years before his death, he handed this slip
over to me with the words: "I am too old to be able to
write this now, so I hand it over to you." For a long time
I was uncertain whether I ought to undertake this task, or
simply keep the idea in mind, in order to pass it to someone
more competent than I. But after Jung's death the problem
allowed me no rest, and I have to thank my friend Barbara
Hannah for having urged me to venture on the undertaking.
This work has thus come into being over a period of more
than six years; it represents no more than a first attempt to
clarify a few questions on this difficult subject.

The book is not mathematical in the strict sense of the
word, nor is it intended to be a study of number symbolism;
rather it is in principle an attempt to observe the phenomenon of number from a new angle, one based on a consideration of the unconscious. Although I had to venture into the
field of mathematics, I remain fully aware that I lack the

equipment to hazard far-reaching expositions in this area. For similar reasons, I have not gone into the relation of number to the logic of language and to the theory of music, although a rich mine of related material lies there for the uncovering.

As well as to Barbara Hannah, I also wish to express my gratitude to the late Dr. Franz Riklin for his support of this work, and also to Arnold and Nora Mindell who, as enthusiastic listeners, helped to clarify my thoughts. I am especially deeply indebted to Nora Mindell for her enormous contribution to the translation. I would also like to thank Professor Konrad Voss of the Eidgenössische Technische Hochschule, who placed himself at my disposal in his capacity as mathematician in order to discuss the basic problems, and helped me to improve on certain amateurish formulations. I must, however, take responsibility for the ideas put forward in this work. My warmest thanks are also due to William Byers Brown, professor of mathematical chemistry at the University of Manchester, for correcting some of my statements and making several valuable suggestions.

In addition, my thanks are due to Dr. Mokusen Miyuki for information on number theories in the work of Fa-tzang. I cannot resist telling the interesting synchronistic phenomenon that occurred in this connection. When I thought I had finished the book I had the following dream: I was at an exhibition of antique Indian art. In a showcase I saw some figurines of demons, approximately thirty centimeters high, which were crying. I knew this related to a story from the life of Buddha, in which he was killed by demons, who, when they saw what they had done, wept and were converted to a more human attitude. A few figurines were missing because a young scholar had taken them in order to give a lecture. I looked into the lecture hall, but it was pitch black. The young savant (unknown to me) then emerged from the room. At this moment, Jung approached him and they began an animated scientific discussion. Jung signaled to me that I should listen in too.

I realized that the scholar (representing my animus or my spiritual and mental side) knew something that might possibly concern my book, but he was reading in the dark; for me his knowledge lay in total obscurity. Since I did not know how to pursue the problem further, I did nothing about it. A few weeks later I met Dr. Miyuki in completely different circumstances. During a pause in the conversation my dream occurred to me and I told it to him. Dr. Miyuki then informed me that there was an esoteric science of numbers in the Hwa-yen Buddhism (a transplantation from India to China), which he had already begun translating for me, but had not finished. He took the trouble to translate the main theme of the text of the patriarch Fa-tzang for me. To my surprise the idea of a continuum therein presented, as well as the idea of a retrograde counting of numbers, formed a far-reaching parallel to my own ideas. My unconscious was thus aware of information which, rationally speaking, it was impossible for it to have known; and in this case cryptomnesia must be ruled out, since the text had not yet been translated into any European language, and I am not acquainted with any Eastern ones. Fa-tzang's statements are based on the all-embracing unity of the archetype of the Self and contain many further metaphysical speculations which I have not included in my work.

Finally, I would like to extend my heartiest thanks to Dr. Elizabeth Rüf and to Dr. Gertrud Roos, who, by procuring for me the necessary books, saved me much time-consuming labor. My thanks are also due to Ernst Klett Verlag and Northwestern University Press for bringing this book out— but mainly to Mr. Fowler McCormick who made this possible by his generous contribution.

MARIE-LOUISE VON FRANZ

PART I

Number as the Common Ordering Factor of Psyche and Matter

CHAPTER ONE

The Problem of the Unity
of Psyche and Matter

IN RECENT YEARS the question of the relation of psyche and matter has come more and more to the forefront of scientific discussion, although we still have to admit that we are dealing with an unfathomable mystery. But a few reflections on certain facts may be ventured in order to clear at least a small stretch of the way into this impenetrable realm of nature.

Along with the discoveries in modern physics, the most important discovery made at the beginning of this century was undoubtedly that of the unconscious. Empirical proof was adduced that our personality consists not only of an ego-centered field of consciousness, but also of an immeasurably wide realm of unconscious psychic activities. Through dreams, visions, spontaneous fantasies, faulty actions, involuntary gestures, physical symptoms, and other factors we are able to obtain a certain degree of indirect information about this realm of the psyche.

C. G. Jung discovered that, while a sector of this unconscious region is indeed personal and consists of personal complexes, a further portion is universally human and appears to have the same structure in every individual. Jung called this layer of the unconscious, which manifests itself similarly in all mankind, the collective unconscious. This layer does not represent merely a psychic appendage of "archaic remains," as Sigmund Freud saw it, but *the* living creative matrix of all our unconscious and conscious functionings, the essential structural basis of all our psychic life.

Within this basic stratum of our psyche certain particular forms may be relatively isolated, which—in a manner comparable to the behavior pattern of animals—dynamically and formally motivate our emotions, imaginings, feelings, and actions. In the face of death, for instance, or of an encounter with the opposite sex, as well as in all other common human situations, such inner archetypal reactions become activated. They are comparable to the instincts, and are similar in all men. Because they appear coupled with typical emotions, their effects also include the physical sphere. It is common knowledge that emotions such as fear, love, enthusiasm, heroic feelings, and so forth, produce immediate physiological and chemical reactions (such as trembling, outbreaks of sweating, and accelerated pulse) within us. Basing himself on Pierre Janet's early work, Jung therefore defined the psyche as a spectrumlike field of reality situated between the "infrared" pole of material bodily reactions at the one end, and the "ultraviolet" pole of the archetypes at the other.

The conscious and unconscious psychic realm

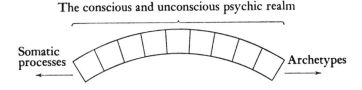

Somatic processes

Archetypes

The center of our psychic inwardness slides along this "spectrum" like a ray of light and is drawn sometimes more to the one end, sometimes more to the other. If one is overcome by an instinctive occurrence, then the emphasis of the ego awareness will slide more to the left, whereas if one is "possessed" by an idea one is more attracted to the right-hand archetypal pole.

It may, however, be surmised, as Jung himself realized, that the two poles partake of one and the same unknown living reality, and are registered only as two different factors in consciousness. If we are affected by the physical or so-called "material" events of the outer world, we call it matter; if we are moved by fantasies, ideas, or feelings from within, we call it the objective psyche or the collective unconscious. Jung then concentrated his attention on investigating the latter phenomenon, and subsequently discovered to his amazement that he had developed thought models and concepts which exhibited an extraordinary correspondence with the models of microphysics. For example, there is the concept of complementarity (in physics between particle and wave and in psychology between conscious and unconscious contents); the necessity for taking the conscious hypotheses of the "observer" into account when describing events; the limitation of only being able to describe the "workings" of nonperceptual structures without grasping their substance "in itself"; and the fact that we can only do justice to phenomena by an interpretation on the level of energetics. Thus there is a certain parallelism of thought models between the two disciplines, although this parallelism does not imply that their subject matters are directly related.

And yet all the indications are that an actual connection does exist between the psychic unconscious and the subject matter of physics. This connection in the first place appears to be statistical-causal, insofar as interactions between them are demonstrable. Bodily physical conditions influence the psyche, and conversely purely mental conceptions can alter the *physis*. Such reciprocal influences can be statistically formulated; psychosomatic medicine has already begun to do research in this field.

Beyond this, however, a further relation appears to exist between psyche and matter which, because it does not fit in with accepted scientific theories, presents a stumbling block to present-day rationalism. When Jung began to investigate the deeper layers of the unconscious psyche, he observed, even before 1930, a form of occurrence which he only much later decided to describe systematically as the phenomenon of synchronicity.[1] This phenomenon consists of a symbolic image constellated in the psychic inner world, a dream, for instance, or a waking vision, or a sudden hunch originating in the unconscious, which coincides in a "miraculous" manner, not causally or rationally explicable, with an event of similar meaning in the outer world.[2] At the time that Jung began to observe more closely this type of phenomenon, he became acquainted with the sinologist Richard Wilhelm who introduced him to the deeper ideas of the ancient Chinese book of oracles and wisdom, the I Ching; Jung was previously acquainted with it only from Legge's inadequate translation. In the final analysis, this book is based entirely on the observation of synchronistic coincidences.

The difficulty for the Western mind in attaining a proper understanding of synchronistic phenomena lies not so much in their occurrence, since every introspective person can easily recognize them,[3] as in their fundamental acceptance

1. Cf. C. G. Jung, "Synchronicity: An Acausal Connecting Principle," *The Structure and Dynamics of the Psyche, Collected Works*, Vol. VIII, hereafter cited as "Synchronicity." (Note: See Bibliography for full information on *The Collected Works of C. G. Jung*, and for publication information on individual volumes. *The Collected Works* will hereafter be referred to as *CW*.) Cf. also Jung, "Ein Brief zur Frage der Synchronizität," *Zeitschrift für Parapsychologie und Grenzgebiete der Psychologie*, Vol. V, no. 1 (1961), and Jung, "Ein astrologisches Experiment," *Zeitschrift für Parapsychologie und Grenzgebiete der Psychologie*, Vol. I, no. 213 (1957–58).

2. By a synchronistic phenomenon Jung understands the coincidence in time of two or more psychic and physical events which are connected, not causally, but by their identical meaning. (See Jung, "Synchronicity," ¶¶ 870, 902 ff., 915.)

3. By synchronistic events are also meant such well-known occurrences as were collected by W. von Scholz, among others. For example, he recounts: "A man is journeying from Norderney to Helgoland. During the crossing, impelled by no outer event, he tells how many years ago the paddle wheel was broken during the same

in the realms of scientific thought. Science is inclined to dispose of them as "pure chance." [4] These phenomena conflict with our preconceived notions that the psyche, as a realm "only subjectively experienceable," differs from matter which is "objectively present in the outer world." This view is only correct, however, if we equate the psyche with ego consciousness. In situations, however, where the collective unconscious, the archetypal realm, is activated such "improbable" psychophysical events are frequently observable. As Jung points out, the lowest collective level of our psyche is simply pure nature, "Nature, which includes *everything,*

---

crossing. At this very moment a crash is heard—the paddle wheel of the ship is shattered." Here the narrator's fancy, coming from within, coincides with the actual event taking place a few seconds later. Another example: "A man brings his wife two doves which had been given to him. She exclaims: 'Oh, if only I might also get one, sometime.' That same day a dove flies into her room and lets itself be caught by her" (W. von Scholz, *Der Zufall und das Schicksal* [Berlin, 1924], pp. 92, 101). J. B. Rhine has tried to understand these coincidences statistically, but I doubt whether statistics is the correct method for this attempt. Cf. M. Rhally, "Varieties of Paranormal Cognition," in *Spectrum Psychologiae: Festschrift für C. A. Meier,* ed. C. T. Frey-Wehrlin (Zurich, 1965), pp. 253 ff., and the literature there quoted. Rhally concludes his paper with the words: "Both laboratory confirmations such as that achieved by J. B. Rhine in his 'willed' dice-throwing experiments (*Psychokinesis*) and spontaneous events such as the stopping of watches at the moment their owners die, would tend to indicate that the physical and psychic worlds are two facets of the same reality" (p. 265). Cf. L. C. Kling, "Archetypische Symbolik und Synchronizitäten im aktuellen Weltgeschehen," *Verborgene Welt,* no. 4 (1965–66). Cf. also L. C. Kling, "Irrational Occurrences in Psychotherapy," *Journal of Existential Psychiatry,* no. 15 (1963).

4. Arthur Koestler, *The Roots of Coincidence* (London, 1972), unfortunately misrepresents Jung's idea completely by projecting into it a sort of causal thinking which is not there. But, as Jung makes clear, the postulate of probability also assumes the existence of improbability (Jung, "Ein Brief," p. 4). See also the discussion of the principle of synchronicity in K. Friedrichs, "Über Koinzidenz oder Synchronizität," *Grenzgebiete der Wissenschaft,* XVI, no. 1 (1967). (There are, however, certain aspects of Jung's ideas which Friedrichs has not understood.) Cf. also P. Urban, "Philosophische und empirische Aspekte der Synchronizitätstheorie," *Grenzgebiete der Wissenschaft,* XVII, no. 4 (1968), 347 ff.

thus also the unknown, *inclusive* of matter." [5] In it the preconscious aspect of the object is to be found, as it were, on
the "animal" or instinctual level of the psyche.[6] It is only
with the activation of *this* level that synchronistic events
appear to be constellated.

Insofar as similar structures manifest themselves through
synchronistic phenomena both in the unconscious psyche
and in matter, the unity of existence (already conjectured
by the ancient alchemists) which underlies the duality of
psyche and matter becomes more comprehensible to us. Jung
applied the term *unus mundus* to this aspect of the unity of
existence.[7]

5. Jung, "Ein Brief," pp. 4 f. He goes on: "To the assumption that
the psyche be a quality of matter or that matter be a concrete aspect
of the psyche I would make no objection, provided that 'psyche'
be defined as the collective unconscious." He also says: "In consequence of the autonomy of the physical phenomena there cannot be
only *one* approach to the mystery of being—there must be at least
two: namely, the physical happening on the one hand, and the
psychic reflection on the other, but it is hardly possible to decide
what is reflecting what!"

6. *Ibid.*, p. 5. Jung continues: "I look upon the latter as the preconscious aspect of the object on the 'animal' or instinctual level
of the psyche. Everything that the psyche asserts or manifests is the
expression of the nature of the object, of which man is also a part.
As in physics the nuclear process cannot be directly observed, so the
contents of the collective unconscious are not directly observable
either. In both cases the essential nature of the thing will only be
perceptible by inference, like the track of a nuclear particle in the
Wilson chamber. Practically speaking the archetypal 'traces' are observed first and foremost in dreams, where they become visible as
psychic forms . . . they can however also appear concretely and
objectively in the form of physical factors. . . ." Even inanimate
objects, meteorological phenomena, for instance, occasionally behave
in this manner. See A. Jaffé, *Aus Leben und Werkstatt C. G. Jungs*
(Zurich, 1968), and the same author's *Der Mythus vom Sinn im
Werk C. G. Jungs* (Zurich, 1967). See also C. A. Meier, "Moderne
Physik, moderne Psychologie," in *Die kulturelle Bedeutung der
komplexen Psychologie*, ed. Psychologischer Club Zürich (Berlin,
1935).

7. See C. G. Jung, *Mysterium Coniunctionis*, *CW*, Vol. XIV,
¶¶ 663, 759, 767. This term should not be confused with E. Neumann's
concept of "oneness of reality," by which he chiefly means the
merging of the individual with his actual physical surroundings. See

In the final analysis the idea of an *unus mundus* is founded, as he says:

> on the assumption that the multiplicity of the empirical world rests on an underlying unity, and that not two or more fundamentally different worlds exist side by side or are mingled with one another. Rather, everything divided and different belongs to one and the same world, which is not the world of sense but a postulate whose probability is vouched for by the fact that until now no one has been able to discover a world in which the known laws of nature are invalid.[8]

Even the psychic world is rooted in the same universe. Jung stresses, however, that there is little or no hope of illuminating this undivided existence except through antinomies. But we do know for certain *that the empirical world of appearances is in some way based on a transcendental background.*[9] It is *this* background which, suddenly as it were, falls into our conscious world through synchronistic happenings. He says:

> I think you are correct in assuming that synchronicity, though in practice a relatively rare phenomenon, is an all-pervading factor or principle in the universe, i.e., in the *unus mundus*, where there is no incommensurability between so-called matter and so-called psyche. Here one gets into deep waters, at least I myself must confess that I am far from having sounded these abysmal depths.
>
> In this connection I always come upon the enigma of the *natural number*. I have a distinct feeling that number is a key to the mystery, since it is just as much discovered as it is invented. It is quantity as well as meaning. For the

---

E. Neumann, "Die Psyche und die Wandlung der Wirklichkeitsebenen," *Eranos Jahrbuch*, XXI (1952), 169 ff. The Jungian concept of the *unus mundus*, on the other hand, denotes a *potential* structure which becomes only sporadically actualized in the real inner and outer worlds.

8. Jung, *Mysterium*, ¶¶ 767–70.

9. In the sense of "transcending consciousness." I will always use the word "transcendental" in this sense.

latter I refer to the arithmetical qualities of the fundamental archetype of the so-called Self (monad, microcosm, etc.) and its historically and empirically well-documented variants of the Four, the $3 + 1$ and the $4 - 1^3$.[10]

Helmut Wilhelm discovered an interesting Chinese parallel to the Western concept of the *unus mundus* in the writings of the philosopher Wang Fu Ch'ih (1619–92). He made an attempt to clarify the mysterious workings of the Book of Changes, the I Ching, from the philosophical point of view. According to Wang Fu Ch'ih's interpretation, all existence is finally based on *an all-containing continuum which is itself lawfully ordered,* but which "in itself . . . is without perceptual manifestation" and is therefore not immediately accessible to sensory perception.[11] (This idea largely agrees with Jung's concept of a *nonperceptual* psychophysical universal background.) In Wang Fu Ch'ih's view the dynamism inherent in this universal continuum differentiates certain images which, in their structure and position, participate in the conformity of the continuum.[12] Since these images are *in themselves ordered* and therefore lawful, *they participate in the world of number and can be grasped in a numerical procedure.* In other words, they enter the playfield of number and can, as legitimate subjects of theory, be numerically structured. These images can of course also be grasped directly, emotionally and experientially, without the benefit of an arithmetical procedure. But number opens up a theoretical and speculative method of approaching the situations represented by such images.

Wang Fu Ch'ih's idea of the two avenues of approach to the nuclei of the unconscious strikes me as exceedingly

10. Jung to Stephen I. Abrams, October 21, 1957, in Jung, *Briefe,* ed. A. Jaffé (Olten, 1973), III, 135.

11. H. Wilhelm, "Der Zeitbegriff im Buch der Wandlungen," *Eranos Jahrbuch,* XX (1951), 333 ff. See also the same author's *Change: Eight Lectures on the I Ching* (London, 1960), pp. 97 ff.

12. He refers to the sixty-four situational images of the I Ching. These "images" correspond to the archetypal images of Jung, the sum of which constitutes the *unus mundus.*

meaningful; the one a purely qualitative approach on an inner psychic level, the other more technorational and related more to the structural arrangement than to the contents of the images. Nevertheless both approaches lead to the same goal, namely, the comprehension of an actual "constellation" in the psychophysical background of existence.

From this background flow the archetypal images, and indeed it was assumed in the I Ching that this flow takes place in a certain order and sequence. "The I Ching," Jung therefore says, "is a formidable psychological system that endeavours to organize the play of the archetypes . . . into a certain pattern, so that a 'reading' becomes possible."[13]

Although the nonperceptual potential continuum or *unus mundus* appears to exist outside time, certain dynamic manifestations of it break through into our ordinary temporal sphere in the form of synchronistic occurrences. To understand the nature of these manifestations is the aim of the I Ching. Its function clearly presupposes a certain "probability" in the existence of synchronistic events.

In his article on the principle of synchronicity, Jung raised the question of whether the phenomena of synchronicity might not ultimately prove to be only a special instance of a more general principle of nature, which he termed "acausal orderedness."[14] The acausal orderedness of certain natural phenomena may actually be observed in matter (for example, in the discontinuities in physics such as radioactive decay) as well as in the psyche (in the just-so uniformity of mankind's associations to natural integer concepts).[15] Both these examples are regular manifestations of

13. Jung, *Mysterium*, ¶ 401.
14. Jung, "Synchronicity," ¶¶ 964–65.
15. *Ibid.* "The meaningful coincidence or equivalence of a psychic and a physical state that have no causal relationship to one another means, in general terms, that it is a modality without a cause, an 'acausal orderedness.' The question now arises whether our definition of synchronicity is capable of expansion, or rather, requires expansion. This requirement seems to force itself on us whenever we consider the above, wider, conception of synchronicity as an 'acausal

an acausal orderedness. As opposed to them, synchronistic events form perhaps only momentary and special instances in which the observer stands in a position to recognize the *tertium comparationis*, namely, a "similarity of meaning." [16] The orderedness which is illustrated in synchronistic happenings, says Jung,

> differs from that of the properties of natural numbers or the discontinuities of physics in that the latter have existed from eternity and occur regularly, whereas synchronistic events are *acts of creation in time*. [17]

These are acts of creation in the sense of a *creatio continua*. They should be conceived of not only as a series of successive acts of creation, but also as the "eternal presence" of the single creative act. In this sense "the contingent," says Jung, "would be taken partly as a universal factor existing from all eternity, and partly as the sum of countless individual acts of creation occurring in time." [18]

"Individual creative acts," therefore, do not occur outside recognizable means of prediction but, on the contrary, take place within certain "fields of probability of acausal orderedness," and the latter do not appear to entirely evade prediction. In the past, to predict the future one usually turned for assistance to some numerical procedure. Jung therefore conjectured that the archetypes of natural num-

---

orderedness.' Into this category come all the 'acts of creation,' a priori factors such as the properties of natural numbers, the discontinuities of modern physics, etc."

16. *Ibid.*, ¶¶ 965 ff.

17. *Ibid.*, ¶¶ 964 ff. and p. 518, n. 17.

18. *Ibid.*, ¶ 968. See also Marie-Louise von Franz, "Time and Synchronicity in Analytical Psychology," in *The Voices of Time*, ed. J. T. Fraser (New York, 1966). Concerning the psychological significance of number, see G. Murphy, "Pythagorean Number Theory and Its Implications for Psychology," *American Psychologist*, XX (June, 1967), 423 ff. Murphy correctly maintains that the abstract idea of probability theory does not apply to psychic phenomena and that we should turn our attention more to discontinuous "types" such as natural numbers. I thank Mr. William Kennedy for drawing my attention to this article.

bers might be specially bound up with the *unus mundus*. For this reason, toward the end of his life he planned to investigate more closely the role of number in connection with the principle of synchronicity. Number, at all events (as his legacy of observation makes clear to us), should not be understood solely as a construction of consciousness, but also as an archetype and thus as a constituent of nature, both without and within. These ideas of Jung and their implications are the ones which will be pursued in this work.

CHAPTER TWO

Images and
Mathematical Structures
in Relation to
the *Unus Mundus*

THE COLLECTIVE UNCONSCIOUS, or the world of the archetypes, is not, as Jung emphasizes, perceptual in itself, and it transcends consciousness for the simple reason that our conscious processes themselves are based on and subject to the archetypes.[1] The archetypes represent an unconscious objective reality

> which behaves at the same time like a subjective one—in other words, like a consciousness. Hence the reality underlying the unconscious effects includes the observing subject and is therefore constituted in a way we cannot conceive.[2]

Whenever the human mind confronts an unknown, it invents symbolic models, drawing on a preconscious process of projection. In the history of mankind we therefore find numerous symbolic representations of the *unus mundus*, a few of which will be more closely examined in due course. Such a survey reveals that the facts presented in Wang Fu

1. Cf. C. G. Jung, *The Structure and Dynamics of the Psyche*, CW, Vol. VIII, ¶ 439.
2. *Ibid.*

15

Ch'ih's speculative model of the universe are confirmed by all other models; they all portray this "one world" as a continuum consisting of images, as a geometrical continuum, or as a numerically structured system. These divisions may even be traced in the works of modern theoretical physicists who continue to attempt to outline speculative thought models of the cosmos. The Einsteinian four-dimensional model of the universe, for instance, is conceived of as a geometrical continuum.[3] In quantum physics, on the other hand, natural numbers are considered to be the ultimate structural element of being.[4]

Niels Bohr has stressed that an important step had been taken toward realizing the ideal "of tracing the description of natural phenomena back to combinations of pure numbers, which far transcends the boldest dreams of the Pythagoreans."[5] This step consisted in a systematic classification of electrons in the stationary states of atoms and in the explanation of the characteristic relations between the physical and chemical properties of the elements (in the Mendelevian system) thereby made possible.[6]

3. Ernst Anrich goes so far as to interpret this Einsteinian continuum as a "field of existence" in general, which contains a structured, lawful orderedness. See *Moderne Physik und Tiefenpsychologie* (Stuttgart, 1963), pp. 126 f.

4. Cf. Sir Arthur Eddington, *The Philosophy of Physical Science* (Cambridge, 1939), p. 75. Quantum physics calculates primarily with nondimensional quantities, i.e., pure numbers. One must, however, admit that it also works with dimensional quantities (e.g., energy, momentum spin, etc.). See also Aloys Wenzl, *Die philosophischen Grenzfragen der modernen Naturwissenschaft* (Stuttgart, 1960), p. 127: "Concentrations of energy and both mass and its equivalent energy express themselves *and* their relationship through the mathematical order of a four-dimensional continuum of a variable metric system. The phenomena are therefore concretizations of a mathematical idea."

5. Niels Bohr, *Atomphysik und menschliche Erkenntnis* (Brunswick, 1958), p. 18. See also G. Holton, "Über die Hypothesen, welche der Naturwissenschaft zugrundeliegen," *Eranos Jahrbuch*, XXXI (1962), 413.

6. On the Mendelevian system, see below, p. 221.

The French physicist Olivier Costa de Beauregard suggests an interesting enlargement of the Minkowski-Einsteinian "universe" by postulating that a coexistent cosmic *infrapsychisme* should be coordinated with the four-dimensional continuum of the relativists. This *infrapsychisme* contains the pictorial representations of the outer world which we produce in our psyche. These images constitute the basic elements for the production of all higher orders (negentropy and information).[7]

Consequently, there seem to be two tendencies at play in the modern scientific viewpoint on the ultimate order of existence, one consisting of images, and the other of geometric or numerical structures.[8] In this connection Jung expressed himself more guardedly by saying that the *unus mundus* contains all the preconditions which determine the form of empirical phenomena.[9] These preconditions must be considered completely nonperceptual and to some extent both pre-image-creating and premathematical. Only when they reach the threshold of psychic perception do they take on the form of images or geometric or numerical structures. By "preconditions" Jung thus refers to the archetypes in their aspect as nonperceptual dispositions latent in the unconscious which are manifest on the threshold of consciousness in regularly appearing images, thoughts, and typical

7. For further details see below, pp. 208–9.
8. In Wang Fu Ch'ih's writings the images are "structured images which, owing to their orderedness, move into the playground of number."
9. C. G. Jung, *Mysterium Coniunctionis, CW*, Vol. XIV, ¶ 769: "The transcendental psychophysical background corresponds to a 'potential world' in so far as all those conditions which determine the form of empirical phenomena are inherent in it." Anrich, on the other hand, denies this type of potential aspect of the "field of existence," as he calls it; for him there is only "occurring existence" (see his *Moderne Physik*, p. 91). Nonetheless it seems to me that a potential aspect also belongs to the wholeness of this field, in order for it to form a wholeness. Like the Eleatics and the existentialists, Anrich here identifies existence with the contents of ego consciousness.

emotional modes of behavior. In this connection Wolfgang Pauli postulated that the "basic intuitions" of mathematics, the idea of an infinite series of whole numbers, for instance, and the idea of a geometric continuum, should be included in Jung's concept of archetypal ideas.[10] Should this observation prove correct, it might throw some light on the question of why certain mathematical ideas prove particularly suitable for describing the regularity of phenomena in the outer world. It is known, for example, that the conic sections sought and discovered in antiquity for duplication of an altar were subsequently proved to be accurate models of planetary courses.

The imaginary magnitudes invented by Cardanus and Bombelli describe in some strange way the characteristic features of alternating currents. The absolute differential calculus which originated in a fantasy of Riemann became the mathematical vehicle for the theory of relativity. And the matrices which were a complete abstraction in the days

10. Wolfgang Pauli, "Naturwissenschaftliche und erkenntnistheoretische Aspekte der Ideen vom Unbewussten," *Aufsätze und Vorträge über Physik und Erkenntnistheorie*, ed. W. Westphal (Brunswick, 1961), p. 122: "In searching for an application of the concept of the archetypes apart from its use in modern psychology of the unconscious, I first came across the historical fact that Kepler expanded and regularly made use of the terms *archetypus* and *archetypalis*, and actually in the same sense as Jung, namely, as 'prototype,' 'primal image.' At all events, Kepler's use of this concept is a special one; he applies it to mathematical ideas exclusively. . . . From my teacher, A. Sommerfeld, I well knew that the Pythagorean elements which appeared in Kepler are still living today. It is that ancient psychic 'dynamic' of number which is still effective today. . . . If therefore the general concept of 'archetype' is made use of today it should be understood in such a way as to include the ideas, among others, of the continuous series of whole numbers in arithmetic, and that of the continuum in geometry. Without doubt it is a question of constantly and regularly recurring concepts. I think it would be of interest to work out more precisely the specific qualities of the archetypal ideas which form the basis of mathematics in comparison with more general archetypal concepts." In my opinion the concept of the archetypes requires no enlargement in order for us to understand these basic mathematical intuitions.

of Cayley and Sylvester appear admirably adapted to the exotic situation exhibited by quantum theory.[11]

If we accept Pauli's contention that certain mathematical structures rest on an archetypal basis, then their isomorphism with certain outer-world phenomena is not so surprising.[12] For we know that the archetypes engender images and ideas in man which lie at the basis of his grasp of the outer world, and that they serve to release generally adequate adaptation reactions (comparable to the patterns of behavior in animals) that are probably not dependent on anything radically different from the basic structure of the physical world itself.

The question then becomes: What is the relationship of mathematics to reality in general? The mathematician Tobias Dantzig discusses this question, defining our subjective reality as "the aggregate of all the sense-impressions of an individual." [13] But, he asks, is there also an objective reality? Henri Poincaré seeks to define the latter as "what is common to many thinking beings and could be common to

11. See Tobias Dantzig, *Number: The Language of Science* (New York, 1954), p. 234. See also the applicability of the Fibonacci series to the problem of leaf distribution in plants.

12. H. Jammer maintains, for instance, that "the reality content of physics is no longer perceived in an objectively accurate reflection of reality, but in a structurally accurate relationship connection." Since this isomorphism allows for no possibility of objectively accurate concepts, the physicist should work with symbols. The formation of thought models precedes theoretical formulation, and that which really connects sense perceptions with concepts cannot be demonstrated by logic. This isomorphism consists, however, of mathematical structures, which returns us once again to the question: How is it possible that mathematical structures coincide with physical processes in the outer world? See H. Jammer, "Die Entwicklung des Modellbegriffs in den physikalischen Wissenschaften," *Studium generale*, XVIII, no. 3 (1965), 169. See also G. Müller, "Der Modellbegriff in der Mathematik," *Studium generale*, XVIII, no. 3 (1965), 156. He maintains that "the origin of mathematical patterns of thought is a process that eludes exact description." As I see it this origin cannot be explained solely on the basis of consciousness, but requires that we postulate the existence of an unconscious psyche, as Henri Poincaré realized.

13. Dantzig, *Number*, p. 242.

all."[14] More recently modern depth psychology has discovered that thoughts which may "be common to all" at any given time are based on the archetypal, preconscious structural disposition of the human psyche. Thus the "commonness" postulated by Poincaré is empirically substantiated. If we take the collective unconscious as the foundation of such "common" experiences, the description of the origin of the mathematical thought models comes an important step closer to realization because we can use dreams to study their psychic prehistory.[15]

In my opinion, not only do the mathematical "basic intuitions" Pauli mentions possess an archetypal nature and arise out of a structural disposition of the unconscious common to all, but even more complicated mathematical systems can also originate from direct inspirations of the unconscious. Various mathematicians affirm that they owe their discoveries to an inspiration from this source. B. L. van der Waerden[16] and Jacques Hadamard[17] have collected a whole series of such testimonies by acclaimed mathematicians. Henri Poincaré's discovery of the "theta-fuchsian series" (now known as the automorphic functions) through an inspiration of the unconscious is a well-known instance. "The role of unconscious work in mathematical discovery seems to me incontestable," he confesses, describing the stages which led to his discovery as follows:

14. Quoted from *Science et Méthode* (Paris, 1947), by Dantzig, *Number*, p. 242.
15. See C. G. Jung, *Psychology and Religion, CW*, Vol. XI, ¶ 419: "It is therefore difficult to understand how people today can still doubt the existence of a collective unconscious. After all, nobody would dream of regarding the instincts or human morphology as personal acquisitions or personal caprices. The unconscious is the universal mediator among men. It is in a sense the all-embracing One, or the psychic substratum common to all."
16. B. L. van der Waerden, *Einfall und Überlegung: Drei kleine Beiträge zur Psychologie des mathematischen Denkens* (Basel and Stuttgart, 1954), pp. 1 f.
17. Jacques Hadamard, *The Psychology of Invention in the Mathematical Field* (Princeton, N.J., 1945).

21 *Chapter Two*

Contrary to my custom I drank black coffee and could not sleep. Ideas rose in crowds. I felt them collide until pairs interlocked, so to speak, making a stable combination. It seems in such cases that one is present at his own unconscious work, made partially perceptible to the overexcited consciousness, yet without having changed its nature. Then we vaguely comprehend what distinguishes the two mechanisms or, if you wish, the working methods of the two egos.[18]

In a letter to Olbers, the famous mathematician Karl Friedrich Gauss also describes how he discovered a long-sought principle of number theory:

Finally, two days ago, I succeeded—not on account of my painful efforts but by the grace of God. Like a sudden flash of lightning, the riddle happened to be solved. I myself cannot say what was the conducting thread which connected what I previously knew with what made my success possible.[19]

Felix Klein, the discoverer of the Kleinian circular figures, similarly admits:

During last night of 22nd–23rd March [1882] . . . around half past two the circular limit theorem . . . as already prefigured . . . by the fourteen-angled figure . . . sud-

18. *Ibid.*, pp. 14 f., quoted from *Science et méthode*, pp. 49 ff. By "unconscious work," Poincaré means work of the ego and the unconscious. The characteristics of the "other" ego are overlaid by the conscious ego. It exhibits measure, the power of discrimination, and "délicatesse"; it can select and judge. As the end result of this preconscious ability of the subliminal ego, the consciousness of the mathematician experiences an "illumination subite" (p. 56). Poincaré propounds the hypothesis that the subliminal ego automatically forms all possible combinations (p. 57), but that only certain of them cross the threshold of consciousness. The screening of possibilities occurs on the threshold of consciousness, through our "sensibilité," by which he understands a *feeling* "pour la beauté mathématique, introduisent de l'ordre" into the complexity of the world (p. 25).
19. *Gauss' Werke* (Leipzig, 1917) X, pt. 1, 25, as quoted by van der Waerden, *Einfall*, p. 1, and Hadamard, *Psychology of Invention*, p. 15. Also published in *Revue des questions scientifiques* (Paris: October 2, 1886), p. 575.

denly appeared before me. . . . I now knew that I had discovered an important theorem.[20]

These types of mathematical discovery have a numinous effect on the discoverer and leave him with a feeling of absolute assurance. For this reason Poincaré and van der Waerden postulated that the unconscious possesses the faculty of mathematical association as well as the power of judgment.[21]

Although the form which Descartes's subsequent evaluation of his vision took cannot be established, his celebrated experience of illumination can also, in my opinion, be traced back to a vision of a complete mathematical order suddenly emerging from the unconscious. The discovery of the Cartesian system of coordinates (a mandala) probably stands in close relation to this experience, since it followed immediately upon Descartes's announcement that a *scientia mirabilis* had been revealed to him. This visionary experience will be discussed more fully in a later passage.[22]

Chinese number theory is quite differently constituted but also traces its basic conceptions back to inspirations from the collective unconscious. In ancient China many arts and sciences (such as music and architecture) were based on certain fundamental numerical patterns. One of these patterns is known as the "Lo-shu" (pattern of the river Lo), a cosmic plan which, according to legend, was said to have been given to the great culture hero Yü by a dragon-horse or a god in the form of a tortoise. It contains a ground plan of the universe in the following form:[23]

---

20. Quoted by A. Speiser, *Die Theorie der Gruppen von endlicher Ordnung* (Basel, 1956), pp. 261 f., from F. Klein, *Gesammelte mathematische Abhandlungen* (Berlin, 1923), III, 584. The Kleinian circular figures are differentiated mandalas. A few are illustrated by Speiser, p. 263.
21. Van der Waerden, *Einfall*, p. 9.
22. See below, pp. 206 ff.
23. Cf. Marcel Granet, *La Pensée chinoise* (Paris, 1968), pp. 148 ff. See also Joseph Needham, *Science and Civilization in China* (Cambridge, 1959), III, 57.

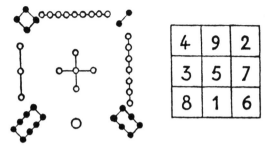

The Lo-shu model [Source: Marcel Granet, *La Pensée chinoise,* © Albin Michel 1936, 1968, Collection Evolution de l'humanité, p. 131.]

Mathematically this pattern is a pandiagonal magic square of the module B-three for which there exists only one possible solution (in eight arrangements).[24] A parallel version, the Ho-t'u model, which originated from a dragon-horse in the Yellow River, looks like this:

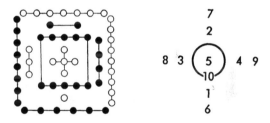

The Ho-t'u model [Source: Granet, *Pensée chinoise,* © Albin Michel 1936, 1968, p. 130.]

24. Cf. F. Meister, *Magische Quadrate* (Zurich, 1952), and the further literature there given. In Greek antiquity as well, the first nine numbers were arranged in a similar mandala field. Cf. W. H. Roscher, *Enneadische Studien* (Leipzig, 1907), p. 112. The ennead is arranged thus:

α	δ	ζ
β	ε	η
γ	στ	ϑ

This nine is called "square" (*tetrágonos*).

The numerical square of the Lo-shu and the numerical cross of the Ho-t'u both possessed a ritual significance. The model of the so-called Yüeh-ling forms another such numerical pattern, an ancient arrangement of the calendar in which the elements were coordinated with the numbers.[25] In the ancient Chinese view the entire time-space continuum of the universe was "organized" according to numerical patterns of this kind.[26] The four basic operations of arithmetic were also derived from the two numerical arrangements of the Lo-shu and the Ho-t'u. The former was visualized in form of a person with the number five at his center, the number nine on his hat, the numbers three and seven to his right and left, four and two on his shoulders, and eight and six on his legs, which both stood on the number one. Out of the various movements resulting from combinations of these numbers originated the operations of multiplication and division, addition and subtraction. The Pythagorean theorem was similarly derived from the Ho-t'u.[27]

Finally, to these examples must we add the numerical system of the I Ching, for which fifty yarrow stalks were originally used as the instruments of divination and reckoning. The famous trigrams of the I Ching are built up on a binary arithmetical basis, and are in their turn associated with the two complementary cosmic models of the universe already referred to.[28] The eight trigrams (pa-kua) are endowed with

25. Granet, Pensée chinoise, pp. 141, 144, 151. Water = 6, fire = 7, wood = 8, metal = 9, earth = 5. On the other hand, in the work known as the Hong-fan, the order was: water = 1, fire = 2, wood = 3, metal = 4, earth = 5. In the Yüeh-ling the values were: winter = 6 = North, summer = 7 = South, spring = 8 = East, autumn = 9 = West (ibid., p. 143).
26. See ibid., p. 157.
27. See further Chin-te-Cheng, "On the Mathematical Significance of the Chinese Ho-t'u and Lo-shu," American Mathematical Monthly, XXXII (1925), pp. 499–504. I am indebted to Mr. Arnold Mindell for drawing my attention to this article.
28. Concerning the binary arithmetic of the I Ching, see Needham, Science and Civilization in China, II, 340. See also A. Rump, "Die Verwundung des Hellen als Aspekt des Bösen im I Ging," Ph.D.

a specific numerical value in their groupings in order to correspond to the Lo-shu or the Ho-t'u.[29] According to legend this set of associations originated with the culture hero Fu Shi who was begotten by a dragon and whose body ended in a snake's tail.[30]

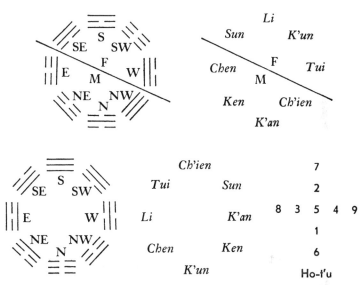

Above, the younger heavenly order; *below,* the older heavenly order [Source: Granet, *Pensée chinoise,* © Albin Michel 1936, 1968, pp. 156, 148.]

These well-known Chinese cosmic numerical patterns possessed a classificatory symbolic meaning which was valid for the whole cultural realm. In them, as Marcel Granet says, number functions as a hierarchically regulating element.

These Chinese patterns can also be regarded as square matrices of the kind introduced by Cayley in his matrix

---

Diss., University of Zurich, 1967. See also the examples in Granet, *Pensée chinoise,* pp. 158 ff.

29. Granet, *Pensée chinoise,* pp. 154 ff. See also pp. 171 ff.

30. *Ibid.,* pp. 156 f.

algebra which has applications ranging from quantum theory to modern technology.[31] The fundamental difference between the Chinese matrices and Western ones lies, however, in the fact that the Chinese regarded the single elements of their matrices as qualities of a "field" instead of pure sets of algebraic quantities, and utilized them accordingly.[32] Nevertheless, these matrices also served to help them understand complex facts. It is noteworthy that according to Chinese legends all these cosmic numerical patterns were said to have been "revealed" by a dragon-horse, tortoise, snake, or other lowly vertebrate. Translated into psychological language, this means they originated from the deepest levels of the collective unconscious. Consequently these patterns, like the mathematical realizations of Poincaré or Gauss, were not the result of conscious reflection but were inspired from the unconscious.

These Eastern and Western examples seem to me to suggest that the unconscious is able spontaneously to produce mathematical structures consisting of natural numbers, and even in certain cases matrices, in order to express a form of orderedness.[33] This hypothesis is met halfway by the mathematician John Kreittner who was deeply impressed by the

31. See G. B. Noble, *Applied Linear Algebra* (Englewood Cliffs, N.J., 1969). A rectangular array of *m* rows and *n* columns of numbers or other quantities is called a matrix. See further A. C. Aitken, *Determinants and Matrices* (Edinburgh and London, 1944).
32. See also Needham, *Science and Civilization in China*, IV, pt. I, 14: "Their [the Chinese] universe was a continuum or matrix within which interactions of things took place, not by the clash of atoms, but by radiating influences."
33. Perhaps this also lies behind the fact that primitive man possessed a kind of "number sense" (for sets of objects) long before he consciously discovered and used words for numbers. See Dantzig, *Number*, pp. 4 ff. Apart from this, discoveries in number theory have been made by a sort of induction, and we can work out the factual connections of many problems for which we are unable to find the proofs (*ibid.*, p. 37). The geometrical pattern interpretation of numbers among the Pythagoreans also points in the same direction (*ibid.*, pp. 42 ff.). In this context "inductive" means proceeding from facts already known.

amazing practical mathematical knowledge of the Sumerians and Babylonians and postulated that a kind of "instinctual mathematics" must exist in man which consists of a "direct perception of the relation between numbers." [34] This perception appears to be more rhythmical than visual—at all events the well-known lightning calculator Professor Aitken said he does not visualize anything during the solution of arithmetical problems but "that the auditory-rhythmic impulse is strong." [35]

If our assumption that the unconscious psyche displays a special relation to the world of number finds broader confirmation, it will underscore Jung's conviction that natural integers contain the very element which regulates the unitary realm of psyche and matter. It will also substantiate his contention that number serves as a special instrument for becoming conscious of such unitary patterns. But before we deal with these considerations at greater length, it is necessary to review the natural number concepts now prevalent. For it strikes me that the bulk of recently developed number theories, with their predominantly abstract definitions, do not provide an adequate means for exploring the laws lying behind the phenomena of synchronicity. The statistics and probability calculus developed from a predominantly quantitative conception of number are not applicable in this con-

34. See "Man's Mathematical Mind," *Main Currents in Modern Thought*, XIV, no. 5 (May, 1958), 111 f. I am indebted to Mrs. Dorcas Arnold for knowledge of this article. Kreittner compares this with the ability of lightning calculators, who work in a kind of trance condition. The fact that certain mentally handicapped persons can often calculate particularly fast and accurately seems to fit in here. See also M. Dehn, "Das Mathematische im Menschen," *Scientia* LII (1932), 125 ff. Dehn likewise tries to trace the existence of a primitive sense of number in man, as does W. Hartner, "Zahlen und Zahlensysteme bei Primitiv- und Hochkulturvölkern," *Paideuma*, II, nos. 6–7 (1940–44), 279 ff.

35. See further F. Karger, "Paraphysik und Physik," *Zeitschrift für Parapsychologie und Grenzgebiete der Psychologie*, VIII, no. 3 (1965), 148–58, and the literature there quoted. Karger quite rightly insists on a search for new patterns of thought before psychology and physics can be brought together.

nection, as various people have already emphasized.[36] In my opinion our concept of number must first be broadened in several respects before we can apply it to the investigation of synchronicity and other parapsychological phenomena.[37] The ideas about number that have developed in the West up to the present day may be divided into three basic tendencies: 1) mathematical theories, 2) attempts at philosophical definitions, and 3) research into number symbolism. Common to the mathematical formulations recently propounded is the general emphasis on formal laws deducible from natural integer concepts; there is less concern for the individual numbers themselves. Although, as Hermann Weyl stresses, the whole structure of mathematics is ultimately erected on the foundations of natural numbers, the individual numbers themselves are only occasionally of interest to mathematicians and then only as alleged "manifolds from which general laws may be deduced." [38]

Nevertheless a certain irrationality about numbers has been repeatedly acknowledged by important mathematicians. Weyl, who emphasized this aspect in his earlier work, later turned more to Hilbertian logic, only to reaffirm in

---

36. These problems will be discussed below (pp. 222 ff.).

37. See the interpretation of the concept of "probability" as either "relative frequency of a type of occurrence in a long series" (= W_e, where e = empirical)—this probability consists of "incompletely verifiable principles"; or "the degree of verification of a hypothesis" (= W_l, where l = logical) (R. Carnap). Here it is not the degree of probability in the actual outer event that is observed, but rather the probability of the affirmative propositions, or the degree of their accuracy. See W. Stegmüller, "Bemerkungen zum Wahrscheinlichkeitsproblem," *Studium generale*, VI, no. 10 (1953), 563 ff. My earlier statement concerns W_e, since it is most often used in science. It is a pure hypothesis which is not verifiable (*ibid.*, pp. 573, 581). Indeed the "real situation" is frequently explained as an "illusory concept" because it cannot be verified by W_e (*ibid.*, p. 582). When I make use of the concept of probability hereafter, it is always in the sense of W_e. Cf. also Eddington, *Physical Science*, p. 95.

38. *Philosophy of Mathematics and Natural Science* (Princeton, N.J., 1949), app. A, pp. 219 ff.

the end, in spite of everything, his recognition of number's incomprehensibility.[39] He says:

The aim of Hilbert's "Proof Theory" was, as he declared, to settle for once and for all the basic questions. In 1926 there was reason for the optimistic expectation that by a few years' sustained effort he and his collaborators would succeed in establishing consistency for the formal equivalent of classical mathematics. But such bright hopes were dashed by a discovery in 1931 due to Kurt Gödel. . . . The ultimate foundations and the ultimate meaning of mathematics remain an open question. . . . "Mathematizing" may well be a creative activity of man, like music. . . . Although the idea of a transcendental world existing and complete in itself is the guiding principle in building up our formalism, that formalism at any fixed stage has the character of incompleteness, inasmuch as there will always be problems, even problems of a simple arithmetical nature, that can be formulated within the formalism and decided by insight, but not decided by deduction within the formalism. We are not surprised that a concrete chunk of nature, taken in its isolated phenomenal existence, challenges our analysis by its inexhaustibility and incompleteness; it is for the sake of completeness, as we have seen, that physics projects what is given onto the background of the possible. But it is surprising that a construct created by mind itself, the sequence of the integers, the simplest and most diaphanous thing for the constructive mind, assumes a similar aspect of obscurity and deficiency when viewed from the axiomatic angle.[40]

Had Weyl not assumed that our conscious mind alone creates the number series, but perceived that behind its creative capacity another preconscious dynamism of the unconscious

39. Cf. P. Beisswanger, "Die Phasen in Hermann Weyls Beurteilung der Mathematik," *Mathematische-physikalische Semesterberichte* XII, no. 2 (1965), 132 ff. I thank Professor Konrad Voss for his kindness in making this article known to me.
40. Weyl, *Philosophy of Mathematics*, p. 219.

is at work, he would not have been so surprised; it is nevertheless very creditable that he formulated the irrationality of number so clearly.

Apart from mathematicians, many philosophers have made repeated efforts to explain the concept of the natural numbers. Gottfried Martin's article, "Methodische Probleme der Metaphysik der Zahl," provides a clear survey of the various lines of inquiry.[41] To the present day, however, none of these philosophical theories have taken the phenomenon of the unconscious into consideration, even when they included psychological considerations in their speculations. Consequently, in their attempts to derive number solely on the basis of man's conscious processes, they have come up against an "alogical" or irrational element in number conception which they are unable to describe further, and which some of them have therefore tried to deny. Others have tried to represent this element as an accepted "alogical medium" or something that they described as being similar to it (while using other terms for it).[42] In this way the truth is satisfied insofar as they grant recognition to the irrational aspect of number but cannot more fully investigate its further implications.

The third tendency at play in number investigations adheres faithfully to the Pythagorean-Platonic standpoint on number in spite of all the opposition of "pure" mathematicians. It consists chiefly of a collection of the mythological and symbolic assertions of mankind concerning numbers contained in various historical works, some of which are of the greatest value. In these collections, however, the part played by the unconscious is once again ignored, leading to

---

41. *Studium generale*, VI, no. 10 (1953), 610 ff. See also Edmund Husserl, *Philosophie der Arithmetik*, Vol. I (Halle a. S., 1891).

42. The term "consistency" (freedom from contradictions) points to the fact that there is also an "inconsistent" background against which the idea of consistency only makes sense. The fact that there are "indistinguishable series" (Kurt Gödel) also points to an irrational element, since a limit is thereby set to the sphere of logical operations.

the erroneous idea that symbolic statements, such as one for example which declares the number three to be "masculine," are absolute truth. The striking uniformity of mankind's assertions on number symbolism have repeatedly attracted the attention of number symbolists,[43] although recently one of them, Werner Danckert, justly pointed out that the ideas of different cultures on this subject also display great variations.[44] Different cultures possess different "sacred numbers" and the same numbers may be considered now more as "spiritual" or "material," now more "masculine," "chthonic-lunar," or "feminine." In this field too knowledge of the part played by the psychic unconscious in the formation of the concept of number is lacking.[45] Of the archetypes of the collective unconscious we know that they—like a crystal lattice in the mother liquid—form structural dispositions in the unconscious, invariable in themselves, although their pictorial and representational appearance in human consciousness exhibits variations. Behind these variations lies a basic

43. Compare this, for example, with V. F. Hopper, *Medieval Number Symbolism* (New York, 1939), and Hermann Weyl, "Über den Symbolismus der Mathematik und mathematischen Physik," *Studium generale*, VI, no. 4 (1953), 221 f. Weyl maintains that, in the last analysis, number magic is based on concepts in number theory.

44. *Tonreich und Symbolzahl* (Bonn, 1966), p. 12. Danckert therefore rejects the theory of the archetypes as dogmatic and erroneous. As he is only acquainted with the work of L. Paneth, *Zahlensymbolik im Unbewusstsein* (Zurich, 1952), he overlooks the difference between archetype and archetypal image. The latter is always variable, but behind these variants stands a constant, nonperceptual pattern. According to Jung a conscious and invariable definition of its meaning is not possible.

45. L. Paneth rightly stressed the importance of this fact. On the other hand, the dream examples on which he bases his interpretation of number symbolism are not open to scrutiny in their context, and in my view the interpretations are far too generalized and often not convincing. Not only dreams and mythology should be included in a descriptive interpretation of the meaning of numbers, but in my opinion, the mathematical qualities of numbers and physical number structures should also be included in such an attempt. Their interpretation will be conducted, as far as possible, in a "neutral" language. Assertions that the number five, for example, simply means Eros place too heavy a value on partial aspects, in my opinion.

archetypal pattern that can be descriptively reconstructed. Here I would include the school of Hans Kayser in the ranks of the number symbolists, although his advocates add a reality aspect to the subject which is lacking among many other exponents.[46] Kayser even speaks of prototypes in a clear parallel to Jung's archetypes. But he emphasizes the fact that, in contradistinction to the latter, his prototypes possess a material basis. He thus overlooks the fact that Jung expressly stated that his archetypes possess a "psychoid" aspect overlapping outer material reality. This declaration renders Kayser's distinction between the two obsolete; it is actually a matter of one and the same thing. In addition Kayser, one-sidedly adhering to a Pythagorean outlook, bases his whole symbolism of numbers on the Pythagorean *lambdoma*, the law of tone intervals, and hypostasizes particular numerical-symbolic meanings in the sense already described. (He speaks, for instance, of "lunar" or "solar" numbers, and so forth.) Despite all its merit his interpretation thus regresses onto the level of historically familiar conclusions regarding number symbolism.[47]

The anthroposophist Ernst Bindel has likewise explored the meaning of natural numbers in connection with the musical scale, a field I do not intend to consider in this book because it would lead too far from my main argument.[48] None-

46. However, Professor Rudolf Haase's studies begin increasingly to meet with our views.
47. W. Preyer's *Über den Ursprung des Zahlbegriffs aus dem Tonsinn und über das Wesen der Primzahlen* (Hamburg and Leipzig, 1891), which came out so much longer ago, seems to be a more serious work. It ends with the convincing argument that the conception of number may well have arisen out of a sense either of tone or of rhythm and frequencies. For this reason Preyer wished to introduce a hexadic system of numbers, which would correspond better to man's psychic tonal sense than a decadic system (p. 19).
48. Ernst Bindel, *Die geistigen Grundlagen der Zahlen* (Stuttgart, 1958) and the same author's *Die Zahlengrundlagen der Musik* (Stuttgart, 1950). See also his *Die ägyptischen Pyramiden* (Stuttgart, 1966). I am indebted to Dr. Fentener van Vlissingen for kindly drawing my attention to this author. I am however not able to accept Bindel's anthroposophical assumptions. Also very much to be recommended in

theless his exposition should be mentioned here in passing.
The whole province of music and its relation to number
seems to me to represent a *feeling* grasp of the same elements
which I shall attempt to formulate consciously. Leibniz once
made the significant remark that music was

> a hidden practice of the soul, which does not know that
> it is dealing with numbers. . . . In a confused and un-
> noticed kind of perception the soul achieves that which, in
> the midst of clearer perceptions, it is not able to observe.
> If therefore the soul does not notice that it calculates, it
> yet senses the effect of its unconscious reckoning, be this
> as joy over harmony or as oppression over discord.[49]

Through the discovery of the unconscious it has now become possible to throw a clearer light on these hitherto
vaguely surmised relationships. If, following Jung's suggestion, we admit that the unconscious participates in the
formation of our representations of natural numbers, then
all statements about them become recognizable as realizations of only partial aspects of the number archetype. In
order to grasp the meaning of these aspects more closely we
must first return to simpler facts, namely, to the individual
numbers themselves, and gather together the sum total of
thought, both technical and mythological assertions, which
they have called forth from humanity. Numbers, furthermore, as archetypal structural constants of the collective unconscious, possess a dynamic, active aspect which is especially
important to keep in mind. It is not what we can *do* with
numbers but what *they* do to our consciousness that is essential.[50] Because of this my subsequent remarks balance to
some extent on the razor's edge between philosophical-

---

this field is M. Ghyka, *Philosophie et mystique du nombre* (Paris,
1971).

49. Leibniz to Goldbach, April 12, 1712, quoted by Bindel, *Die
ägyptischen Pyramiden*, pp. 26 f.

50. Cf. also H. Plenk, *Das Metaphysische in Mathematik, Physik,
und Biologie* (Vienna and Munich, 1959), p. 52. Plenk looks on numbers as dynamic entities in an objective universe.

mathematical and numerical-symbolical statements. But individual number, its unique and fundamental factual material, stands always at the center of my attention,[51] because
in the final analysis *it* has given rise to mankind's most varied
assertions.

51. For this reason I have not "counted" beyond the number four
in this work. My chief purpose is to expound a *new* principle whose
applications are not yet fully explored. The specialist in a particular
discipline may eventually be alarmed at the way in which I mingle
mathematical, scientific, and psychological statements. But if he keeps
in mind the fact that we are examining what number "does" to our
mind in every instance, he will easily recognize the common denominator among these divergent streams of thought.

CHAPTER THREE

Number as the
Basic Manifestation
of the Mind
and as the Unalterable
Quality of Matter

S IR ARTHUR EDDINGTON, who made a clear-sighted attempt to formulate the epistemology of physics, differentiated three kinds of "knowing": 1) direct knowledge, as, for example, sensations of pain, 2) sympathetic understanding, as when I imagine another's pain in similar terms, as if it were mine, and finally, 3) structural knowledge of the physical universe in the narrower sense of the word. As the last-named type is a faculty of our conscious knowledge and memory of the structures of our sense perception, it belongs equally to the province of sympathetic knowledge. In this sense "sympathy" is based on the community of special thought patterns conscious to different persons.[1]

1. Sir Arthur Eddington, *The Philosophy of Physical Science* (Cambridge, 1939), pp. 190 ff. In a similar vein, Wolfgang Pauli states: "I am in agreement with Bohr that the objectivity of a scientific interpretation of nature should be defined as broadmindedly as possible. Every way of thinking that can be taught to others, that can, with the necessary previous knowledge, be made use of by others, and that can be discussed, may be called objective" ("Naturwissenschaftliche und erkenntnistheoretische Aspekte der Ideen vom Unbewussten," *Aufsätze und Vorträge über Physik und Erkenntnistheorie* [Brunswick, 1961], p. 95). Cf. also Werner Heisenberg, "Wolfgang

Patterns of thought of this kind, perceptions "which are or could be common to everyone" (Poincaré), originate, according to Jung, in certain structural constants of the collective unconscious.[2] Naturally we must accept the limitation of not being able to comprehend the collective unconscious "in itself." We can only observe its active manifestations on the threshold of individual consciousness in the form of dreams, creative inspirations, and the like. The mathematical illuminations referred to in the last chapter belong to this category of observable facts. The relation of mathematical conceptions to reality has led to numerous discussions which I cannot examine in detail here.[3] Both the applicability, already mentioned, of certain purely "mentally" discovered theorems to the description of physical reality and the question of the origins of our axiomatic basic intuitions pose some knotty problems for the mathematician—when he possesses no knowledge of the unconscious. In my view the Swiss philosopher and mathematician

Paulis philosophische Auffassungen," *Zeitschrift für Parapsychologie und Grenzgebiete der Psychologie*, III, nos. 2–3 (1960), pp. 120 f.

2. In this connection Pascual Jordan says: (If Jung's concept of the collective unconscious is accepted) "we become aware that in everyday waking life, situations are present which are fundamentally just as amazing as the more infrequent unusual manifestations of telepathy. . . . The curious fact that my normal field of consciousness is identical with that of others can therefore no longer be explained by saying that we all perceive the same "real outer world," but has to be accepted as a basic reality" (*Verdrängung und Komplementarität* [Hamburg, 1947], p. 79). According to the Jungian view the archetypes of the collective unconscious are responsible for this possibility of conscious agreement on human perception.

3. See Pauli, *Aufsätze*, pp. 91 f.: "F. Gonseth's dualistic attitude to the 'dialogue between experiment and theory' seems to be an exception to the more general relation of inner (psychic) and outer (physical). In the case of epistemology it is a question of the knower and the known. . . . With reference to Plato's philosophy, I would like to suggest that the process of understanding nature be interpreted as a correspondence of preexistent inner images in the human psyche with outer objects and their behavior. . . . The sought-for bridge between sense perceptions and ideas or concepts seems to be conditioned *by regulating factors*" (my italics).

Ferdinand Gonseth formulated the problem convincingly by stating that mathematics exists in a field of knowledge which lies

> between two complementary poles: one the world of reality called exterior, the other, interior. These two worlds are transcendental i.e., beyond consciousness. They cannot be perceived "in themselves," but only by the traces which they leave in the field of our consciousness.[4]

By these two poles he means the same two transcendental spheres of reality commonly termed "matter" and "spirit" (mind). Jung, like Gonseth, remarks that:

> Matter and spirit both appear in the psychic realm as distinctive qualities of conscious contents. The ultimate nature of both is transcendental, that is, irrepresentational, since the psyche and its contents are the only reality which is imparted directly to us.[5]

According to Jung, number appears to display an exact relation to *both* spheres. Number forms not only an essential aspect of every material manifestation but is just as much a product of the mind (meaning the dynamic aspect of the unconscious psyche). It appears in our mental processes as a purely archetypal preconscious basic structure. When observed in the abstract, in itself, a natural integer exhibits characteristics which express an a priori acausal just-so-ness. For instance, it is immediately evident to us that six is the first numeral of the series to represent the sum of its divisors (one, two, and three). This quality determines, so to speak, the "form" or "structure" of the number six.[6] Such characteristics are inherent to a number, independent of the

4. Private communication quoted by Marie-Louise von Franz, "The Dream of Descartes," *Timeless Documents of the Soul* (Evanston, Ill., 1968), p. 71, n. 68 (translation modified).

5. *Structure and Dynamics of the Psyche, CW*, Vol. VIII, ¶ 420. Cf. also Pauli, *Aufsätze*, p. 116.

6. Cf. Ernst Anrich, *Moderne Physik und Tiefenpsychologie* (Stuttgart, 1963), pp. 126 f.

objects it enumerates. They appear to be absolutely self-evident to us, which means that number's own nature forces such declarations upon us.

We must, therefore, concede that from the psychological point of view number is an archetypal content, since the latter are known for their capacity to motivate such "necessary" amplificatory statements.[7] With regard to these "self-evident" qualities, the numbers of the first decade, and following ones, are markedly individual.[8] Recently various mathematicians, such as Poincaré, Weyl, and Philip J. Davis, have again drawn attention to the fact that the natural integers possess a "personality," an "individual character," [9] and are by no means the abstract quantities or sets still posited by Gottlob Frege and Bertrand Russell, among others. They thus hark back to Plato's statement that "this number is Socrates, this number is Kallias." [10] Aristotle, of course, found this statement laughable because numbers for him were merely homogeneous units. His viewpoint on number is more in the nature of a subsequent construct of consciousness. Jung, however, took up again the Platonic idea of the individuality of numbers when he stated that:

> the infinite series of natural numbers corresponds to the infinite [i.e., very large] number of individual creatures. That series likewise consists of individuals, and the properties of even the first ten members represent—if they

7. Cf. C. G. Jung's explanations in *Memories, Dreams, Reflections* (London, 1963), pp. 287 f.

8. According to Jung, number is thus recognizable as both an invention and a discovery. He pointed out that it has never really been determined whether number was invented or discovered. Certainly, on the one hand it involves the idea of counting, the idea of quantity, but on the other hand it involves also *the* number present at this moment, which has always been there.

9. See Hermann Weyl, *Philosophy of Mathematics and Natural Science* (Princeton, N.J., 1949), pp. 7 f., and Philip J. Davis, *The Lore of Large Numbers* (New York, 1961), pp. 82 f.

10. See J. Stenzel, *Zahl und Gestalt bei Plato und Aristoteles* (Homburg a.H., 1959), p. 7.

represent anything at all—an abstract cosmogony derived from monad.

One, as the first numeral, is unity. But it is also "*The unity*," the One, All-oneness, individuality and non-duality —not a numeral but a philosophical concept, an archetype and attribute of God, the monad. It is quite proper that the human intellect should make these statements; but at the same time the intellect is determined and limited by its conception of oneness and its implication. . . . Theoretically, the same logical operation could be performed for each of the following conceptions of number, but in practice the process soon comes to an end because of the increase in complications, which become too numerous to handle.

Every further unit introduces new properties and new modifications. Thus, it is a property of the number four that equations of the fourth degree can be solved [i.e., through radicals], whereas equations of the fifth degree cannot. The necessary statement of the number four, therefore, is that, among other things, it is an apex and simultaneously the end of a preceding ascent. Since with each additional unit one or more new mathematical properties appear, the statements attain such a complexity that they can no longer be formulated.[11]

If we now reexamine the examples presented in chapter one, it becomes clear that certain mathematical structures can originate in the unconscious and that Western number theory follows a very different path from that taken in the East. The Western mathematician seeks quantitative, structural connections in number theory while the Oriental looks more for qualitative and feeling-toned relationships. In a state of preconscious awareness about number this opposition probably did not exist; rather it evolved in the course of the development of human consciousness. Western arithmetic deals with number mainly in terms of quantity or

11. Jung, *Memories*, pp. 287 f.

order, abstracting from the latter all it can of general valid arithmetical, geometrical, and algebraic formal laws.[12] Eventually our Western idea of mathematical "order" came to consist of these laws. Lately we even find exponents of the view that the whole of Western mathematics may finally be interpreted as a series of theorems based on the concept of natural integers;[13] even the logical forms in which mathematics moves are entirely, at least in Hermann Weyl's view, dependent on the concept of natural number.[14]

The most important basic concepts are those of zero, number, and successor (Péano), and thus numbers are nowadays regarded primarily in the light of set theory.[15] Bertrand Russell even goes so far as to define these sets as logical, definable characteristic qualities of constructed "fictions."[16] He says:

> The only thing that is arbitrary about the various orders of a set of terms is our attention, for the terms themselves have always all the orders of which they are capable.[17] Accordingly, the Western theory of numbers in general ignores as much as it possibly can of the nature of the quantities to be classified. Indeed, the exact amount is unimportant in comparison with the relation between the terms of the quantities[18] and their so-called structures. Of the latter it is assumed that in certain circumstances they can also agree with some objective data of the outer world

12. See for instance Bertrand Russell, *Introduction to Mathematical Philosophy* (London, 1956), pp. 14 ff. On p. 213 Russell denies number's aspect as a "quantity" and describes it, rather, as an ordering factor.
13. *Ibid.*, pp. 5 ff.
14. Tobias Dantzig, *Number: The Language of Science* (New York, 1954), p. 230.
15. Russell, *Mathematical Philosophy*, p. 5.
16. *Ibid.*, p. 184.
17. *Ibid.*, p. 30. The next part of the quotation, beginning with the word "Accordingly," is added from the more extensive German version: Bertrand Russell, *Einführung in die mathematische Philosophie* (Darmstadt and Geneva, n.d.), p. 41.
18. *Ibid.*, p. 30 (English version).

*with the exception of the variations which belong to the
essence of individuality* and which is irrelevant to science.[19]

Whereas Western number theory has thus on the whole
always turned its attention solely to the quantitative or abstract structural aspect of the number series, Chinese theory
has followed a completely different course. In his standard
work on Chinese thought, Marcel Granet emphasizes that
numbers are quite definitely not quantitative sets for the
Chinese but "emblems."[20] (Granet uses this word in the
same sense as Jung uses the term "symbol.") As with us,
numbers serve in China to describe the "regular relations
among things" (*des rapports réguliers des êtres*) but in the
sense of hierarchical categories or "concrete modalities of
orderedness" instead of quantitative categories.[21] These hierarchical modes of order, in the last analysis, mirror the
basic mathematical pattern of the universe, which in its details provides us, through numbers, with a classificatory symbolism. Numbers thus serve chiefly to make visible the circumstantial individual aspects of the cosmic unity or whole.[22]

The most important words in this connection are "circumstantial individual aspects," because they reveal a new
and essential line of thought, *a relationship of number to
time.* By definition, the great cosmic unity cannot be subdivided into a plurality of "quantities"; it can only reveal
itself in the course of time (always as the same whole) in
various qualitative aspects (or, as Manfred Porkert translates
it, rhythmical phases of transformation) which are "circumstantial"—literally translated as by that which stands
around.[23] In China, numbers signify organizations which

19. *Ibid.*, pp. 74, 75 (German version). Concerning the latter, Russell is of the opinion that it has no significance for science.

20. Marcel Granet, *La Pensée chinoise*, (Paris, 1968), p. 127 (*des
emblèmes*, "symbolic rubrics").

21. *Ibid.*, pp. 145, 135, 137.

22. *Ibid.*, p. 236: "les nombres servent avant tout à figurer *les for-
mes* circonstancielles de *l'Unité ou, plûtot, du Total.*"

23. "Circumstantial" from *circum-stare!*

vary in time, or transient "ensembles" of inner and outer factors within the world-totality. Each number, as well as the already mentioned matrices of the Ho-t'u and the Lo-shu, always represents a totality. The single numbers of the matrices are not subdivisions but illustrations of the "phases of transformation" that form the time-bound aspects of the whole.

This time-bound aspect of number is closely connected with the general outlook of early Chinese thought, which was oriented to the principle of synchronicity instead of causality.[24] It is therefore worth our while to outline the basic difference between our causal and their synchronistic mode of thought.

Jung describes it in his "Foreword to the I Ching" as follows:

> Just as causality describes the sequence of events, so synchronicity to the Chinese mind deals with the coincidence of events. The causal point of view tells us a dramatic story about how D came into existence: it took its origin from C, which existed before D, and C in its turn had a father, B, etc. The synchronistic view on the other hand tries to produce an equally meaningful picture of coincidence. How does it happen that A', B', C', D', etc., appear all at the same moment and in the same place? It happens in the first place because the physical events A' and B' are of the same quality as the psychic events C' and D', and further because all are the exponents of one and the same momentary situation. The situation is assumed to represent a legible or understandable picture.[25]

The thought model for causality presupposes a "linear" lapse of time, a succession of events engendered by the "flow" of

A——B——C——D——→   Linear casual thinking

24. See Manfred Porkert, "Wissenschaftliches Denken im alten China," *Antaios*, Vol. II, no. 6 (1961).
25. In *Psychology and Religion, CW*, Vol. XI, ¶ 973.

a function (causal succession in time A B C D).The Chinese model is more that of a field, as shown in the next diagram.

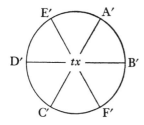

The field of synchronistic events A′B′C′D′, etc. They are grouped around the time moment *tx* and its specific qualities. They are contained in the qualitative "field" of the moment *tx*.

Both the Eastern and the Western concepts are based on a psychophysical model of the world, since in Western microphysical experiments the observer and his mental model, which propels him to set up the experiment, must be taken into account. In the East, the whole subjective psychic condition of the experimenter is even considered to form an aspect of the qualitative "field" or the moment.[26] In Western

26. *Ibid.* More exactly, a synchronistic coincidence should be described as follows:
I. a) A mental image or picture engendered by the unconscious comes through to consciousness directly (i.e., illustrating the outer event) or
   b) indirectly (i.e., hinting symbolically at the outer event) in the form of a dream, sudden idea or presentiment.
II. This coincides with the perception of an outer objective state of affairs without there being any possibility of causally explainable long-distance communication. When, for example, the unconscious image emerges exactly *prior* to the event, one cannot conclude that the occurrence was operative before it took place, or that the psychic image was responsible for bringing about the macrophysical event. The foreknowledge of an event in the unconscious appears, moreover, not to be conditioned like other knowledge we may possess, but resembles something in the nature of a pictorial representation without a subject. "It is not cognition but, as Leibniz so excellently calls it, a perceiving which consists—or to be more cautious, seems to consist—of images, of subjectless simulacra" ("Synchronicity," *The Structure and Dynamics of the Psyche, CW*, Vol. VIII, ¶ 931).

physics the experimenter makes a "cut" by arbitrarily undertaking to isolate the phenomena to be observed.[27] In Eastern divination a "cut" is also made in order to determine
the time moment by throwing coins or dividing yarrow
stalks.[28]
While in Western probability calculus number is used to
describe statistically significant relationships in nature, in
China number serves to determine the quality of synchronistic *kairoi* more accurately.[29] And just as we can observe an
isomorphism between the quantitative number series and a
"linear time sequence," [30] in China individual numbers were
considered to form a true reflection of qualitatively imagined time.[31] The necessary assumption for this concept was
that time is not an "empty" frame for the events taking
place within it, but

> a concrete continuum containing qualities or fundamental
> conditions which can be manifested relatively simultane-
> ously in different places, in a not causally explainable
> parallelism. As, for instance, in cases of the simultaneous
> appearance of identical ideas, symbols, or psychic situa-
> tions.[32]

27. See also Pauli, *Aufsätze*, pp. 114 f.
28. The choice of the "cut" in physics occurs relatively consciously,
the throwing of the coins unconsciously, even if a question is consciously formulated in one's mind as a datum point for an answer.
29. The "magically" right moment.
30. See G. J. Whitrow, *The Natural Philosophy of Time*, 2d ed.
(London and Edinburgh, 1961), pp. 155 ff. See also Rudolf Carnap,
Physikalische Begriffsbildung (Darmstadt, 1966), p. 15: "In the last
analysis all counting originates in the counting of a temporal succession of experiences."
31. Jung has called special attention to the fact that mantic procedures hitherto used for the understanding of synchronistic phenomena are almost all based on some numerical method. Consultation of
the oracle in the Chinese I Ching, for example, takes place by counting off yarrow stalks or by throwing three coins and adding up the
values of obverse and reverse. Western geomancy is based on counting off grains, small stones, or other objects—to mention only two
important examples ("Synchronicity," ¶ 870).
32. C. G. Jung, "Nachruf auf Richard Wilhelm," *Chinesisch-deut-
scher Almanach* (Frankfurt a. M., 1931), p. 9. In China the qualita-

The famous Book of Changes is built up entirely on such assumptions and its numerical procedure for the determination of the time moment is directed toward the understanding of such a "formal factor" in the flow of time. Whether number is quantitatively employed, as in the West, for the calculation of quantitative probabilities, or employed, as in China, for the building up of qualitative and symbolic elements of order to help us understand synchronistic events, one thing remains common: it serves to apprehend regularities or establish orderedness. Jung therefore says that number is the most fitting instrument our mind can utilize for the understanding of order. "It may well be the most primitive element of order in the human mind . . . thus we define number psychologically as an *archetype of order which has become conscious*." [33] In this instance "mind" should be understood as a dynamism operating in the unconscious, whose aspect of order, when it becomes conscious, appears to the inner vision as the idea of number.

In his paper on synchronicity Jung designated number not only as the primal manifestation of the mind or spirit, but also as an unalterable quality of matter. When all its other properties or characteristics such as mass, color, consistency, and so on have been subtracted, he says, the numerical aspect of matter remains the most primitive basic element.[34] This concept has been substantially confirmed by

---

tive interpretation of time went so far that the quality of a creature (an immortal genius, for instance) was wholly determined by the time and place in the cosmos that brought him into being. "On the day of his coming forth," as it says of a genius, "therein is his true essence testified" (Granet, *Pensée chinoise*, p. 133).

33. "Synchronicity," ¶ 870 (my italics).

34. *Ibid.* K. Menninger also says: "Everything that is really distinguishable can be counted." Long before man learned to count consciously, he possessed a feeling for number, and long before he was able to formulate the abstraction of "empty" numbers he used the first four numbers as adjectives to characterize specific groupings; or else he tried to explain a quantity of objects to himself by bringing the objects to be counted into relation with a row of similar objects (rods, fingers, nails, strokes), so-called auxiliary numbers. The separa-

progressive discoveries in modern physics. The atomic character of matter, electricity, and electromagnetic radiation have led to the idea that the energy fields underlying observable phenomena have associated with them discontinuous quantized units whose countability connects them directly with the natural numbers.[35] Already in 1919 the physicist A. Sommerfeld wrote:

> What we hear today in the language of the spectra is a real music of the spheres of the atom, a concord of whole numbers, numerical relations, a progressive order and harmony of all diversities. For all time the theory of spectral lines will carry the name of Niels Bohr; another name will also always be associated with it, that of Planck. In the final analysis all whole-number laws of the spectral lines and the atom are derived from quantum theory. It is the mysterious organ on which Nature plays the music of the spectra and according to whose rhythm it controls the structure of the atom and the nucleus.[36]

Although the situation has become more complicated since these remarks were made, and the significance of many numerical values more uncertain, Pauli points out that Sommerfeld must still receive the credit for having classified the harmonies which he discovered within the new conceptual system of quantum and wave mechanics.[37] Sommerfeld's pupil, Werner Heisenberg, retained an interest in the Pythagorean view of numbers and often stressed their impor-

---

tion of the concept of number from concrete objects is clearly a late cultural achievement. See *Zahlwort und Ziffer: Eine Kulturgeschichte der Zahl* (Göttingen, 1958), pp. 17, 21 f., 29 f., 43 f.

35. I owe this formulation to the kindness of Professor W. Byers Brown. Cf. also Anrich, *Moderne Physik*, p. 8 (the dependence of whole-numbered multiples of ℏ). "Physical existence thus seems to have a specific existential connection with number as such, as a unity and a totality." For further material concerning this relation of quantum physics to number or to mathematical "form," see *ibid.*, pp. 128–31, 142, and the literature there quoted.

36. A. Sommerfeld, *Atombau und Spekrallinien* (Brunswick, 1919).

37. Wolfgang Pauli, "Sommerfelds Beiträge zur Quantentheorie," *Die Naturwissenschaften*, XXXV, no. 5 (1948), 192, 32.

tance,[38] while Rudolf Carnap goes so far as to maintain that the meaning of every physical quantity consists in the fact "that specific physical objects can be coordinated with specific numbers." [39]

Not only does the discontinuous manifestation of physical energy establish a relation to number, but further developments in physics led to the concept of *proportional number*, revealing a new aspect of the number concept. The atomic shell-structure has its "magic numbers," 2, 10, 18, 36, 54, 86, 118, . . . which correspond to the number of electrons in the very stable rare gases, He, Ne, Ar, Kr, Xe, Rn. . . . They were discovered and explained over the period from Mendeleev to Bohr (1923). Another dramatic case is the problem of the magic nuclear numbers.[40] It is well known that certain numbers play a special role in the structure of the atomic nucleus, namely those numbers appearing time and again in the structure of the stable nucleus, in their binding energies, in the distribution of the isotope- and element-quantities, in the captured cross sections of nuclear reactions and in the "delayed emitters," in the spin of the nucleus with an unpaired proton, and in still further characteristic processes.[41] Maria Göppert-Mayer, one of their discoverers (along with J. H. D. Jensen), herself described these numbers as "magic numbers." The numbers in question are 2, 8, 20, 28, 50, 82, 126, and so on. Interestingly, she discovered these numbers in the same manner as Poincaré and Gauss, by a sudden intuitive revelation from the

38. Werner Heisenberg, *Physik und Philosophie* (Stuttgart, 1959), pp. 52 f. See also "Über den Formenreichtum in der mathematischen Naturwissenschaft," *Transparante Welt: Festschrift für Jean Gebser* (Bern and Stuttgart, 1965).
39. Quoted by Anrich, *Moderne Physik*, p. 142.
40. I owe this information to Professor Byers Brown.
41. Cf. J. H. D. Jensen, "Zur Interpretation der ausgezeichneten Nukleonenzahlen im Bau der Atomkerne," *Die Naturwissenschaften*, XXXV, no. 12 (1948), 376, and XXXVI, no. 5 (1949), p. 155. Quoted by F. Hund, "Denkschemata und Modelle in der Physik," *Studium generale*, XVIII, no. 3 (1965), *passim*.

unconscious.[42] She describes how she had long been puzzled as to why certain elements, especially the stable isotopes, had the same number of neutrons in their nuclei. One day she was in Fermi's workroom in the University of Chicago, discussing this problem when the telephone rang. Turning to the instrument Fermi remarked: "By the way, is there any possibility at all there of spin-orbit-coupling?" "When he said that everything fell into place. In ten minutes I knew it." She then outlined the atomic nucleus as a group of onionlike skins lying one inside the other, the inner containing two protons or two neutrons, the next eight, and so on right through the sequence. This type of number appears to have a determining effect on structure[43] and recently has been termed "proportional number," since it expresses proportional relations. Ernst Anrich, who is much to be commended for his attempt, in *Moderne Physik und Tiefenpsychologie*, to bring about a *rapprochement* between the two disciplines,[44] also saw this aspect of number very clearly:

> This number must be unequivocally distinguished from the infinitesimal number of the linear, ever-renewed and continuing or dividing numbers and measurings, as also from number as cipher, and from number which might give rise to the idea that it had originated in pure logical abstraction. . . . Rather, it means that every single thing is characterized and ruled by a specific numerical effective ordering factor.[45]

42. Cf. *Newsweek*, November 18, 1963.

43. For further explanations of the possible numerical subdivisions, see Linus Pauling, "Structural Significance of the Principal Quantum Number of Nucleonic Orbital Wave-Functions," *Physical Review Letters*, XV, no. 11 (Sept. 13, 1965), 499.

44. P. 131. In order to bring the results of research in these two fields closer together, Anrich suggests describing quantum numbers as "hierarchical" numbers. He rightly notes that they do not simply constitute one of the continuously flowing cipher numbers; they contain a crucial element pointing to more than a purely quantitative factor. The stress lies in their specific ability to take on form and thus quality (p. 135).

45. *Ibid.*, pp. 140–41, 142.

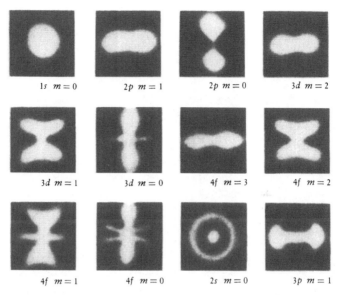

1s m = 0	2p m = 1	2p m = 0	3d m = 2
3d m = 1	3d m = 0	4f m = 3	4f m = 2
4f m = 1	4f m = 0	2s m = 0	3p m = 1

Outline of the charge distribution in the hydrogen atom. The light part is a measurement of the intensity of the waves and thus, according to Schrödinger, of the distribution of electron charge. The single states are characterized by their quantum numbers. Foremost is the main quantum number n; in the series the letters s, p, d, and f denote the values of the angular momentum, $1 = 0, 1, 2, 3$. Behind them stands the value of the magnetic quantum number m. The various locations of the nodal areas should be noted. [Source: Ernst Zimmer, *Umsturz im Weltbild der Physik* (Munich, 1961), p. 391, reproduced by permission of Carl Hanser Verlag.]

Such harmonies cannot be constructed, they can only be encountered; number is determining, not "predetermination." [46] Every hierarchical number is an "individual statement," the expression of an "objective correlation of forces in nature." [47] Anrich therefore maintains that these qualita-

---

46. *Ibid.* In the final sentence Anrich gropes toward an acausal principle.
47. *Ibid.*, p. 144.

tive aspects of number should be examined in order to formulate a physics "which would be able to base all its descriptions on a concept of wholeness." [48] He nevertheless leaves out the relation of number to time, and to the principle of synchronicity, and does not himself pursue the essential meaning of qualitative numbers further.

In light of the existence of such "hierarchical" or proportional numbers in physics, it is evident that number really represents an unalterable quality of matter, both as a quantitative factor and as the form (and thus a qualitative structure) of an effective factor of orderedness. In Maria Göppert-Mayer's extemporaneous designation of the numbers of the atomic nuclei as "magic numbers," something of the ancient archetypal numinosity of number radiates forth. And the fact that her discovery emanated from a sudden illumination of the unconscious seems of great importance to me, because it demonstrates *ad oculos* a connection between the unconscious and microphysical structures.

The reconstruction (p. 49) of the wave patterns of electrons in order of increasing frequency is perhaps the clearest illustration of the numerical structure of this extremely small building-unit of matter. As Victor Weisskopf says:

> The lowest state, the ground state, is the simplest one; the higher the frequency, the more involved the pattern. The ground state has spherical symmetry. The next ones have a "figure eight" form. The higher ones are usually more complex, although we also find simpler ones among them.[49]

These patterns, he adds, are of the greatest importance in nature.

> They are the shapes, and the *only* shapes, that the electron "motion" can assume under the conditions prevailing in

48. *Ibid.*, p. 146. Here Anrich is clearly trying to find his way to the idea of the *unus mundus*.

49. Victor Weisskopf, *Knowledge and Wonder*, 2d ed. (New York, 1966), p. 125.

atoms—that is, under the influence of a central force. The patterns . . . determine the behavior of the atoms; they are the basis of the orderly arrangement in molecules and also of the symmetrical arrangement of atoms or molecules in crystals. The simple beauty of a crystal reflects on a larger scale the fundamental shapes of the atomic patterns. Ultimately all the regularities of form and structure that we see in nature, ranging from the hexagonal shape of a snowflake to the intricate symmetries of living forms in flowers and animals, are based upon the symmetries of atomic patterns. . . . One electron added or removed makes so much difference in the atomic world. The pattern of the last electron added determines the configuration of the atom. This in turn determines the way the atoms fit together, whether they form a crystal, a liquid, or a gas. . . . Quantity becomes quality in the atomic world; one electron more may lead to a complete change of properties.[50]

The strict mathematical order of crystals has particularly stimulated researchers to search for a relationship between their orderedness and mental functions. Werner Nowacki recognized the possible connection between crystal forms and Jung's concept of the archetypes, and in the structure of the latter perceived forms of physical as well as psychic

---

50. *Ibid.*, p. 27. Cf. A. Magnus, "Mathematik und ihre Anwendung in der Chemie," *Studium generale*, VI, no. 11 (1953), 629 ff. The standard work on biology for this purpose is D. W. Thompson, *On Growth and Form*, 2 vols., 2d ed. (Cambridge, 1963), which will be referred to here.

It has been recently discovered that these particles that are known to us are by no means the smallest units of matter, but are divisible into infinitely smaller units. It is believed that the smallest units could be energetically excited components of the fundamental geometry of space in fields which are in a constant state of fluctuation. Cf. *New York Times* "News of the Week," Feb. 5, 1967. Furthermore, so-called hadronic matter is formed in the vicinity of the boiling point, where each hadron consists simultaneously of all the others, and none can lay claim to being the elementary one. Thus further splitting reveals nothing new.

reality.[51] He goes so far as to affirm that the symmetry element in the crystal is something spiritual:

> Symmetries are formal factors which regulate material data according to set laws. A symmetry element or a symmetry operation is in itself something irrepresentational. Only when—as in the present case—it has an effect upon something material does it become both representational and comprehensible. As *primal images* the symmetry groups underlie, as it were, crystalized matter; they are the essential patterns according to which matter is arranged in a crystal.[52]

Crystal lattices are based, according to their symmetry, on a sevenfold axial system. Nowacki goes on to say that "The analogy between symmetry elements and the archetypes is clearly unusually close. This is the pivot of the structure of reality." [53] He claims that the archetypes and symmetry elements should therefore be examined together as "groups of ordering factors" which organize psychic as well as material reality.[54] In my opinion these symmetry elements of a crystal are by no means the only analogy to archetypal ideas, but a special instance of a far more general principle of nature.

To sum up: numbers appear to represent both an attribute of matter and the unconscious foundation of our mental processes. For this reason, number forms, according to Jung, that particular element that unites the realms of matter and psyche. It is "real" in a double sense, as an archetypal image and as a qualitative manifestation in the realm of outerworld experience.[55] Number thereby throws a bridge across the gap between the physically knowable and the imaginary. In this manner it operates as a still largely unexplored mid-

51. See Werner Nowacki, "Die Idee einer Struktur der Wirklichkeit," *Mitteilungen der Schweizerischen Naturforschenden Gesellschaft in Bern.* New Series, XIV (February, 1957), 141 ff.
52. *Ibid.,* p. 153.
53. *Ibid.*
54. *Ibid.,* p. 157.
55. See C. G. Jung, "Flying Saucers: A Modern Myth," *Civilization in Transition, CW,* Vol. X ¶¶ 775–76.

point between myth (the psychic) and reality (the physical), at the same time both quantitative and qualitative, representational *and* irrepresentational.[56] Consequently, it is not only the parallelism of concepts (to which Bohr and Pauli have both drawn attention) which nowadays draws physics and psychology together, but more significantly the psychic dynamics of the concept of number as an archetypal actuality appearing in its "transgressive" aspect in the realm of matter.[57] It preconsciously orders both psychic thought processes *and* the manifestations of material reality. As the active ordering factor, it represents the essence of what we generally term "mind."

> Indeed [says Jung], this ordering capacity or quality of the mind also inheres in the other realms; physics can create order in the psychic, and the psyche in the realm of matter, but in principle both are subject to the mind or spirit, in other words—number.[58]

In "The Phenomenology of the Spirit in Fairytales" Jung describes the nature of the spirit, when it becomes observable in a psychic manifestation, as that unknown element embodying a spontaneous principle of movement in the unconscious psyche which engenders, autonomously manipulates, and orders inner images. Number is, as it were, the most accessible primitive manifestation of this transcendental spontaneous principle of movement in the psyche.[59]

---

56. See *ibid.*, ¶¶ 776–79.
57. See *ibid.*, ¶ 780, and cf. Wolfgang Pauli, "Die Wissenschaft und das abendländische Denken," *Internationaler Gelehrten-Kongress: Europa—Erbe und Aufgabe* (Mainz, 1956), pp. 71 ff. For this reason the mathematician Jacobi has stated: "Among the Olympians eternal number reigns." In this statement the views of the old Pythagoreans and of the Mayans, both of whom considered numbers to be divine cosmic powers, survive.
58. This is a rendering of a discussion at the C. G. Jung Institute. I am only giving the content, therefore, and not the text. The discussion was mimeographed and distributed to the participants.
59. *The Archetypes and the Collective Unconscious, CW*, Vol. IX, pt. 1, ¶ 393.

The question then becomes: In what form is the "spirit," or mind, i.e., the dynamic ordering factor of the unconscious, bound up with matter and psyche? Probably it operates (precisely in the form of number) in the background of these two regions, but it does not have a causal effect on them (otherwise the spirit would have to be partly material and partly psychological, or we would have to fall back on the old conception of a subtle body). Most likely number expresses an essential quality of phenomenon, and phenomenon represents an essential quality of the spirit, and it is precisely these facts that let us guess the existence of a unitary reality (*unus mundus*). In the last analysis, the mystery of the *unus mundus* resides in the nature of number. The means by which we experience the hieroglyphs of the *unus mundus* is always a numerical value; a pile of stones, for instance, simply lies there and an observer is present who perceives them. This in itself is our most direct experience of the *unus mundus*. I shall try in the following chapters to clarify these abstract formulations of Jung's.

The diagram on p. 55 may be useful in clarifying epistemologically the processes of cognition I have been describing. By consciously turning away from physical reality (matter) the psychologist observes the so-called psychic reality (shaded area A). The physicist, on the other hand, observes the psychic images of physical reality or relations among physical data (crosshatched area B) through the elimination of the psychic, experienced by him as a "personal subjective element." But for the psychologist, another unknown lurks behind observable psychic reality, since he cannot define psychic reality while he himself is enveloped by it. Behind that which the physicist calls matter there probably also lies a "reality," unrecognizable in itself (the two hatched outer rings).[60] It is probable, as Jung points out, that the un-

60. Eddington correctly emphasizes (*Physical Science*, p. 17) that a purely objective outer world could not be observed. He calls the procedure of modern physics "selective subjectivism." By this he means that its epistemological postulates lie entirely in the subject, or

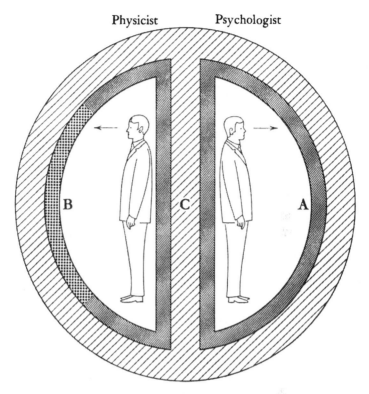

Physicist   Psychologist

B   C   A

knowns in both fields ultimately partake of the same reality.
As the common unknown, the *unus mundus* thus confronts both physicist and psychologist. Operating as the dynamism of motivation, it suggests a "pattern of thought" to
both (hatched center line C). This may be detected in their
dreams. If the two men possess an extraverted attitude,

that its so-called natural laws have an epistemological origin. They
are the result of certain "thought forms" which—whether acquired or
inborn—originate in an inescapable condition which cannot be separated from the phenomenon of consciousness (p. 132). Subjective
feelings, emotions, and individual experiences are naturally excluded.
But in this circumscribed field of thought in physics there are also
"certain quantities" which are and will remain manifestly "unobserva-
ble" (p. 32).

observing mainly their scientific "objects," they observe the unknown as A—B (within the darker inner ring). But if they orientate themselves in an introverted way to their dreams, they no longer practice "science" in the limited and literal sense of nineteenth-century rationalism; they allow themselves to be motivated by admissible evidence from C as well. A more comprehensive and conscious scientific attitude in the future will certainly entail making both aspects simultaneously conscious, and correspondingly formulating its theories in duplicate. These new formulations will not be hopelessly "subjective," because the unknown (the hatched area C) is at bottom common to all men.

Most probably the archetypes of natural integers form the simplest structural patterns in C that manifest themselves on the threshold of perception. The examination of such patterns therefore provides the best avenue of approach to the transcendental realm of the *unus mundus*.

PART II

The Structure of the First Four Integers

CHAPTER FOUR

Number as a Time-bound Quality of the One-Continuum

T HE GREAT PROBLEM posed by the application of natural numbers to the understanding of synchronistic phenomena is, as already mentioned, the fact that a qualitative aspect, rarely taken into account in modern Western number theory, must be attributed to them. At the same time, this aspect lends a new character to the concept of a numerical continuum, since every individual numerical form or structure qualitatively represents an indivisible whole. This continuum should not, however, only be conceived of as an indivisible whole, but as a continuum in which every individual number represents the continuum in its entirety.

When the series of natural numbers is considered primarily from the standpoint of set theory it is discontinuous, inasmuch as it consists of a series of defined units, a sequence in which one represents the basic element.[1] Proceeding from

---

1. In his "Who's Who" of natural numbers, Philip J. Davis says: "1 = unit, 1^n and triangular." A number is triangular when it is the sum of successive natural numbers beginning with one, for instance $6 = 1 + 2 + 3$ (*The Lore of Large Numbers* [New York, 1961], pp. 92 f.) In Western definitions of number, this quantitative description well-nigh holds a monopoly. Locke, for instance, defines number as

this idea Western mathematics works primarily toward the "generalization and enlargement of the concept of number," as A. N. Whitehead formulates it.[2] He points out that any limitation whatsoever of the generality of theorems, evidence, and interpretation is repugnant to mathematical instinct. "These three notions of the variable, form and generality compose a sort of mathematical trinity which presides over the whole subject." [3]

To my mind, however, this viewpoint omits the fourth, irrational, "just-so-ness" of individual natural integers. This element has certainly been recognized time and again, but no one quite knows what to make of it. Henri Poincaré, for instance, says: "Every whole [natural] number is detached from the others, it possesses its own individuality, so to speak; each one of them forms a kind of exception, for which reason also general theorems of number theory are but seldom forthcoming." [4] Nevertheless, this individual as-

---

"a collective idea, i.e., the idea of several collections of units, distinguished one from another." Cf. Edmund Husserl, *Über den Begriff der Zahl* (Halle a. S., 1887), p. 12. Leibniz defines number as a group of units ("numerum definio unum et unum et unum etc. seu unitates"), a plurality of units (*ibid.*, p. 168). In definitions such as these it is, indeed, often implied that the whole consists of more than a mere conglomeration of its parts and the idea of a specific kind of relationship of parts creeps in (*ibid.*, p. 14). Husserl himself therefore maintains (*ibid.*, pp. 62 f.) that the concept of number is based on the idea of a certain something and on collective unification. When "discrete contents" are simultaneously conceived of in an aggregate we are always dealing with an analogous act of summarizing interest and observation. See also Edmund Husserl, *Philosophie der Arithmetik*, Vol. I (Halle a. S., 1891).

2. Alfred North Whitehead, *Eine Einführung in die Mathematik* (Bern, 1958), p. 41. (Note: this material, as well as that cited in n. 3, is not contained in the English edition.)

3. *Ibid.*, p. 47.

4. Translated from *Science et méthode* (Paris, 1927), p. 36. Hermann Weyl, *Philosophy of Mathematics and Natural Science* (Princeton, N.J., 1949), pp. 7 f., likewise says: "Within the domain of natural numbers, 1 is an individual, for it is the only such number which does not follow upon any other. *Indeed, all natural numbers are individuals.* The Mystery that clings to numbers, the magic of numbers, may spring from this very fact, that the intellect, in the

pect of number appears to contain the mysterious factor that enables it to organize psyche and matter jointly.

The number one possesses these unique qualities to a particular degree. In contradistinction to all other numbers it does not multiply by itself, or reduce itself by division because it is the *divisor* of all other numbers. It is the only number that yields more by addition with itself than by multiplication with itself ($1 + 1 = 2$, but $1 \times 1 = 1$). The well-known number of Mersenne ($2^p - 1$) ($p =$ prime number) and that of Fermat ($2^{2^p + 1}$) cannot be formulated without one. The number one also forms the marginal number of Pascal's triangle:

$$
\begin{array}{ccccccccc}
 & & & & 1 & & & & \\
 & & & 1 & & 1 & & & \\
 & & 1 & & 2 & & 1 & & \\
 & 1 & & 3 & & 3 & & 1 & \\
1 & & 4 & & 6 & & 4 & & 1 \\
\end{array}
$$

It is the first triangular and also the first square number $\left(n \cdot \dfrac{(n + 1)}{2} \right)$ and (N^2). It is the only natural integer which does not follow another; that is, it has no predecessor. In

----

form of the number series, creates an *infinite manifold* of well-distinguished individuals. Even we enlightened scientists can still feel it, e.g., in the impenetrable law of the distribution of prime numbers. On the other hand it is the free constructibility and the individual character of the numbers that qualify them for the exact theoretical representation of reality" (my italics). When he adheres to the idea that the human intellect creates numbers, Weyl really contradicts himself, because by describing them as individual beings he indirectly characterizes them as "entia," to which an irrational something clings that simply cannot be invented by the intellect. He goes on to say that this exists in contrast to space, the intuitive homogeneity of which is expressed in geometric figures. It seems to me that this problem would be solved if we simply conceived of qualitative number as an aspect of the one-continuum. M. Fierz, "Zur physikalischen Erkenntnis," *Eranos Jahrbuch*, XVI (1948), 450, also points out: "Mathematically speaking every whole number also possesses an individual qualitative character: the whole numbers are far from being mere quantities."

this sense it does not yet "count"; if it did it would be the first uneven prime number. Actually, in mathematics the number one is not reckoned among prime numbers, and in multiplication it is excluded as a neutral element in order to avoid the difficulties involved in its exceptional position in division theory. Interestingly enough, there are scientific grounds for this omission; in the so-called Chladni figures dealing with the wave configurations of sand vibrations on thin plates of metal, all prime numbers figure with the exception of the one.[5]

In China, as in occidental number symbolism, one signifies the indivisible Whole, the *hen-to-pan*, the All-One.[6] The purely mathematical fact that the number series begins with the one, but extends on to infinity, indicates that this number is also conceptually bound up with the infinite. It thus possesses the following complementary dual aspect: quantitatively it forms the unit, qualitatively it contains the whole sequence of natural numbers. Its "unit" character arises through a kind of *kenōsis* (2 Cor. 8: 9) out of the All-Unity, and in this manner the one becomes the *principium individuationis*. In it a paradox appears: One is unique and, at the same time, one among many.[7]

5. See M. D. Waller, *Chladni Figures: A Study in Symmetry* (London, 1961), p. 31: "Fermat defined a positive prime number as any number greater than 1 which has as its divisors (without remainder) only 1 and the number itself. The exclusion of 1 from the series is a matter of convenience. But the law of vibrating plates in showing that when $n = 1$ there are only two classes instead of four classes provides a physical reason for so doing."

6. See also Marcel Granet, *La Pensée chinoise* (Paris, 1968), p. 232. According to K. Menninger, *Zahlwort und Ziffer: Eine Kulturgeschichte der Zahl* (Göttingen, 1958), pp. 31 f., Stevins postulates that when I subtract a non-number from 3, then 3 remains; since, however, $3 - 1 = 2$, one is not a non-number. In my opinion, however, this argument operates on the assumption that the number series already exists. In it one naturally appears to be the unit, thereby invalidating his argument, since the foregoing interpretation proceeds from the primal one as it is manifest when it appears *alone*. Mathematically, Stevins' argument is also nonsense.

7. This paradox is already contained within the Pythagorean cosmogony in the idea that the one, as the monad, sometimes represents

Plato and many of the number theorists who followed him in antiquity considered all further numbers to arise by *diairesis* (division) of the monad.[8] As indeterminate *dyas* in the Pythagorean sense, the duality does, in Plato's view, occupy an exceptional position, because it is either a halving *or* a doubling of the monad. Only when it confronts the primal unity does it become a finite two.[9] This *diairesis* idea of Plato's is based on a quantitative type of intuition, and it is therefore the point at which I—departing from the traditional, Pythagorean-Platonic outlook on number—wish to propound another view. Instead of assuming a division of the monad, I prefer to consider the latter running right through the whole number series.[10] One can compare it to a "field" in which the individual numbers represent activated points.

This continuum, which I suggest calling the one-continuum, differs fundamentally from the recognized continuum theories of Cantor, Dedekind, and Bolzano-Weierstrass, in the sense that the latter are constructs of consciousness in which natural numbers are *not* topologically distinguished

---

the one original *archē* of the world and sometimes reveals itself as the generating single seed (thus revealing only one side of its two antithetical series). In this it only represents the first odd number. See also J. E. Raven, *Pythagoreans and Eleatics* (Amsterdam, 1966), *passim*. The Gnostic Markos distinguishes the All-One from the numerical unit by the terms "Monotes" and "Henotes." He says: "With the Monotes stood also the Henotes. From them proceeded two emanations: the 'Monas' and the 'Hen.' This makes two times two" (H. Leisegang, *Die Gnosis* [Leipzig, 1924], p. 336). In *Le Symbolisme des nombres* (Paris, 1948), R. Allendy calls "the oneness of the one" a synthetic element and the numerical one an analytic element.

8. This has been convincingly demonstrated by J. Stenzel in his outstanding book, *Zahl und Gestalt bei Plato und Aristoteles* (Homburg a. H., 1959).

9. *Ibid.*, p. 52.

10. To Plato the two is *aōristos*, indefinite, because it can result from a division or a multiplication of the one (*ibid.*, pp. 52 f.). It is still without a "thesis," (i.e., it is directionless). Only when it is confronted with the original monad does it become determined. A trace of my idea of the one-continuum is recognizable here, but it has already been transformed into a quantitative form.

from real numbers,[11] and are not differentiated in their individual characteristics.[12] If we accept the monad as an expanding element running through the whole series, then a new interpretation of the evolution of the number series comes into being: from the quantitative point of view, it consists of an ever-repeated addition of one unit, while from the qualitative viewpoint we must postulate that the one-continuum always remains the same.[13] According to this new hypothesis, for instance, the number two is not a halved or doubled monad (or the class of elements which, after the deduction of an element, yields the unitary element), but the symmetry aspect of the one-continuum. If this property of the number two is intellectually hypostatized and confronted with the undifferentiated primal one, the number three arises out of this confrontation as their synthesis, or as the symmetrical axis in the bipolarity of the one-continuum. According to this view the three then represents the unitary aspect of the bipolar one-continuum that has become conscious. Strictly speaking this intellectual step from two to three is a retrograde one, a reflection leading from two back to the primal one. In principle this procedure can be repeated with all subsequent numbers.[14] The retrograde

11. In the so-called topological continuum, on the other hand, natural numbers are defined as the smallest elements.

12. This presupposes another differentiation between infinity and totality. David Hilbert, for instance, identifies the word "totality" with infinity, in my opinion. He says: "The function left to the infinite . . . is merely that of an idea—if with Kant, one understands by an idea a concept of reason [*Vernunftbegriff*] transcending all experience and supplementing the concrete in the sense of totality" ("Über das Unendliche," *Mathematische Annalen*, XCV, no. 1 [1925], 190, quoted by Weyl, *Philosophy of Mathematics*, p. 62, and St. Körner, *Philosophy of Mathematics* (London, 1960), p. 137. It appears to me that the idea of a totality is projected here onto the concept of infinity. If the two are separated there is no longer any reason to deny that every concrete single number is also a totality.

13. J. Stenzel also calls the Platonic "monad" a "continuum of meaning."

14. For this reason Jung says, in the quotation referred to above (p. 39), that the progression of the first decade represents the emergence of a sort of cosmogony out of the monad.

counting step leading from the number three to four has even been made historically famous by Maria Prophetissa's alchemical axiom. It runs: "Out of the One comes Two, out of Two comes Three, and from the Third comes the One as the Fourth." This means that the number three, taken as a unity related back to the primal one, becomes the fourth. This four is understood not so much to have "originated" progressively, but to have retrospectively existed from the very beginning. The next step to number five is also described in medieval natural philosophy. It is included in the concept of the "philosophers' stone" as the *quinta essentia.* The latter is not merely a fifth element added on to the four known ones, but represents their realized unity of existence. Examples such as these can be multiplied at will. In China, for instance, eleven is the number of Tao, but it is not taken in the quantitative sense of ten plus one. Rather it signifies the unity of the decade in its wholeness.[15]

In this way every individual number possesses an overlapping aspect. Through its retrograde relationship to the primal monad each number "reaches across" to its successor. This *hen-to-pan* aspect, as Jung points out, is specific to every number.[16] This fact can be illustrated as follows:

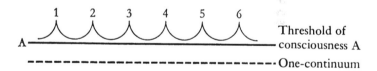

Whereas numbers above the threshold of consciousness appear to be quantitative discontinuities and qualitative individual numbers, in the unconscious they interpermeate and overlap (as do all the other archetypes of the collective unconscious), participating in the one-continuum which runs

15. Cf. Granet, *Pensée chinoise*, p. 166. In the Mayan culture, for instance, so-called seven-one-gods play an outstanding role.
16. Handwritten note by Jung in my possession.

through them all. From this viewpoint all numbers are simply qualitatively differentiated manifestations of the primal one. The latter is a mathematical symbol of the *unus mundus*, isomorphic to the collective unconscious. I shall endeavor to illustrate later on that it actually possesses a relatively homogeneous "field" aspect.

When Edmund Husserl stresses the fact that "a repeated act of concentrated attention" is involved in the concept of number,[17] and Heinrich Rickert speaks of a "homogeneous medium" underlying our number concept,[18] they are groping toward similar formulations. But they incorrectly ascribe these facts to the arithmetical faculty of our ego consciousness. In reality, modern formalistic mathematics proves that our conscious ego may utterly neglect these aspects. The "homogeneous medium" consists rather of an aspect of the *unconscious* psyche which—when its archetypal preconscious basis is taken into account—partakes of our conceptions about numbers, and is responsible for their aspect of wholeness.

17. *Philosophie der Arithmetik*, p. 62.
18. *Das Eine, die Einheit und die Eins*, 2d ed. (Tübingen, 1924), *passim*. This "homogeneous medium" is alogical, an objective "something" which is encountered (pp. 7, 10 ff.). The one is a latent multiplicity. It unites quantity and quality undivided within itself (p. 17). More curiously, Rickert designates this medium as "Logos" and as a nonpsychological element. He was led to this conclusion because in his day the psyche was still identified with ego consciousness. Since the discovery of the unconscious it would be better to say that this medium signifies the Logos aspect of the unconscious psyche. See also H. Wigge, *Der Zahlbegriff in der neueren Philosophie* (Langensalza, 1921). Wigge takes up Rickert's concept, but reduces it to the "alogical medium" of number. However, he speaks in general terms of a "number medium" which cannot logically be further reduced (*ibid.*, p. 33). It stands for a "minimum of the alogical." In *Accent on Form: World Perspectives* (New York, 1954), p. 19, L. L. Whyte also says: "The unexpectedness of a mathematical result gives us the feeling that it is not our own creation, that the world of number exists of its own right, while its necessity and symmetry are balm after the ragged edges of life, or pure joy to those who do not yet know them. The appeal of mathematical form reaches deep into human character."

In their qualitative aspect as configurations of such a one-continuum, all numbers become part of an indivisible wholeness. The quality of a natural number is then no longer attached to its single units, but only to its wholeness, which includes an irrational element.

As a visual aid, natural individual numbers may be conceived of in terms of the rungs on a ladder:

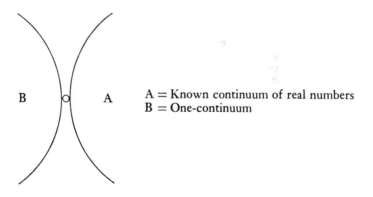

A = Known continuum of real numbers

B = One-continuum, of which each natural number represents an aspect or a time phase[19]

Or we can illustrate a natural number as a point between two continua:

B   A   A = Known continuum of real numbers
                B = One-continuum

19. By the formation of substatives in *-ās* (*monās, dyās, triās*) Plato (as Hultsch has already established) expressed an awareness of the "pure meaning of duality in its essence." When this meaning of duality is present (*parousia*), the ordinary two, three, and so on can be once again generated through participation (*methexis*) at any given time (*Phaidon* 101C, 105C. Cf. Stenzel, *Zahl und Gestalt*, p. 34).

Participation in continuum A means that every number is a particular unit, but no natural numbers are differentiated from real ones, or qualitatively delineated. By participation in B, however, every natural number becomes endowed with a quality of wholeness and meaning.

Another aid to visualizing the role of natural numbers in the continuum is provided by the following schema, a circular periphery that fixes all its numbers at an equal distance from the primal one. This diagram makes it easier to visualize the fact that every number represents an individual aspect of the same primal one:

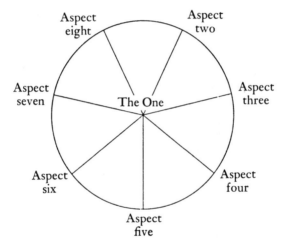

This wholeness adhering to each number was alive in primitive number concepts. If one places two groups of matches, one group containing three matches and the other two matches, before a primitive man and asks "What is this?" he will answer, quite correctly, "three matches and two matches." If one match is then transferred from the group of three to the group of two and the question is repeated he will reply, "two three-matches and two two-matches with one three-match." Every element is qualitatively delineated in terms of its membership in a set. I believe that this aspect of natural numbers should be examined anew. Just as Georg Cantor actually hearkens back to primitive concepts of magnitudes in his discovery of different infinite sets of different powers,[20] so, in my opinion, we would benefit from reconsidering the primitive qualitative character of number, namely its wholeness aspect.[21]

20. Compare also the qualitative view of number among primitives. P. Sergescu, in "Histoire du nombre," *Conférences du Palais de la découverte*, series D, no. 23 (1949), p. 2, says: "In the minds of primitive people, number appears to be an all-encompassing (global) idea, qualitative, not quantitative." I am indebted to Mr. Arnold Mindell for drawing my attention to this article. See also E. Fettweis, *Das Rechnen der Naturvölker* (Leipzig and Berlin, 1927), pp. 2 ff. In the Aztec language (Nahuatl), the numbers are named differently according to the types of objects they serve to count: one type of number word is used for animated objects (pieces of wood, blankets, paper, spheres, tortillas, etc.), another for round objects, another for things that are arranged in a row, and so on. See Fray Alonso de Molina, *Vocabulario Nahuatl-Castellano, Castellano-Nahuatl*, 2d ed. (Mexico City, 1966). I owe this information to the kindness of Dr. José Zavala.

21. One definition of the continuum may be traced back to Eudoxus. According to him, every real number was given, as a line is, as the ratio of two given segments of a geometrical continuum. In this way, real numbers were not differentiated from natural ones. They are both deflected off the same reflections of a "becoming" continuum. See Weyl, *Philosophy of Mathematics*, pp. 39 ff. Carried over to the natural number series the same ratio is characterized by the following qualities: two segment ratios $a:b$ and $a':b'$ are equal to each other if, for every arbitrary natural number m and n, the fulfillment of the condition in the first line below invariably entails the validity of the corresponding condition in the second line:

$$\text{I} \begin{cases} na > mb \\ na' > mb' \end{cases} \qquad \text{II} \begin{cases} na = mb \\ na' = mb' \end{cases} \qquad \text{III} \begin{cases} na < mb \\ na' < mb' \end{cases}$$

Hence what is characteristic of the individual number a is the cut that it creates in the domain of rational numbers, by dividing fractions m/n into three classes. Richard Dedekind subsequently reversed this law and formulated it as follows: any arbitrary given cut in the domain of rational numbers, that is to say, any division of rational numbers into three classes, I, II, and III, determines a real number (cf. *ibid.*, p. 40). According to Dedekind, *Was sind und was sollen die Zahlen* (Brunswick, 1888), pp. 21 ff, quoted by Weyl, *Philosophy of Mathematics*, p. 48, a series C of numbers is said to be isomorphic with the chain of natural numbers if for every number x contained in C its image $x' = x + 1$ likewise belongs to C. Every chain which contains 1 as an element is identical with the whole series N.

A known procedure for the definition of an individual real number is, for instance, its representation as an infinite sequence of nested division intervals of increasing level, whereby for every value of n, the nth interval of the sequence a and the nth interval of the sequence β partially or wholly overlap.[22] This, as Hermann Weyl suggests, is a more differentiated version of the Platonic *diairesis* concept. I cannot enter into a more detailed discussion at this time of the existing continuum derivations that have been erected on such insights. The objection has been repeatedly raised (rightly) that they illegitimately conceive of an infinite series of elements when, at the same time, they treat this whole in terms of a single individual.[23] Weyl even goes so far as to distinguish continuum theories from number theory.[24] In existing continuum concepts, moreover, natural numbers are not topologically distinguished. They can, indeed, be distinguished algebraically, but they are not then characterized as individuals; only their common denominators are expressed.[25]

22. Weyl, *Philosophy of Mathematics*, pp. 23, 35, 52 f., 62ff. A description of real numbers such as this can be traced back to the mathematician Brouwer, who regarded every number as the limit of a nested division interval (see also Tobias Dantzig, *Number: The Language of Science* (New York, 1954), pp. 168, 176 f. The succession of such intervals forms what Cantor calls an arithmetic continuum (*ibid.*, p. 169).
23. Weyl, *Philosophy of Mathematics*, p. 24. See also G. Gentzen, *Die gegenwärtige Lage in der mathematischen Grundlagenforschung* (Darmstadt, 1969), and W. Böhm, *Die metaphysischen Grundlagen der Naturwissenschaft und Mathematik* (Vienna, Freiburg, and Basel, 1966), especially pp. 65 ff.
24. Recently, P. J. Cohen demonstrated that the idea of the continuum is not deducible. (This was done with special reference to the problem of the power of an infinite series.) See "The Independence of the Continuum Hypothesis, I," *Proceedings of the National Academy of Sciences*, L (1963), 1143, and II, LI (1964), 105.
25. Moreover, the continuum concept underlying this definition is that of a "becoming" continuum (Weyl, *Philosophy of Mathematics*, p. 52), i.e., it is not an aggregate of stable elements, but a "medium of free becoming" (Leibniz). Similarly, in Brouwer's idea

If the Brouwerian continuum (the infinite sequence of nested division intervals of increasing level) is more closely examined, natural individual numbers appear in it only because an observer counts them off by marking one of the "wave tips": he therefore makes a *cut* in the series when he begins to count them:[26]

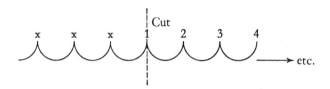

When the natural number is derived in this way, the implication remains that we have "three from a vast number, or five from a multiplicity, etc." But when, on the other hand, we consider the number two, for example, "in itself" (the *dyas* in Plato's sense), or consider two objects as merely forming a set, we imply more an idea of wholeness, the *hen-to-pan*. In both cases, nevertheless, a natural, individual number only emerges when human consciousness perceives a group of objects as a quantity. In mathematics an absolute limit is set at "ego-extinction," as Weyl calls it,[27] indicating

of the continuum subdivisions exist only in terms of possibility, not actuality. Gassendi's postulate that "nothing is separable which is not already separate" is also applicable here (*ibid.,* p. 54).

26. Naturally it is not the Dedekindian cut which is meant here, but a cut in the generally accepted sense of the word.

27. Weyl, in *Philosophy of Mathematics,* p. 75, says: "The problem becomes a serious one when the point-field is infinite, in particular when it is a continuum. A conceptual fixation of points by labels of the above-described nature . . . is here possible only in relation to a *coordinate system,* or frame of reference, that has to be exhibited by an individual demonstrative act. The objectification, by elimination of the ego and its immediate life of intuition, does not fully succeed, and the coordinate system remains as the necessary residue of ego-extinction." In this the commencement of a numeration is equal to the setting up of a coordinate system.

that there, as in modern physics, the role of the observer initially making a "cut" cannot be excluded.[28] Whereas most mathematical assumptions deal with pure acts of consciousness, with mathematicians doing their utmost to imply nothing beyond their formulated assumptions, in the case of natural numbers and sets of objects found in nature we are dealing more with a priori facts of nature, which are not created by human consciousness. This fact applies whenever it is a question of the numerical structure of matter, or of "natural" numbers perceived in the preconscious number sense of the unconscious. Such numbers were "discovered"; they are not arbitrarily posited by our consciousness. They therefore possess a "content" which can only be subsequently derived. In other words, they behave in the realm of the psyche like all other symbols produced by the unconscious. In this sense the natural number is an "encountered" natural phenomenon.[29] The English number theorist G. H. Hardy goes so far as to say:

> The theory of numbers more than any other branch of mathematics, began by being an experimental science. Its most famous theorems have all been conjectured, sometimes a hundred years and more before they were proved; and they have been suggested by the evidence of a mass of computations.[30]

Lately Gert Müller has also stressed that "in mathematics the province of natural integers plays the role of a reality which has to be explored." [31]

As a result of modern number theory, natural numbers are

28. Cf. Wolfgang Pauli, "Naturwissenschaftliche und erkenntnistheoretische Aspekte der Ideen vom Unbewussten," *Aufsätze und Vorträge über Physik und Erkenntnistheorie* (Brunswick, 1961), pp. 16 f., for the part played by the "cut" in physics.

29. Ernst Anrich likewise points out that the numbers of material structure also signified a "beginning of quality" (*Moderne Physik und Tiefenpsychologie* [Stuttgart, 1963], pp. 142 f.).

30. Quoted from Dantzig, *Number*, p. 57.

31. "Der Modellbegriff in der Mathematik," *Studium generale*, XVIII, no. 3 (1965), 155.

nowadays considered in quite a different light; they are taken to be logical abstractions. But they could only have arisen after the experience of "number" had already become a conscious idea. This step could hardly have been achieved if the phenomenon of number did not exist previously and we had not then become gradually familiar with its a priori existence. Even in consciously formulated (i.e., posited) mathematical theorems it is often impossible to exclude number's aspect of preconscious orderedness, which only subsequently was made conscious. This is apparent in the fact, for example, that axioms are initially considered to be "reasonable." Heinrich Hertz once remarked:

> One cannot escape the feeling that these mathematical formulae have an independent existence and an intelligence of their own, that they are wiser than we are, wiser even than their discoverers, that we get more out of them than was originally put into them.[32]

But this only becomes possible when, along with our conscious assumptions, we bring them into play as genuine symbols in the psychological sense. In depth psychology we make a distinction between "signs" used conventionally to designate contents contained strictly within the conscious sphere[33] and "symbols" inspired by the unconscious which invariably remain pregnant with meaning. Symbols can propagate in our thoughts an unlimited series of further intuitions and insights.[34]

If we concede that natural integers are true symbols in this sense, and this means acknowledging their origin in archetypes, then they must contain the psychic dynamism of the

32. Quoted from Dantzig, *Number*, p. 78.
33. As an example, the winged wheel emblematic of the railway is a "sign" and not a symbol.
34. From the age-old symbol of the "tree of life," for instance, human consciousness has derived diverse outlooks on life and growth processes in nature, individuation, the continuum, measurement of time, enlightenment, death, death of a god, the manifestation of a divine natural law, the maternal womb of life and death, and many more.

latter. In other words, they also possess the autonomy of an archetype. By virtue of its dynamism an archetype is able to produce assertions of its own, as Hertz so pertinently observes in connection with mathematical intuitions. In Jung's view numbers actually do possess this autonomy and are therefore capable of instigating mathematical or psychological statements.[35] They consist of a sort of self-amplificatory or preconscious unfolding of aspects. In order to get at the context of their own workings, both in nature and in our own psyches, we must look at them just as though they were dynamic natural phenomena under observation.[36] The question of what purpose we ourselves can use them for as instruments should be put aside.[37] Numbers then become typical psychophysical patterns of motion about which we can make the following statements: One comprises wholeness, two divides, repeats, and engenders symmetries, three centers the symmetries and initiates linear succession, four acts as a stabilizer by turning back to the one as well as bringing forth observables by creating boundaries, and so on. We are dealing here first of all with the principle according to which number, taken qualitatively, is understood to function

35. Jung to Pauli, October 10, 1955, in Jung, *Briefe,* ed. A. Jaffé (Olten, 1973).

36. This aspect was indeed noted by F. Zitscher, *Philosophische Untersuchungen über die Zahl* (Bern and Leipzig, 1910). He suggests interpreting number as an "active dynamic unit," but he deduces no further consequences from it.

37. In *Number Theory and Its History* (New York, Toronto, and London, 1948), p. 25, Oystein Ore remarks: "The origins of the study of number properties go back probably almost as far as counting and the arithmetic operations. It does not take long before it is discovered that some numbers behave differently from others; for instance some numbers can be divided into smaller equal parts and others not." This corresponds somewhat to the utterance: "It has been noticed that pheasants and swans behave somewhat differently; the former can be eaten, the latter cannot." Logically it would be better to ask: what do the dynamics of number themselves consist of? In my opinion J. S. Mill's idea of number (ridiculed by Husserl) follows along the lines of my thought. He saw number as an "objectively present action," not an instrument for our consciousness to manipulate.

as a preconscious psychic principle of activity; each number must be thought of as containing a specific activity that streams forth like a field of force. From this standpoint numbers signify different rhythmic configurations of the one-continuum.

Human consciousness can naturally appropriate this type of numerical activity when dividing by two, constructing the third reconciling form of an antithesis through ratiocinative reflections, and so forth. But this secondary activity does not deprive the number concept of its primary energetic character; it alone forms the preconscious requisite for our arithmetical thought processes.

When we look at a number in this way *four* principal aspects result. The number consists of:

Quantity = Specific coordination
to the multitude of
things, Cantorian
continuum, etc.

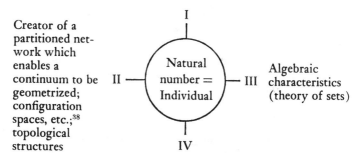

Creator of a partitioned network which enables a continuum to be geometrized; configuration spaces, etc.;[38] topological structures

I

Natural number = Individual

II   III

Algebraic characteristics (theory of sets)

IV

Quality = Pattern of movement
or individual rhythmic
manifestation of the
one-continuum

38. Cf. Weyl, *Philosophy of Mathematics,* p. 90: "In order to subject a continuum to mathematical treatment it is necessary to assume that it is divided up into 'elementary segments' . . . (which, in the one-dimensional case, consists of the bipartition of each elementary segment). The effect is that the continuum is spun into a sub-dividing net of increasing density."

I. Quantity,

II. Geometric capacity in the formation of time and space parameters,

III. Algebraic capacity (theory of sets), and

IV. Qualitative rhythm of the one-continuum or the aspect of meaning.

Aspects I through III may all be associated with factors present in outer nature, for instance:

1. Nuclear numbers,

2. Crystals,

3. Laws of crystal combinations in numerical sequences of fixed development, such as the time-bound processes of chromosome division, auxin effects in plants, signaling processes by chain reactions (RNA, DNA), etc.,

4. Retrogressive connection of all phenomena qualitatively with the whole, through an aspect of meaning.[39]

What, however, does this qualitative aspect of number mean practically? And how can we represent it? In the Lo-shu and Ho-t'u models, the Chinese clearly sought to make use of matrices of a kind, which must be interpreted as "qualitative fields." Their internal numerical structures should not be taken quantitatively; rather they represent

---

39. When my concept of the qualitative one-continuum existing behind the number series is not consciously realized, it slips into scientific discussion through the back door. For example, this slip occurs, as G. J. Whitrow remarked, whenever the continuum concept prevalent among mathematicians is applied by physicists dealing with the summarization of discontinuous phenomena. Whitrow therefore draws special attention to the fact that "in statistical mechanics the symbol dN denotes a number of particles and therefore strictly speaking should be integral. Or again in electrical problems dq denotes an element of charge, despite our knowledge of the quantum nature of electricity. However objectionable these apparently self-contradictory procedures may seem to the logically minded, they are never queried by physicists who, if challenged, would argue that they are justified because of the smallness of dN compared with the total number of particles under consideration, and of dq relative to the total charge in question" (The Natural Philosophy of Time [London and Edinburgh, 1961], p. 158).

time phases of the field's dynamic internal structure.[40] The Chinese concept of number was consistently based on this idea. Marcel Granet says:

> The ontological and logical ordering [of numbers] is translated into rhythmical and geometrical images. On account of their descriptive power, as the exponents of a concrete analysis, numbers are *classificatory*, and are for that reason used to identify concrete sets. They can serve as rubrics, for they indicate the various types of organization which are imposed on things when these are manifest in their proper order in the cosmos. If one desires to awaken the feeling of a progression, numbers are used in their linear sequence; but, as already mentioned, no other distance is imagined between the beginning and the end of the progression than that which separates the whole [*un total*], which is comprehended in its unity, from the "ensemble" which one wants to understand, and which is always seen as something integral. In order to clarify the idea of such a progression, *which in the last analysis is static* and only serves, so to speak, to elucidate the symbolic aspects of a finite cosmos by hierarchically ordered categories—it is not necessary to invoke the numerals as elements of an infinite series; it is better to imagine them as the *"ensemble" of a finite series—in which each number is completely capable of representing the whole series*.[41]

For this reason "numbers serve to make manifest relations and proportions, and to make the manipulation of relations or a play of proportions possible." [42]

---

40. In his translation of Granet's work into German, M. Porkert calls the single Chinese symbols for numbers "phases of transformation" (*Wandlungsphasen*). I hope to demonstrate further on the apparent isomorphism between this time-phase structure of Chinese numbers and the archetypes of the collective unconscious, as the latter are known in modern depth psychology. See also E. H. Gräfe, *I Ging: Buch des Stetigen und der Wandlung* (Oberstedten, Oberursel, 1967), pp. 32, 37.

41. Granet, *Pensée chinoise*, p. 138 (my translation and my italics).

42. *Ibid.*, p. 231.

In China, as we see, the number series and its subsets were not only thought of as a continuum in which the primal one variously manifested itself but as a continuum with two- and three-axes persisting right through the entire number series in a manner similar to the primal one. According to the Chinese, for instance, the progression of numbers, after the formation of the three, proceeds in duplicate along two contrasting rows of even and odd numbers, which correspond to the cosmic rhythms of Yin and Yang.[43] One remains the point of departure for this symmetrical process:[44]

$$1 \begin{cases} \nearrow & 3 \to 5 \to 7 \to 9 \quad \text{Yang A} \\ \searrow & 2 \to 4 \to 6 \to 8 \quad \text{Yin B} \end{cases}$$

A new idea, which strikes me as particularly significant, is contained in this schema: the odd numbers comprise and engender the even ones. The latter always represent a mere double projection (Yin-Yang) of the uneven ones. Neither the odd nor the even are additively tacked onto the even ones. Rather the even ones convert a merely centered or hierarchical orderedness of the whole into symmetrical orderedness.[45] This duplicate progression also modifies the number series in a qualitative way: its hierarchical ordered-

43. "All even numbers have the value of representing a symmetrical arrangement and all odd ones of representing a hierarchical order. Furthermore, the odd numbers are symbols of a whole or of the [cosmic] unity in its more or less complex aspects. One is *the* whole and each odd number, that is, a sort of whole, is one. . . . The transition from every even to every odd number is not a transition from something limited to something illimited or from the undetermined to the determined, but a transition from the symmetrical to the centralized, from the nonhierarchical to a hierarchical order" (*ibid.*, p. 234).

44. *Ibid.*, p. 233. This viewpoint offers a certain analogy to Plato's idea of the diairetic construction of the number sequence. For further information on this subject see Stenzel, *Zahl und Gestalt*, pp. 24 ff, 31 ff.

45. Every even number can be divided into two symmetrical halves and every odd one can also be divided into two halves, plus a midpoint.

ness pays particular attention to the center (**⦙**), while its symmetrical orderedness illustrates the polar nature of the number series. All the higher numbers represent complex examples of these two cosmic orders. Interestingly enough, in pure formal mathematics these two sequences are distinguished in an important way: both sequences are "well-ordered," but they are not symmetrically related to each other. The lower series B, for example, contains only *one* prime number, two; all the other prime numbers belong to series A. No matter how many elements of series B are added together, B elements result. The same holds true for their multiplication. When, on the other hand, the elements of series A are added together the results of all even groups of addition fall into series B. According to Goldbach's theorem (as yet unproved) every element of series B, starting with six, consists of the sum of two prime numbers, while every element of series A starting with nine consists of three prime numbers.

The Chinese idea of constructing two such rhythmically different Yang and Yin sequences is based on the assumption that the one-continuum in all its characteristics (such as polarity, centeredness, symmetry, dynamics, etc.), is constantly present in each number and among all the individual integers. In other words, all numbers, according to the Chinese, are simply different qualitative configurations of the same one-continuum.[46]

An important version of this one-continuum concept of the number series in China was brought to my attention by Dr. Mokusen Miyuki. It is to be found in the doctrine known as Hwa-yen Buddhism, founded by Fa-tzang (A.D. 643–712), the third patriarch of his line.[47] Fa-tzang's treatise

---

46. In the language of the Kunjara tribe (Upper Nile) the word "one" is actually identical with "all" (see Fettweis, *Das Rechnen*, p. 59).

47. Dr. Miyuki was kind enough to translate the relevant text into English for the first time for me. It is called *Hua-yen i-cheng chiao fen-ch'i chang*, "A Treatise expounding the Essence of the Significance and Teaching of the One Vehicle of the Hwa-yen Sutra."

comments on two aspects of the psychic state in which Buddha taught the Hwa-yen Sutra. The problem, if I understand the text correctly, is concerned with the fact that on this occasion Buddha spoke in a state of the most exalted enlightenment (Deep-Sea Impression), which raises the question of whether the "Othernesses" he addresses do in fact exist. Fa-tzang distinguished two aspects of the condition he reached. The first is ineffable and bears no relation to the human realm; it is called "the Realm of the Ten Buddhas." The second belongs to the realm of the Bodhisattva Samantabhadra and is called "that which brings about perfection." Dr. Miyuki compares the first aspect to the Jungian concept of the *unus mundus;* this first aspect symbolizes the "Deep-Sea Impression enlightenment," in other words, the realm of the archetypes as such, in their eternal, timeless, totally transcendental aspect. The second condition portrays the same realm but deals with the form in which it can be experienced by individuals, and therefore described.

While the first aspect represents a continuous totality of reciprocally interpermeating elements, the second can be described in similes. For this purpose Fa-tzang makes use of the symbol of ten copper coins (*ch'ien*), in which ten here signifies the whole inexhaustible multiplicity of existence. The ten coins possess distinct substance (*i-ti*), identical substance (*t'ung-ti*), pervading continuous identity, and at the same time reciprocal interpermeation. From the standpoint of continuous identity no Otherness exists, but from the standpoint of reciprocal interpermeation only "Otherness," instead of individual Self, exists. These two aspects are basically the same; only in temporal experience do they become mutually exclusive. The effect produced by reciprocal interpermeation is that either the *one,* all-embracing Self or unalloyed Othernesses exist. Although these two aspects cannot temporally coincide, they contain each other reciprocally. In terms of the simile this means that the number one represents the primal number without which no other number can exist. Ten, however, represents the ten in one, ten integrated by one. This aspect is called "numbers in progression." We also find "numbers in regression," according to which ten contains the one because the one could not be set up without the ten. One contains no power (*wu-li*) in itself and is therefore integrated into the ten, while still remaining the one and not the ten. (This idea of "numbers in regression" is analogous to the "retrograde counting steps" by which I derive qualitative numbers.)

Psychologically this text is concerned with an attempt to explain the paradoxical multiplicity and unity of the Self archetype which denotes psychic wholeness. It certainly seems to me to be more than a matter of chance that Fatzang refers to the continuity and discontinuity of the number series in this connection. Through it the concept of a continuum underlying the number sequence is clearly brought out.

In the West this concept of number is *expressis verbis* hardly ever represented. It merely glows dimly in the background of certain numerological speculations. There is one exception, however. An original author at the end of the eighteenth century, the archevist and privy councillor to the Count Palatine, Ludwig von Eckhartshausen, published *Zahlenlehre der Natur* which draws on cabalistic (and in my opinion Fluddian) sources as well as other works on number symbolism, formulating the idea he found in them of a continuum in a clearer and partially new way. Von Eckhartshausen makes a distinction between the mathematical "analysis," used merely for quantity measurement, and his "number theory of nature." [48] All nature, he says, forms an "unbroken chain" whose links rest "on an immutable law of the progression of a universal power which is the unity of all things." [49] This progression is based on the action of time. It is concerned not with the world of outer appearances but

48. L. von Eckhartshausen, *Zahlenlehre der Natur* (Leipzig, 1794), p. 7. In his opinion the principles of mathematics then known were based solely on quantities and relationships (*ibid.*, p. 13).
49. *Ibid.*, pp. 11, 12.

with the laws existing *prior* to the formation of quantity.[50]
Whereas the numbers of ordinary arithmetic signify a multiplicity of material units, this progression knows "only one
unity," according to which numbers are progressively generated. This type of thinking is oriented toward determining "the relations of conceivable objects within an imagina-
ble totality." [51] Accordingly, numbers form a midpoint
between the material and the spiritual (extrasensory); they
give us "true perspicuity about extrasensory facts." [52] The
element of unity itself is the active principle, and number is
the passive one.[53] (This idea goes right back to Proclus who
speaks of the generating power of the monad.[54]) For the
numbers to lie in their proper order means that they indicate
their relationship to the one; when they depart from their
order they lose their true relationship to the one.[55]

Concepts of the continuum similar to that of von Eckhartshausen, were already in existence in Greek antiquity, although, as we are forced to admit today, they intermingled

50. *Ibid.*, pp. 14, 17.
51. *Ibid.*, pp. 18, 72. In other passages Heinrich Rickert (*Das Eine*)
pays special attention to this problem.
52. Von Eckhartshausen, *Zahlenlehre*, p. 25.
53. *Ibid.*, p. 74. One is the source of all numbers, the origin and
primal number of all numbers, containing everything within itself.
The Unity is never mingled with the multitude; it is always the
same and remains immutable. When it is multiplied it produces no
other number than itself. The Unity is therefore the beginning and
the end of all numbers. "It is the source of all things." "The laws of
Number and sequence arise from the Unity's progression in the
generation of numbers" (p. 73).
54. Stenzel, *Zahl und Gestalt*, p. 38.
55. The one thing to be regretted about this ingenious theory is its
all too concrete conception of numerical relations. Progression is
ascribed to an operative force, the emanation of a divine *dynamis*
which also creates matter. The whole theory thus acquires a ma-
terialistic tinge. As Jung stresses, it is not wise to transcend the immediate psychic context in order to speculate on the material or
spiritual significance of the unknowable.

my qualitative concept of a one-continuum with the beginnings of the quantitative continuum concept deduced by
modern mathematicians.[56] In Plato's work, for instance, the

Intuitive cabalistic speculations most certainly influenced von
Eckhartshausen. He speaks in his *Zahlenlehre* (p. 84) of the "mysteries
of the Hebrews" and gives the order of the *sephiroth* once again:

1		1. Love	
3	2	3. Wisdom	2. Truth
5	4	5. Righteousness	4. Goodness
	6	6. Beauty	
8	7	8. Sensual nature	7. Spiritual nature
	9	9. Attributes	
	10	10. Totality	

It is common knowledge that in the cabala the ten primal numbers,
the *sephiroth*, are considered to be emanations of divine immaterial
origin in the sense that the "original one" remains far removed from
all things and only manifests its various aspects in each single
sephira. The cabalistic doctrine of numbers is in itself a revival of
ancient Gnostic ideas about numbers. In the latter doctrine numbers,
as *archōn*s or divine powers, continually stream forth from the unknowable *archē* of the one. All are manifestations of single aspects
of the primal one. For this reason the first ten numbers of the
sephiroth system are designated by the word *sephira*, instead of the
ordinary word for numbers (*mispar*). They are "spheres" and "to-
talities" of the unknowable primal one. I am indebted to Dr. S. Hurwitz for kindly giving me this information.

Credit is due to von Eckhartshausen for having attempted, in contradistinction to ancient traditional philosophers, an abstract formulation of the number continuum and for trying to comprehend it as a
basic mathematical structure, even though he quickly slipped back
into purely mythological speculations.

56. A more interesting attempt to deduce the existence of natural
numbers may be found in the work of a modern author writing
under the pseudonym of Mathesius, *Weg zu Gott: Erlebnisse eines
Mathematikers* (Zurich and Stuttgart, 1959). Mathesius proceeds
mainly from the concept of mathematical infinity to differentiate
first so-called nonsets or unsets (i.e., undifferentiable infinite sets)
from an entity that, repeatedly established, becomes a series of identical ones. By being named (the ordinal number), these open sets
thereupon become the series of natural numbers as we know them.
Taking his point of departure from mathematical infinity, Mathesius
postulates that this infinity comprises a complete orderedness which
was not invented but discovered. Recognition of this order within
infinity makes possible all further mathematical understanding for
the first time. He says: "Thus pure mathematics rests on the recogni-

number one still possesses a substantial nature and, as Stenzel has shown, it is taken in many passages to constitute a kind of "continuum of meaning." The "unbounded" duality of the large-small (duplication or halving of the monad) forms, on the other hand, a kind of "continuum of becoming" for all numbers, except prime numbers.[57] Through the idea of *diairesis*, however, Plato's duality slips over into the quantitative realm.[58] In my opinion, Plato moves away in this manner from formulating the continuum nature of all numbers because, in conformity with the general outlook of antiquity, he still thought in terms of static numerical *figures* and not of rhythmical configurations.[59] His work thus demonstrates a blend of quantitative and qualitative standpoints,

---

tion of the infinite as a basic and incomprehensible concept. It contains a complete orderedness, which also operates in the finite so that man can participate in it: only imperfectly, to be sure, but with the certainty that this imperfection appertains to an all-embracing and perfect order" (p. 261). The author also describes this ordered infinity as a "superordinated spirituality" and looks on it as something divine (pp. 162 ff.).

This idea of an alleged infinity which contains a "perfect order" exhibits a surprising degree of conformity to Wang Fu Ch'ih's idea of a continuum behind the I Ching hexagrams, although in contradistinction to the latter it is not to be understood as a qualitative-dynamic entity. My one-continuum proposal likewise resembles Mathesius' concept of an "ordered infinity" in many respects, but with the difference that I do not merely assume that single numbers can be quantitatively extracted from it in sets. Rather I suggest that individual numbers, as dynamic configurations, *are identical with the whole continuum at the same time, and that the qualitative aspect of the number concept should be sought in this identity*.

57. Cf. Aristotle, *Metaphysics* 987B. 20 and Stenzel's interpretation, *Zahl und Gestalt*, p. 6.

58. "Plato's endeavor," as Stenzel points out, "is directed toward defining every individual number absolutely clearly as a new unit, a totality of some characteristics or other" (*Zahl und Gestalt*, p. 35).

59. See *ibid.*, p. 35. In contrast to Plato, Aristotle emphasizes the idea that all numbers represent the unification of similar units combinable through operations (p. 7). This is a purely quantitative definition of number which has been one-sidedly accepted in modern times.

comparable to the magical-causal thinking of earlier times.[60]

Looking back today, we can trace a mixture of causal and synchronistic thinking in this type of thought. The gradual development of occidental scientific thinking proceeded by the sifting of a more rigorously defined idea of causality out of the "magical" ideas of the past, and at the same time the pursuit of a purely quantitative definition of number through the elimination of its qualitative aspect. This one-sided development has reached its peak today. For this reason Jung suggested coining the term "synchronicity," so that certain aspects of reality which are not included in the causal description of nature can be interpreted as synchronistic events without the necessity of regressing into an archaic form of magical-causal thinking. Similarly, it seems to me desirable to introduce a new qualitative concept of number to complement our hitherto prevailing quantitative number concept, without falling back into magical-numerological speculations on this account.

60. As Stenzel remarks (*ibid.*, p. 9), in Plato every number is seen on the one hand as "a totality determined with regard to its contents," and on the other, it is like an idea (*eidos*); thus it is both a unity and a multiplicity, sharing these characteristics with the logos (*ibid.*, pp. 12, 21).

CHAPTER FIVE

The Number Two
as the One-Continuum's Rhythm
by Which Symmetries and
Observables Are Engendered

Wolfgang Pauli once expressed the wish that we might find a "neutral" language by which to describe both psychic and physical phenomena at the same time. Perhaps the motion patterns of number can be expressed in such a manner as to render their formulation applicable to both fields. We shall now attempt this formulation in describing the first four numbers, with the number one serving simply as the essential representative of the continuum.

The number two, in the first place, plays a very important role in mathematics. The mathematician Brouwer, like Plato, even looks on the concept of two-oneness as the root of mathematical thought.[1] From the purely formal point of view two inaugurates the class of all real numbers that can be multiplied or divided by themselves. It is the basis of the formation of ordered pairs, and lies behind every two-digit relation of order. Furthermore, two is the only existing even prime number.[2] It is also the only number that yields the

1. See Hermann Weyl, *Philosophy of Mathematics and Natural Science* (Princeton, N.J., 1949), p. 63.
2. See also Philip J. Davis, *The Lore of Large Numbers* (New York, 1961), p. 92.

same result when multiplied by or added to itself.[3] When the sum of the reciprocal divisors of a number equals two we are dealing with a so-called perfect number.[4]

The archetype of duality, taken as a preconscious mental dynamism, lies behind the operations of repetition and division.[5] For this reason the word for two in certain primitive languages is related to the word "to split," and in others to the words "to follow" and "to accompany."[6] The act of repetition engenders mathematical symmetry.[7] The archetype of the number two also stands—in the case of bilateral symmetry—behind the operation of mirroring or reflection as an involutive[8] permutation of number.[9] It lies as well behind the principle of duality in plane projection geometry, where the only concept of relation is the incidence of point and line (points lie on a line and lines go through points).[10] As an archetypal thought pattern two also stands behind the division of even and odd numbers, constituting in geometry the directional axis for right and left, on the basis of even or odd permutations of vector numbers.[11]

The archetype of two stands, furthermore, behind the discovery of complex numbers. This term is used to designate any pair of real numbers.[12] Weyl says: "Concerning the

3. The Pythagoreans discovered the first irrational number in $\sqrt{2}$.
4. See O. Gmelin, "Über vollkommene und befreundete Zahlen" (Dissertation, University of Halle a. S., 1917), pp. 9 f.
5. Cf. Weyl, *Philosophy of Mathematics*, p. 30.
6. Cf. E. Fettweis, *Das Rechnen der Naturvölker* (Leipzig, 1927), p. 59.
7. Cf. W. von Engelhardt, "Symmetrie," *Studium generale*, II, nos. 4–5 (1949), 203 f. See also V. Fritsch, *Links und Rechts in Wissenschaft und Leben* (Stuttgart, 1964), p. 22. A set M is considered to be symmetrical if G (G is the symmetry group) contains more than its identical image.
8. The term "involutive" means that diversity results from a single repetition, and identity from the second one. An identical image is thus called involutive when it is not f, but $f \times f'$, which forms an identical image.
9. Weyl, *Philosophy of Mathematics*, pp. 26 f.
10. *Ibid.*, and p. 33.
11. *Ibid.*, p. 84.
12. Cf. W. R. Hamilton, *Lectures on Quaternions* (Dublin, 1853).

complex numbers, the rules of operation e = (1,0) play the part of unity in the complex domain, since its multiplication by any complex number (a, β) reproduces (a, β). And (0,1) is that imaginary unit i which satisfies the equation $i \cdot i = -e$." [13] The operations become no longer consistently valid with hypercomplex numbers (more than one pair). "In this respect the complex numbers denote a natural boundary for the extension of the number concept." [14]

The so-called Hermitian matrices, in which half the number complexes appear to be mathematically imaginary, could also be used to illustrate the combination of conscious-unconscious, since in the psychic realm, too, every conscious psychic content is accompanied by an unconscious "shadow" content.

Although, from the mathematical point of view, the number two, in the concept of bilateral symmetry, is undetermined in content (in other words, it is merely a question of mathematically distinguished points), time and again the idea of polarity has been associated with it. This is especially the case in physics, where the symmetry principle has been brought into connection with positive and negative electricity and magnetism. Actually, in recent times the basic identity of these polar manifestations has been proven, which has resulted in a general contemporary tendency to replace the concept of polarity with that of symmetry. [15] But when the number two is taken to be a dynamic pattern of human thought, polarity becomes once again a suitable image for the expression of numerous phenomena of life, even though the two poles are often identical, according to the law that extremes meet. [16] In his paper "Symmetrie und Polarität," Karl Lothar Wolf demonstrates how in nature

13. Weyl, *Philosophy of Mathematics*, p. 32.

14. *Ibid.*, p. 32 (amplification in which the rule of norm products still holds good).

15. Cf. Fritsch, *Links und Rechts*, pp. 24 f.

16. Regarding symmetry and antisymmetry in mathematics and physics, see A. Lautmann, *Symétrie et dissymétrie en mathématiques et physique* (Paris, 1946), pp. 14 ff.

polarity most frequently steps forth hand in hand with symmetry.[17] He presents diverse biological and physical evidence, to which I refer the reader.

Historically since Pythagorean times the number two has been symbolically equated with matter as an *increatum*.[18] This ancient identification of matter and the number two is of significance again today, because we now know that when man calculates with "counted" material phenomena, or physical energy in electronics, binary arithmetic, as an image of our bivalent logic, proves to be the most suitable system of reckoning. In addition, the above mentioned series of "magic numbers" which distinguishes atomic structures begins with two.[19] When "light" is converted into matter a

17. *Studium generale*, II, nos. 4–5 (1949), 221 f.

18. As the All-Unity and as counting unit (Monotes-Henotes). This double aspect of the number one already contains the two *in potentia*. Regarding its contents, the primal one was characterized (in Gnostic number speculation, for instance) as the divine "Father-Mother," "Silence-Force," etc. See C. A. Baynes, ed., *A Gnostic Coptic Treatise* (Cambridge, 1933). The Paracelsian and alchemist Gerhard Dorn applied himself particularly to the problem of the two, the four, and matter. His idea was that when God divided the upper from the lower waters on the second day of creation, the number two became independent. This was the beginning of all confusion, dissension, and strife. The *quaternarius* then proceeded from the *binarius*. The number two appertained to Eve. For this reason the devil first tempted her. A secret relationship thus arose between the number two, the devil, and woman, and Dorn deductively endowed the number four with an equally negative, "heathen" value on the basis of two. Two was even considered to be the devil himself. Dorn calls him a "quadricornutus binarius." This devilish principle of duality sought to build a creation in opposition to God, striving against the Trinitarian world order. Dorn's theory is exhaustively described by Jung in *Psychology and Religion, CW*, Vol. XI, 2d ed. (1968), ¶¶ 262 ff. A modern variant of the same archetypal idea is contained in Pascual Jordan's cosmogonic theory, according to which the universe is supposed to have come into being through a pair of neutrons. Cf. B. Bavink, *Weltschöpfung in Mythos und Religion, Philosophie und Naturwissenschaft* (Basel, 1951), pp. 80, 102.

19. See Wolfgang Pauli, "Naturwissenschaftliche und erkenntnistheoretische Aspekte der Ideen vom Unbewussten," *Aufsätze und Vorträge über Physik und Erkenntnistheorie* (Brunswick, 1961), p. 133. The number described in the index of the wave function of a single particle amounts, for electrons, to the number two, "so that

pair of electron twins (one electron and one positron) results. In such connections the number two no longer seems to be merely arbitrarily associated with matter in our speculative consciousness, but *appears to be connected with an order already present in nature itself*. Two, however, often exhibits a curious factor of uncertainty, as to which is one, or the other. In physics two identical particles, electrons, for instance, are in principle indistinguishable, so that if at one instant the positions are labeled, at the next they may have changed places. Unless this feature is built into the theory, the theory disagrees with the experimental results.[20] Altogether the archetype of two plays an enormous role in the principle of parity and symmetry[21] (the latter defined as uninfluenceability by variations of the referential system, rotation of the system of coordinates, for instance, time reversal, and so on). Symmetry becomes thus practically equivalent to invariability,[22] on which the describability of a system is mainly based.

But the number two not only appears to form the basis for our possible range of perceptions on the physical level; it also applies to the psychic level. Besides its specific relation to the structural binary basis of matter, two possesses an equally important relationship to the so-called threshold phenomena of consciousness. Identical duplications of objects in dreams, for instance, or in myths, point to the fact that a content *is just beginning to reach the threshold of*

---

the configurational space for N electrons has $3N$ spatial dimensions and N power of two indices." The number series which governs the so-called Chladni figures also begins with two. As Professor Byers Brown pointed out to me, the Pauli principle is also based precisely on two, and holds a dominant position in physics and chemistry. It limits a wide range of possible permutation symmetries in nature to one.

20. Professor Byers Brown kindly gave me this explanation.

21. Cf. the survey of this problem in Fritsch, *Links und Rechts*, pp. 157 ff.

22. This parity is broken in weak interactions; the parity principle therefore only possesses *relative* validity in nature. See *ibid.*, pp. 157 ff.

consciousness as a recognizable entity, taking the first step, as it were, toward manifestation.[23] Jung says:

> Conscious perception means discrimination. Thus, structures arising from the unconscious will be distinguished when they reach the threshold of perception; such structures then appear to be doubled, but are two completely identical entities—the one and the other—since it has not yet become clear which is the one and which is the other.[24]

In practically all cultures and religions of the world two identical demons or divine figures are found acting as the symbolic guardians of the entrance to the Beyond. In psychological language this realm refers to the collective unconscious. The Egyptian double lions, gate-guarding sphinx figures, may serve as one example. In Egypt the might (*mana*) of the king was originally represented by a lion which, as a dual figure, sat at all temple entrances and signified, among other things, the eastern and western horizons.[25] The Egyptian word for lion therefore also stood for eastern and western horizon, the darkness of the night, and the Beyond. At the threshold of this region, which we today would call the unconscious, sat the double lion, Routi, meaning "yesterday and today." [26] Later he was called "Aker," which had earlier been the name of an underworld divinity; he guarded the sun during its death and rebirth cycle in the Be-

23. Cf. C. G. Jung, *Seminar über Kinderträume*, Eidgenössische Technische Hochschule Lectures (Zurich, 1938–39), p. 72, and S. Hurwitz, *Die Gestalt des sterbenden Messias*, Studien aus den C. G. Jung Institut, Vol. VIII (Zurich, 1958), p. 221.

24. Translated from Jung, *Kinderträume*, p. 72. While in the western islands of the Torres Strait the word for one means "the other," in Encounter Bay it means "the one without the other" (see Fettweis, *Das Rechnen*, p. 59). Werner Danckert in *Tonreich und Symbolzahl* (Bonn, 1966), p. 17, demonstrated that a two-tone melody is the typical musical form for those primitives who, from the ethnological point of view, are at a particularly primitive cultural level (which Danckert calls the fossil culture). On this level man's first *conscious* musical ability begins.

25. Cf. Constant de Wit, *Le Rôle et le sens du lion dans l'Egypte ancienne* (Leiden, 1951), p. 71.

26. *Ibid.*, p. 72.

yond.[27] "His powers are mysterious," says one text, "in him lie the deepest mysteries," he has "concealed his forms," he is "the one full of mystery, who is not known" or, "that which brings about the resurrection of the sun." [28] The great Egyptian primal god Atum was also considered a lion who engendered the two lions (Shu and Tefnut), signifying eternity and infinite time, respectively. This double lion (Shu-Tefnut) is clearly Atum himself.[29] Constant de Wit says: "The double lion, the two horizons, the two world mountains, are different images symbolizing the crossing from life to death, from day to night and vice versa. They are the guardians, the gates, the threshold to the Beyond. . . ." [30] It is therefore not surprising that they sometimes stand for the Beyond itself and sometimes for the powers which effect its mystery.[31] The double lion Routi is the divine principle which, recreating itself in death, rises up from the dead.[32] Psychologically this lion symbolizes psychic energy, *in its latent unconscious condition, and its reappearance on the threshold of consciousness.*

Whenever a latent unconscious content pushes up into consciousness, it appears first as a twofold oneness. For this reason nearly all cosmogonies begin their tales of the emergence of world-consciousness with a duality: creator twins, a god and his "helper," or, as in Genesis, the earth "without form, and void," over which the Spirit of God moved.[33] The

27. *Ibid.*, pp. 91 ff., 95.
28. *Ibid.*, pp. 97, 99, 103, 106.
29. *Ibid.*, pp. 113, 117, 133.
30. *Ibid.*, p. 157.
31. The marble table on which the corpse was embalmed was also fashioned into a double lion with a head at each end. See also *ibid.*, pp. 464 f.
32. *Ibid.*, p. 465.
33. Concerning the polar aspect of the number two, Karl Menninger, *Zahlwort und Ziffer: Eine Kulturgeschichte der Zahl* (Göttingen, 1958), p. 24, also says: "Our mind explains the world in terms of Heaven and Earth, day and night, light and darkness, right and left, man and woman, I and you, and the more intensely we experience the tension between these poles the more powerfully shall we

traditional association of duality, on the one hand with matter, and on the other with the rise of consciousness, is not a matter of pure chance; material manifestations and contents of our consciousness have in common the fact that they are both relatively discrete, discontinuous, and "invariable." Because of these characteristics they are thrown into sharp relief against a background of undifferentiable wholeness, appearing either as observable physical phenomena or as comparatively separable representations in our inner field of vision.

Considered as a rhythm of movement, the number two represents a repetition, in the form of an oscillation or pulsation,[34] which forms the basis for our perception of time (not the perception itself initially). It probably produced the idea, repeatedly postulated in antiquity, that time and number are related. This concept will be discussed later, and I

---

also experience their unity. . . ." For this reason many languages possess a special term for duality which emphasizes the specific oneness of two. The fact that this form of twofoldness refers, time and again, to the primal one has been felt very intensely by many peoples. In Irish, for instance, two eyes are designated as a whole (di suil), while one eye, on the contrary, is called a "half" (leth-suil). Menninger continues: "With two we experience the nature of number more strongly than with the other numbers, namely, the characteristics of combining the many into one, and simultaneously being both a multiplicity and unity. To divide the united, to unite the divided—time and again language has refuted this antithesis of separateness and togetherness by its use of the word two; as in the English 'diploma' and 'dispute,' and 'twin' which means both 'one of two born at a birth' and 'to divide, part, separate,' in the German Zwist, dissension, discord, quarrel, and Zwirn, thread, twine, and in the Turkish ikiz, twin and ikilik, dissension (from iki = two). An especially interesting example is proferred in Old Armenian where erku, the word for two, is used to form the pair of opposites, erkin ('heaven') and erkir ('earth')." See also Fritsch, Links und Rechts, who cites mainly the modern philosophical systems which think in pairs, i.e., complementarily. See further Ernst Anrich, Moderne Physik und Tiefenpsychologie (Stuttgart, 1963), p. 124.

34. Cf. the Pythagorean cosmogony which came into being because the finite monad "breathed in" the infinite, thereby engendering the number series. J. E. Raven, Pythagoraeans and Eleatics (Amsterdam, 1966), p. 149.

shall also describe some historical mandala structures that are specifically models of the time structure of the universe. It is not by chance that these models frequently take the form of *double* mandalas. They all represent attempts to throw light on the transcendent unity of existence in both a time-less and a time-bound aspect. The fact that more differen-tiated models of the *unus mundus* are double mandalas, and that they are especially liable to appear when the problem of time and synchronicity becomes constellated, is presumably related to the function of number two as a threshold phe-nomenon.

The ancient Chinese actually divided their whole psycho-physical cosmos into a periodic twofold rhythm, a reciprocal enantiodromial Yin-Yang motion. Yin and Yang are not, as often maintained, cosmic principles, but rather, as Marcel Granet suggests, a symphony of alternating rhythms in which spatial elements (in front–behind) and temporal ele-ments (before-after) are not separable. For, Granet states, *there is not the slightest difference between matter and rhythm.*[35] Thus, making use of musical similes, it is said: Yin and Yang play in concert (*tiao*) and harmonize (*ho*). "The whole universe has a rhythmical basic structure." [36]

In the aforementioned "older or primal heavenly order" of the Chinese Book of Changes, likewise, there are two dy-namisms, a progressive and a regressive movement.[37] In other words, linear or cyclical time does not initially exist.[38] This older heavenly order contains a rhythmical internal move-ment which, however, in its entirety remains static. An old text says that "the powers confront one another, but they do not conflict," meaning that they counterbalance one another

35. *La Pensée chinoise* (Paris, 1968), pp. 121, 107 ff.
36. *Ibid.*, p. 121. *Ho* means the harmony of a piece of music and the harmonious flavor of a broth. The ideas of substance and rhythm are thus closely united (*ibid.*, p. 189, n. 189).
37. *Ibid.*, p. 440, and Richard Wilhelm, trans., *I Ching or Book of Changes*, English trans. C. F. Baynes, 2 vols. (London, 1960), I, 285 ff.
38. Wilhelm trans., *I Ching*, p. 288.

in a symmetrical double movement.[39] In this context, two-ness signifies oscillation and rhythm, but not yet linear time. This confirms the fact that the appearance of identical paired images indicates a content in the act of detaching itself from the unconscious continuum and approaching the threshold of consciousness; it is on the threshold that the phenomenon of a symmetrical mirroring (or duality) first arises.[40]

In the two-continuum we do not confront an ordered sequence or the concept of true seriality to begin with. But it is hardly possible to establish a duality without at the same time acknowledging the impulse to declare whether it involves an identity or an "otherness" of two. This distinction cannot be made conscious unless one confronts two with the original one,[41] which automatically implies a "threeness." [42] In the number two we are dealing first of all with a polarity that manifests itself dynamically as an oscillatory or systolic-

39. *Ibid.*, p. 286.

40. L. E. J. Brouwer, one of the founders of the intuitionist theory of mathematics, based his construction of natural numbers on the conceptual multiplicity of intervals of time, the latter forming a primary intuition of the human intellect (see G. J. Whitrow, *The Natural Philosophy of Time* [London and Edinburgh, 1961], p. 116). To my way of thinking, however, the opposite premise seems justified: number, as the dynamic manifestation of an archetype, unifies our time experience (our perception of intervals and instants).

41. Curiously enough, this is confirmed by quite another source. In his pure set-theoretical research into symmetry, Wolf von Engelhardt asserts that multiple relations can generally be reduced to binary relations and that "all sciences seem to be mostly based on binary relations." Here, too, the act of becoming conscious of connections in nature seems to be basically linked up with a dualistic viewpoint (see "Sinn und Begriff der Symmetrie," *Studium generale*, VI, no. 9 [1953], 531).

42. This kind of overlapping phenomenon, connecting 0, 1, 2, and 3, is based on the continuum nature of the natural number series discussed above. In quantitative calculations of binary arithmetic a similar consideration must also be taken into account. Quantitatively two serves as the basis of ordered pairs, but when—and this is important in the construction of computers—*ba* is not meant to equal *ab*, they have to be differentiated by a third element.

diastolic rhythm.[43] Its numerous repetitions then engender a "path," and thereby a time- or space-vector, the third element. This threeness is implicitly contained in the number two, but not yet explicitly indicated by its (two's) presence.

Jung has explained the step from one to two and from two to three in the following way:

> The number one claims an exceptional position, which we meet again in the natural philosophy of the Middle Ages. According to this, one is not a number at all; the first number is two. Two is the first number because, with it, separation and multiplication begin, which alone make counting possible. With the appearance of the number two, *another* appears alongside the one, a happening which is so striking that in many languages "the other" and "the second" are expressed by the same word. Also associated with the number two is the idea of right and left, and remarkably enough, of favourable and unfavourable, good and bad. The "other" can have a "sinister" significance—or one feels it, at least, as something opposite and alien. Therefore, argues a medieval alchemist, God did not praise the second day of creation, because on this day (Monday, the day of the moon) the *binarius*, alias the devil, came into existence. Two implies a one which is different and distinct from the "numberless" One. In other words, as soon as the number two appears, a unit is produced out of the original unity, and this unit is none other than the same unity split into two and turned into a "number." The "One" and the "Other" form an opposition, but there is no opposition between one and two, for these are simple numbers which are distinguished only by their arithmetical value and by nothing else. The "One," however, seeks to hold to its one-and-alone existence, while the "Other" ever strives to be another opposed to the One. The One will not let go of the Other because, if it did, it would lose its character; and the Other pushes itself away from

43. As this was also represented in the "primal" matrix form of the two Chinese diagrams dealing with the cosmic order.

the One in order to exist at all. Thus there arises a tension of opposites between the One and the Other. But every tension of opposites culminates in a release, out of which comes the "third." In the third, the tension is resolved and the lost unity is restored. Unity, the absolute One, cannot be numbered, it is indefinable and unknowable; only when it appears as a unit, the number one, is it knowable, for the "Other" which is required for this act of knowing is lacking in the condition of the One. Three is an unfolding of the One to a condition where it can be known—unity becomes recognizable; had it not been resolved into the polarity of the One and the Other, it would have remained fixed in a condition devoid of every quality.[44]

These "Pythagorean reflections," as Jung himself calls them, are not formally arithmetical, but they belong to those "necessary" assertions the number archetype compels us to make. Considered from this angle the number one continues, after the emergence of the two, to be linked up with the "other" or "second" in the original one and remains, so to speak, eternally on the point of becoming two.[45] This means that one, like two, continues to be interwoven in the same one-continuum.[46]

This twofold oneness has been preserved in the symbolism of card games; in them the deuce and ace were originally the same, god of luck who is both one and two, in other words a twin.[47] Insofar as the number two recapitulates a relative "disruption" of the original unity, it, curiously

44. *Psychology and Religion,* ¶ 180.

45. *Ibid.,* p. 136, n. 9.

46. The understanding of "pairedness" was highly developed by the natives of the Torres Strait because they employ a binary method of calculation, although they possess no genuine understanding of counting or of number (according to Curr). See Tobias Dantzig, *Number: The Language of Science* (New York, 1954), p. 15, and E. Kramer, *The Main Stream of Mathematics* (New York, 1951), pp. 11 ff.

47. See M. Riemschneider, *Von 0–1001: Das Geheimnis der numinosen Zahl* (Munich, 1966), p. 16.

Acorn deuce: German playing card, B. Merkle, Nuremberg, 1583 [Source: M. Riemschneider, *Von 0–1001: Das Geheimnis der numinosen Zahl* (Munich, 1966), p. 16, reproduced by permission of Heimeran Verlag.]

enough, possesses a certain affinity to zero; at times both two and zero take on the aspect of the "other" opposed to the one. In the binary arithmetic of the I Ching, the Chinese represented plus and minus elements by one (Yang) and two (Yin), three and four following as Heaven and Earth, while the system invented by Leibniz consisted of zero (= *le rien*) and one (= God).[48] Helmut Wilhelm stresses that Leibniz' reversed order and relatively more negative evaluation of the "not-one" element stands in significant relation to the general differences between East and West.[49] In the East the

48. G. W. Leibniz, "Abhandlung über die chinesische Philosophie," *Antaios*, VIII (1967), 144 f.
49. Cf. H. Wilhelm, "Der Zeitbegriff im Buch der Wandlungen," *Eranos Jahrbuch*, XX (1951), 328. See also the outstanding article by

"not-one" is an existing, positive element (nirvana), while in the West it is experienced as "the nothing of the unformed chaos." [50]

The dualism of plus, minus (hit, miss) also plays a hidden role in Bernoulli's theorem and in probability theory, in that results range between the two threshold values, zero and one. [51] The dualism of zero and one, or one and two, furthermore, contains within itself the potential concept of fourfoldness (0–1–1–2), as well as that of three (0–1–2), if one is taken to be the mid-axis between zero and two. This may also be seen in the electron frequency patterns illustrated above, four appearing as a repeated two-pattern, and three as an axially modified twoness with an emphasized mid-line. Once again we can observe how our thought forms coincide strikingly with structures found in nature. According to Jung they are probably not causally linked, but stem back to an identical ordering factor, namely, the archetype of number.

F. Vonessen, "Reim und Zahl bei Leibniz," *Antaios*, VIII (1967), 99 ff.

50. Leibniz himself was convinced of the conformity of the two systems, and even hoped by the use of his calculus to interpret Chinese philosophy anew (bogged down as it was by Chinese historians' lack of understanding), reconciling it with the Christian religion. See R. F. Merkel, *Leibniz und China* (Berlin, 1952), pp. 19 f.

51. Wolfgang Pauli formulates this as follows: To all pairs of positive numbers (ϵ, θ) there always exists a large number N with the following properties: "The chance that a fraction of the number of possibilities among which the event takes place will ever deviate more than ϵ from P, from N possibilities onward is smaller than θ. The assumption is, however, that among all repetitions of the experiments the chance of the event coming off should always be the same" (*Aufsätze*, p. 19). This "tacit" assumption is, however, *not* empirically valid for affectively charged psychic events, because repetition diminishes their charge, in such a manner that P converges toward zero. Insofar as every physical observation is primarily a psychic event, an additional factor slips in, which can only be successfully ignored in dealing with macroscopic conditions (and here too, only to a limited degree, because of the law of entropy). A hidden problem consequently lurks between zero and one, which has been ignored in the forms of probability theory prevailing up to now.

CHAPTER SIX

The Number Three
as a Rhythmic Configuration
of Progressive Actualizations
in Human Consciousness
and the Material Realm

From a purely formal point of view the number three possesses the following characteristics:[1] It is the first odd prime number, as well as the first triangular one, i.e., the sum total of digits of the preceding numbers, beginning with one. It is a perfect number and is often considered the first "counting" number. Like the number two it increases by

1. Although I attempt to describe the qualities of the various number continua in terms of their orderly succession in the number series, I do not mean to imply that they appear or develop solely in this sequence. It seems to me far more likely that the dynamics of the archetypes manifest themselves in completely individual numerical formations. In other words, the latter are essentially related to the contents of specific archetypes. As Jung observed, all quaternary numbers, for instance, are essentially bound up in a qualitative way with the symbols of the process of "becoming conscious of wholeness," and triadic numbers are similarly connected with the principles of intellectual and physical movement. All single numbers—quite apart from their position in the number series—are direct manifestations of the one-continuum. They do not presuppose the existence of preceding numbers, but rather imply them. Each in its own right is an "archetypal ordering factor." A comparison of preceding and succeeding numerals in the number series is only advisable when we attempt to become conscious of their individual functional qualities through discursive thought processes. In principle this step is not necessary.

multiplication, and no so-called perfect or defective number can possess the factors of two and three simultaneously. All uneven, nondefective numbers of the third and fourth order always contain the factor three.[2] Addition of the first three numbers, $1 + 2 + 3$, yields the same result (6) as does their multiplication.

Jung gives a psychological description of the qualitative three-continuum in "Psychology and Religion," in his portrayal of the tension between "the One and the Other," of which I would like to repeat the following part:

> But every tension of opposites culminates in a release, out of which comes the "third." In the third, the tension is resolved and the lost unity is restored. Unity, the absolute One, cannot be numbered, it is indefinable and unknowable; only when it appears as a unit, the number one, is it knowable, for the "Other" which is required for this act of knowing is lacking in the condition of the One. Three is an unfolding of the One to a condition where it can be known—unity become recognizable; had it not been resolved into the polarity of the One and the Other, it would have remained fixed in a condition devoid of every quality.[3]

Accordingly, the number three stands behind dynamic actualizations of the one-continuum in time-space dimensions and in our consciousness. The Chinese concept of number provides us with a parallel to Jung's description of the three-continuum. Marcel Granet outlines it as follows:

> The Unity cannot be One, because it is the Whole, and cannot be distinguished from Two, for it resorbs in itself

2. Cf. O. Gmelin, "Über vollkommene und befreundete Zahlen" (Dissertation, University of Halle a. S., 1917), pp. 15 ff.

3. Jung continues: "The relation of threeness to oneness can be expressed by an equilateral triangle, $A = B = C$, that is, by the identity of the three, threeness being contained in its entirety in each of the three angles. This intellectual idea of the equilateral triangle is a conceptual model for the logical image of the Trinity" ("A Psychological Approach to the Trinity," *Psychology and Religion, CW*, Vol. XI, ¶ 180 (end).

all contrasting aspects, opposing and uniting with one another, such as right and left, high and low, in front and behind, round and square, the ensemble of Yang and Yin. Every ensemble, Unity, and Pair, the Whole, when one wishes to express it in a numerical form, is to be found in all the uneven numbers beginning with the number three (1 plus 2).[4]

The number series thus begins with three.[5]

Modifying the alchemical saying, already quoted, about the emergence of the four, we can also say of the number three: Out of one comes two, but from the pairing of these two comes the third.[6] The "progression" takes place retrogressively here too, by relating our thoughts back to the unity and hypostatizing the latter to a new content of consciousness. In electronic methods of calculating, the step from two to three has similarly been realized in order to achieve more exact results. In order, for example, not to confuse 36 with 63, a third column is introduced in the form of a central axis inserted between the two members of the pair.[7] In relation to this axis the various members cannot turn right or left at will. This axis sets up a positional relation to the original unity and signifies at the same time the number three's "moment of birth."[8]

Taken as rhythm or dynamism, three thus introduces a directional element into the oscillatory rhythm of two,

---

4. Marcel Granet, *La Pensée chinoise* (Paris, 1968), p. 239, 233.

5. In China three is therefore the symbol of "unanimity," just as in the West we assert that the Trinity represents "perfect harmony," an aspect particularly emphasized in the image of the Holy Ghost as the *vinculum amoris* (love bond).

6. The Son proceeds from the Father; the Unity of Father and Son is the *vinculum amoris,* and this constitutes the Holy Ghost, the Third.

7. The model is derived from N. Wiener and C. Kuratowski and is given by W. U. Quine in "The Foundations of Mathematics," *Scientific American,* CCXI, no. 3 (September, 1964), 115.

8. Which in this case is not produced by the addition of another unity but by referring back to the one, or by a more exact discernment of the two's position in relation to the one.

whereby spatial and temporal parameters can be formed. This step involves the interference of an observing consciousness, which inserts a symmetrical axis into the two-rhythm, or else "counts" the latter's temporal and spatial succession. In terms of content the number three therefore serves as the symbol of a dynamic process.[9] In the mythological productions of the unconscious psyche, underworld divinities are particularly likely to appear in triadic form.[10] According to Jung, they represent *the flow of psychic energy*,[11] indicating a *connection with time and fate*.[12] During the course of his quest the hero of myths and fairy tales frequently arrives at three identical or relatively similar intermediatory situations or places (he meets three hermits or witches, or goes to the sun, moon, and night wind, for instance),[13] followed by the decisive climax of action at a fourth station. Such triadic situations or locations thus indicate the dynamic flow of events.

9. R. Allendy, *Le Symbolisme des nombres* (Paris, 1948), pp. 41–43, points out: "Three definitely is the dynamic principle itself," and " 'three,' says Balzac, 'is the formula of all creation.' " Ibn Gabriol says: "The One is not the root of the whole, for the One is only form and the whole is form *and* matter combined, but three is the root of the whole for the One symbolizes form and two represents matter." In the tarot cards the number three is the Empress.

10. More triadic examples may be found in W. Kirfel, *Die dreiköpfige Gottheit* (Bonn, 1940), D. Nielsen, *Der dreieinige Gott* (Copenhagen and London, 1922), and F. Kretschmar, *Kerberos und Hundestammvater* (Stuttgart, 1938), *passim*, to mention but a few.

11. *Seminar über Kinderträume*, E.T.H. Lectures (Zurich, 1938–39), p. 144.

12. For instance the three Norns, three Parcae, three Gorgons, three Hecates, etc., the god Trimurti, or Brahmā-Vishnu-Siva, and others. According to Jamblich three is the number of the Demiurge. Further triads may be found in V. F. Hopper, *Medieval Number Symbolism* (New York, 1939), pp. 5 ff. The sex of the three figures represented can vary. In the oldest form of Pythagoreanism, for instance, the interpretation was that 1 = nous, 2 = man, 3 = woman, in contradistinction to other systems where the values were 1 = father, 2 = mother, 3 = son. See P. Kucharski, *Etude sur la doctrine pythagoricienne de la tétrade* (Paris, 1952).

13. For examples see H. von Beit, *Symbolik des Märchens*, 2d ed. (Bern, 1960), I, 785.

These triadic structures of gods and mythological figures fall into two main categories: either they consist of three identical equally important figures (such as three Parcae, etc.: see n. 12) or a constellation of *one* main figure flanked by two companions (such as Christ between the two thieves or Mithras flanked by the Dadophores). The first category represents more the preconscious dynamism of the archetype, the second, a realization of the unity of its inner opposites[14] and the emergence of the one in time-space, or consciousness. This is the reason that, among certain American Indians, the word for "three" also means the "center of one." [15]

The I Ching oracle, whose rudiments, as already explained, originated in the "revelations" of lowly vertebrates, symbolizing the unconscious, is based on a double constellation of triple lines (e.g., ☷ ☵ ☶ ☳ ☰). Eight possible arrangements result from combinations of these triple lines, known as the *pa-kua*. They depict the basic structures of the whole of existence. Where they are doubled into a hexagram they signify sixty-four possible aspects of the *unus mundus*. One cannot escape the impression that these numerical combinations are introspective representations of fundamental processes in our psychophysical nature; indeed, the modern science of genetics has discovered that the biological genetic code of deoxyribonucleic acid (DNA) consists of *four bases* (adenine A, thymine T, guanine G, and cytosine C) combined into three. These groups constitute the code for building up the twenty amino acids that form all our bodily proteins.[16] From the four bases ($4^3 =$) sixty-four different triplets come

14. All the logical synthetic steps of three phases are based on this schema.

15. Among the Nez Percé and Shahaptian Indians. See E. Fettweis, *Das Rechnen der Naturvölker* (Leipzig, 1927), p. 61.

16. See W. Botsch, *Morsealphabet des Lebens* (Stuttgart, 1965), p. 57. It has, however, not yet been explained how these sixty-four triplets are combined into the twenty amino acids; it is possible that an amino acid possesses several triplets.

into being. Information of the genetic code is passed on by the so-called messenger RNA to the ribosomes of the cells saturated with ribonucleic acid. These cells are constructed similarly to deoxyribonucleic acid.[17]

The messenger RNA likewise uses triplets to form the basic figures of its code.[18] In these genetic findings we are confronted with an exchange of "information" in living cells that corresponds exactly to the structure of I Ching hexagrams.

This astonishing correspondence seems, more than any other evidence, to substantiate Jung's hypothesis that number regulates both psyche and matter. The same numerical model, a pattern underlying the basic processes of human memory and transmission (and thereby also the substratum of our entire conscious processes), has been discovered, first in China through an introspective examination of the unconscious psyche, and then in the West through genetic research into the living cell.

In "neutral" language, therefore, three signifies a unity which dynamically engenders self-expanding linear irreversible processes in matter and in our consciousness (e.g., discursive thought). With the number three, as Karl Menninger formulates it, the step toward the capacity to count, and toward the processes of defining numerical results, is actually achieved in consciousness. He says:

> With three something new in the concept of number makes its appearance. In the I-You situation the ego is

17. In contrast to the DNA, the RNA contains uracil (instead of thymine) as its fourth basic element. Ribose is a simple sugar possessing one oxygen atom more than deoxyribose. I am much indebted to Dr. Alfred Ribi for this information. Cf. Botsch, *Morsealphabet*, p. 63 and (better) G. and M. Beadle, *The Language of Life* (New York, 1966), pp. 154 ff. Mr. Fowler McCormick kindly recommended and procured this book for me. See also C. Bresch and R. Hausmann, *Klassische und molekulare Genetik*, 2d ed. (Berlin, 1970), p. 243. I owe the knowledge of this book to the kindness of Mr. H. P. Novak.

18. Botsch, *Morsealphabet*, p. 64. This basic sequence of the messenger RNA is probably the exact negative of the DNA chain, which is conceived of as a double helix.

still held in tension with the You, but that which is above it, It, the Third, the Many, is the world. This thesis, in which the psychic, the linguistic, and the numerical come together, might serve as a rather vague paraphrase of early man's conception of number. One—two—many, is it not mirrored exactly in the numerical forms of the substantives singular, dual, plural?[19]

Three is the "beyond," the "trans-." An attempt has been made to bring together *tres-*, "three," and the Latin *trans*, "across" (the participle of *trare*, "to penetrate, permeate");[20] compare *intrare*, "to invade, pierce, penetrate" (German *eindringen*), in relation to the French *trois* and *tres-*, and the English "three" and "through," etc. In many forms of writing, a plurality is indicated by three strokes.

> The step to three is a step over the dark threshold, prior to which number was still deeply rooted in the psychic, a step out into the sober but clear light of objectivity. Number's power to segregate elements is thereby weakened, namely, its capacity to lend an individual character to things. But in exchange its power to construct a useful system of unimagined range in the form of the number series increases.[21]

Nevertheless, three is still used as an adjective, which expresses its particular quality of unity. Although a relative step toward the formation of the number series and the possibility of realizing a quantitative plurality is accomplished by the number three, in many respects it clearly maintains its oneness. Numerous medieval speculations concerning the Trinity, as well as Maria Prophetissa's aphorism undeniably prove this.[22]

19. *Zahlwort und Ziffer: Eine Kulturgeschichte der Zahl* (Göttingen, 1958), pp. 27 ff.

20. See Tobias Dantzig, *Number: The Language of Science* (New York, 1954), p. 5.

21. Menninger, *Zahlwort und Ziffer*, p. 29.

22. Joannes Mennens, for instance, adds matter to the Trinity as a fourth element. "Nomen itaque Dei quadriliteram sanctam Trinitatem designare videtur et *materiam* quae etiam triplex existit . . . quae

The idea of connecting spatial and temporal succession with the number three and double three (six) can perhaps best be illustrated by the dream of a modern physicist. On the eve of the dream he was amusing himself in arranging various schemata of his life. He depicted them in the form of a double triangle (star of David) on whose points he inscribed the essential elements of his inner life. He then dreamt:

> A Chinese woman (elevated to the rank of a "Sophia") is present with two men. I am the fourth. She says to me: "You must allow us to play every conceivable combination of chess." In a subsequent half-waking fantasy she announced to the dreamer, in a numinous voice: "In your drawings one element is perfectly correct and another transitory and false. It is correct that the lines number six, but it is false to draw six points. See here—" and I saw:

a square with clearly marked off diagonals. "Can you see now finally the four and the six? Four spatial points and six lines or six pairs out of four points. They are the same six lines that exist in the I Ching. There the six, containing three as a latent factor, are correct. Now observe the square more closely: four of the lines are of equal length, the other two are longer—they are "irrationally related." There is *no* figure with four points and six equal lines. *For this reason symmetry cannot be statically produced and a dance results.* The *coniunctio* refers to the exchange

et umbra eius dicitur et a Moyse posteriora Dei" (*Theatrum Chemicum*, ed. L. Zetzner [Frankfurt, 1622], V, 334). (The four letters of the name of God seem to signify the Trinity plus matter, which also forms a triplet . . . it is called God's shadow or (by Moses) God's posterior.)

of places during this dance. One can also speak of a game or rhythms and rotations. *Therefore the three, already contained in a latent form in the square, must be dynamically expressed.*[23]

The most significant aspects of this dream will become self-explanatory in the context of the following chapter, which is devoted to the number four and Jung's double pyramidic model of the Self. For now it is important to note the emphasis on the number three, or six, as the figure of a dynamic process enabling the totality symbol to manifest itself, in all its latent possibilities, in a temporal succession so that it does not congeal into a static symmetry or harmony.

In a study of the possible cyclic relations of objects of a class of similarities, Wolf von Engelhardt very significantly identifies six extension relations.[24] This double-triplet structure also seems to be of particular importance for spatial classification.

Even if the six inner relations could, perhaps, be reduced to three[25] (since in a way two of them are really identical), we would still be dealing with an illustration of the relationship between the number three or double-three and describable extensions in space, in contrast to the above examples which are more concerned with temporal extensions. Threefold rhythms are most probably connected with processes in space and time or with their realization in consciousness. In physics also one of the most important groups is that

23. Report of the dreamer in my possession. The statement that there is no figure with four points and six equal lines is only valid for two-dimensional structures. The number six, as is well known, possesses the following characteristic: its aliquot elements (1, 2, 3), taken together, yield the number itself. Other than the "perfect" number six, all product numbers of the second order are so-called defective numbers, i.e., numbers the sum of whose factors is less than the duplication of the said number. See Gmelin, "Vollkommene Zahlen," p. 15.
24. "Sinn und Begriff der Symmetrie," *Studium generale*, VI, no. 9 (1953), 524 ff.
25. As was pointed out to me by Prof. Konrad Voss.

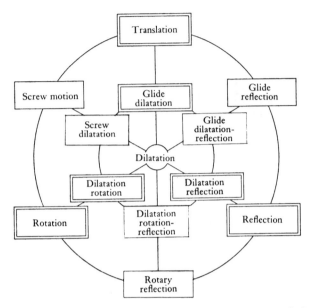

Schema of positional space relations. The relations of the outer ring contain identity as their inner relation. The relations of the inner ring contain dilatation. Dilatation itself is a purely inner relation. [Source: W. von Engelhardt, "Sinn und Begriff der Symmetrie," *Studium generale*, VI, no. 9 (1953), 524, reproduced by permission of Springer Verlag and W. von Engelhardt.]

of rotations in six dimensions. There are fifteen independent planes of rotation in six-dimensional space (corresponding to the three independent planes of rotation in three-dimensional space). If the ex officio element of each group is added, we have a structural group of sixteen elements, or six sets of five (pentads), each member being associated in conjugate pairs.[26]

Another allusion to the dynamic structure of the number three is to be found in kymatology, the field of empirical

26. Sir Arthur Eddington, *The Philosophy of Physical Science* (Cambridge, 1939), pp. 140–41.

research into macrophysical oscillation and wave phenomena. Concerning his endeavors in this field, Hans Jenny concludes that

> Structural moments always occur during an oscillation process and a kinetic effect, just as kinetic and dynamic processes do; and the whole exhibits a periodic character. . . . The three domains—the periodic as basic element along with the two poles of structure and dynamic—invariably appear as one. They are unimaginable without one another.[27]

This threefold unity of structure, dynamics, and periodicity, which Jenny considers to lie at the basis of kymatology, provides a further illustration of the archetype of three, and in it once again three's dynamic element is of decisive importance.

27. Hans Jenny, *Kymatik* (Basel, 1967), p. 176.

.

CHAPTER SEVEN

The Number Four as the One-Continuum's Model of Wholeness in All Relatively Closed Structures of Human Consciousness and in the Body

Considered formally, four is the first nonprime numeral of the number series, namely the first square number and the first of all power numbers (2^2). It represents the sum of

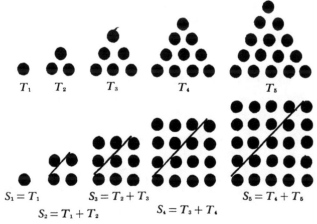

$$S_1 = T_1 \qquad S_3 = T_2 + T_3 \qquad S_5 = T_4 + T_5$$
$$S_2 = T_1 + T_2 \qquad S_4 = T_3 + T_4$$

[Source: Tobias Dantzig, *Number: The Language of Science,* © 1930, 1933, 1939, 1954 by The Macmillan Company, reproduced by permission of Macmillan Publishing Co., Inc., and George Allen and Unwin Ltd.]

the first two triangular numbers $(1 + 3)$, and thus inaugurates the law of sequence $S = T_1 + T_2$.[1]

The famous Pythagorean tetractys consists of the sum of 1, 2, 3, and 4 $(= 10)$.[2] Every square number can be divided by four, resulting in no remainder or a remainder of one,[3] and conversely, if the prime number factors of N_0 are two or possess the form $4n + 1$, every ordinary natural number can be represented by two square numbers. Lagrange demonstrated that every natural number can be represented as the sum of four squares at the most.[4] In Euclidean geometry four points produce the first three-dimensional body. In physics the quaternions of Hamilton and Jakobi are used to control the rules for rotating a rigid body in space.[5] We can take a step toward the qualitative approach with the mathematical declaration that equations beyond the fourth degree can no longer be solved by radicals.[6] The number four thus signifies (as Menninger points out) a peculiar border number.[7] This boundary aspect of the number four is reflected in many figures of speech. Many languages, for instance, possess a trial and quaternal case beyond the dual, but never more.[8] Also, in all languages the numerals up to four are

1. See Tobias Dantzig, *Number: The Language of Science* (New York, 1954), p. 43, and Philip J. Davis, *The Lore of Large Numbers* (New York, 1961), p. 92.

2. See P. Kucharski, *Etude sur la doctrine pythagoricienne de la tétrade* (Paris, 1952).

3. See Oystein Ore, *Number Theory and Its History* (New York, Toronto, and London, 1948), pp. 31, 270.

4. Dantzig, *Number*, p. 22, and Ore, *Number Theory*, pp. 198–99.

5. See Hermann Weyl, *Philosophy of Mathematics and Natural Science* (Princeton, N.J., 1949), p. 32. W. R. Hamilton is one of the inventors, together with J. J. Sylvester and A. Cayley, of the matrix concept. For the description of the product of two complex numbers through i, i^2, i^3, i^4 and $\sqrt{1}$, -1, $-i$, $+1$, etc., see Dantzig, *Number*, p. 180.

6. See E. Kramer, *The Main Stream of Mathematics* (New York, 1951), p. 289. Evariste Galois demonstrates this by means of group theory. Another proof of the same fact was produced by the Norwegian Abel.

7. Karl Menninger, *Zahlwort und Ziffer: Eine Kulturgeschichte der Zahl* (Göttingen, 1958), pp. 33–34.

8. *Ibid.*, pp. 21–22.

etymologically formed as adjectives, but never higher ones.[9] Latin *octo*, "eight," refers to the dual case (of four), and in German *neun*, "nine," is related to "new": one begins "anew." [10] In Czech one says that $1 + 1$ *are* 2, $2 + 2$ *are* 4, but $2 + 3$ *is* 5 (beyond five the singular verb is used). Only beginning with number five do we find, as Menninger states, genuine "empty" numbers, detached from their objects.[11] Up to the number four, the archaic character of the number concept has been tenaciously preserved.[12]

Since Jung devoted practically the whole of his life's work to demonstrating the vast psychological significance of the number four, I must refer the reader to his writings in this connection. I can only touch on several essential aspects of his work here. The fact that mankind's repeated attempts to establish an orientation toward wholeness possess a quaternary structure appears to correspond to an archetypal psychic structural predisposition in man. For spatial orientation we divide the compass into four or eight points. In all models of the universe and concepts of the divine, from sources as widely separated as the Chinese, the North and South American Indian, the Asiatic Indian, the Incan and Mayan, and such cultures as pre-Christian antiquity and the Mediterranean, a fourfold structure dominates. In the Middle Ages of our culture the number four remained—in spite of the Trinity—*the* number of the elements, aggregate states, alchemical steps, temperaments, and so forth.

Minkowski's and Einstein's four-dimensional model of the universe makes its appearance in present-day theoretical physics. It is also generally accepted today that there are only four distinct forces in nature: the nuclear, the electrical, the weak (beta decay) interaction, and the gravitational.[13] Sir Arthur Eddington likewise assumes four di-

9. *Ibid.*, pp. 33 f.   10. *Ibid.*, p. 34.   11. *Ibid.*, p. 36.

12. After the fourth child the Romans bestowed no further personal names on their children—they merely counted them: Quintus, Sextus, Septimus, Octavius, etc. (*ibid.*, p. 36).

13. Formulation by Professor Byers Brown. See also Ernst Anrich, *Moderne Physik und Tiefenpsychologie* (Stuttgart, 1963), pp. 514 f.

mensionless constants of nature.[14] Dirac showed that to satisfy both quantum mechanics and relativity, the electron must be described by a wave vector with four components, and this automatically explains electron spin and the positron.[15] If four different coins are laid on a table the operation of combining them into pairs (inclusive and exclusive of their obverse or reverse positions) constitutes the same group structure described above as rotation in six dimensions. In geometry the same pattern also results from so-called Kummerian quartic areas, in the theory of the theta functions, and last but not least, in the specification of elementary particles in their base states, including charge and spin, described above.[16]

Even in purely technical matters the number four serves the function of a numerical boundary. For the "error-free transmission of information" one uses a Galois field consisting of four elements: 0, 1, A, B (whereby $A-B$ can represent any required content, coupled with the binary basis 0–1).[17]

14. *The Philosophy of Physical Science* (Cambridge, 1939), p. 58, by the elimination of our three arbitrary units of measurement, which accordingly yielded seven constants.

15. See also A. Lautmann, *Symétrie et dissymétrie en mathématiques et physique* (Paris, 1946), p. 12. The fourfold vectors of electric current in complex fields, which vanish identically in real fields, should be mentioned here. Cf. Wolfgang Pauli, "Naturwissenschaftliche und erkenntnistheoretische Aspekte der Ideen vom Unbewussten,"*Aufsätze und Vorträge über Physik und Erkenntnistheorie* (Brunswick, 1961), p. 139.

16. Eddington, *Physical Science*, p. 141.

17. The figure on the left is used for addition, that on the right for multiplication.

	0	1	A	B
0	0	1	A	B
1	1	0	B	A
A	A	B	0	1
B	B	A	1	0

	0	1	A	B
0	0	0	0	0
1	0	1	A	B
A	0	A	B	1
B	0	B	1	A

[Source: W. W. Sawyer, "Algebra," *Scientific American* (September, 1964), p. 78, copyright © 1964 by Scientific American, Inc. All rights reserved.]

Control by four is the sharp boundary for complete transmission of information.[18] Lastly, we must recall that the
triple codes of the genetic substance DNA and memory
substance RNA are built up on a *quaternio* of bases which
can be combined in $4^3 = 64$ variations.[19]

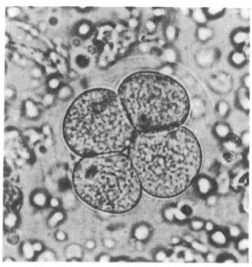

The quaternary structure of the morula, after a male gamete
has met the female oozyte [Source: Cover photo, *Selecta*
6, Vol. XIII (February 8, 1971), reproduced by permission
of Schering AG.]

Quaternally structured "information" also turns up in an
age-old tradition. The Islamic technique of geomancy (possibly originating in India), which spread throughout Europe and as far as West Africa, depends on a quaternary
system. Since this technique is not generally known, a brief
description of it follows. The oracle is determined by dividing pebbles, nuts, and similar material into arbitrary rows

18. Cf. W. W. Sawyer, "Algebra," *Scientific American*, CCII, no.
3 (September, 1964), p. 78.
19. See above pp. 105–6). Pauli made the amusing suggestion that this
would have warmed the heart of every ancient Pythagorean!

of points. The geomancer (working from right to left) lays out four rows of dots, arbitrarily selected on an unconscious basis. He then subtracts pairs from these four rows until he is left with a remainder of one or two dots. This operation is repeated sixteen times. In this manner, four figures, called *matres*, "mothers," take shape.[20] The arrangement of dots in

the first "mother" is then used, counting from top to bottom, to construct the top lines of four *filiae*, "daughters." The lines of the second "mother" go to make up the second line of the four daughters, and so on. From the "daughters," *nepotes*, "nephews," are built up.[21] Ultimately the points of the ninth, tenth, eleventh, and twelfth figures are combined in a similar manner to obtain two witness figures (*testes*), who, when paired, result in the decisive figure of the *iudex* or "judge." The single figures are qualitatively associated with astrological symbols in order to make a "reading" of the situation possible.

This divinatory technique survived not only in Islamic North Africa and the West African coast, but was also widespread in Europe. One of its final advocates, Robert Fludd, developed a noteworthy "explanation" of the process. Conrad Josten recently called attention to its psychological significance.[22] According to Fludd, man's soul possesses, beyond the powers of conscious intellect and reason,

20. In doing this he is not supposed to count them consciously. A good example of this technique may be found in Conrad Josten, "Robert Fludd's Theory of Geomancy and His Experiences at Avignon in the Winter of 1601 to 1602," *Journal of the Warburg and Courtauld Institute*, XXVII (1964), 327 ff.
21. One pairs the first and second "mothers" and subsequently one pairs the first, second, third, and fourth "daughters."
22. Josten, "Robert Fludd's Theory," pp. 327 ff.

a *mens* (the higher intelligence of the unconscious) which rules like a king over the remaining partial functions. For the most part these functions know nothing of its mysterious motives. This *mens* in man consists of the same essence as the divine spirit, and elevates the *mens humana* through its rays to the heights of true prophecy.[23] The human *mens* can, however, operate without divine assistance through geomantic procedures. This means, of course, that we can only estimate the workings of the *mens* empirically and *ex effectu*. Fludd calls this center of action in the soul "unitatem et ipsius mentis punctum" (!) It can only be attained by abandoning the body in a state of ecstasy. In this central point, in the *unitas*, lies the knowledge that is revealed in geomancy.

I mention this theory only because it approaches a psychological interpretation of this phenomenon. Fludd goes so far as to say that in the number and proportion of points to the sixteen signs a prophetic message of the soul lies concealed, which only secondarily takes shape in astrological signs.[24] The hand movements which generate the points are therefore not fortuitous; they proceed from the soul, the true essence of man.

In our context only the numerical structure is important. In geomancy it consists of the quaternios of single figures,[25] which are completed in a threefold step (two *testes* plus one *iudex*). The total number of figures is fifteen (the symmetry number of the Chinese Lo-shu model). The sum total of possibilities is 256 (or else 240). The figures are arranged in either of the forms shown on p. 120.[26]

The binary arithmetical basis, which corresponds to the I Ching, and the predominance of the numbers three and four

23. This is a variation of the *intellectus activus* (*nous poiētikos*) in God and the *intellectus passivus* in man, employed in Scholasticism.

24. Cf. Josten, "Robert Fludd's Theory," p. 329.

25. Not triadic, as in the I Ching, probably because the "movement" is undertaken by the interrogator himself.

26. See, for instance, F. Hartmann, *Geomancy* (London, 1913), p. 53.

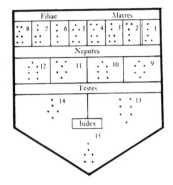
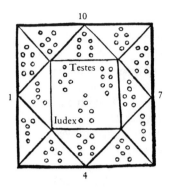

[Source: *left*, Conrad Josten, "Robert Fludd's Theory of Geomancy and His Experiences at Avignon in the Winter of 1601–1602," *Journal of the Warburg and Courtauld Institute*, XXVII (1964), reproduced with permission from the Warburg Institute and Dr. Conrad Josten; *right*, F. Hartmann, *Geomancy* (London, 1913), revised by the author.]

are of chief importance. Indeed, Western technique proceeds from the number four in order to arrive at a triadic figure of "judgment," while the East proceeds from the three in order to reach a quaternary model for a result.[27] Their complementary relationship in this area is probably bound up with the more general phenomena of the complementary outlook of the two cultures. It is as if we are more inclined to ask the unknown "What shall I *do?*," while the East prefers the question: "To what total order does my conduct belong?"

In China the number five possesses the same significance as four does with us, because it is taken to represent the centered four (⦂•⦂). This concept is also found in the West, in the alchemical idea of the *quinta essentia*. The *quinta essentia* is not additively joined onto the first four as a fifth element, but represents the most refined, spiritually imag-

27. Two so-called nuclear trigrams are contained within the two trigrams of each sign, which means that one must take four trigrams into account in every sign. At the beginning of our era the Chinese scholar Yang Hsiung tried to evolve a new form of the I Ching, in which the signs consisted of tetragrams (four lines) (T'ai Hsuan Ching, "The Classic of the Great Dark"). See H. Wilhelm, *Change: Eight Lectures on the I Ching* (London, 1960), p. 86.

inable unity of the four elements. It is either initially present in and extracted from them or produced by the circulation of these elements among one another. Whereas the pentagon

with its five angles geometrizes the number five in its quantitative and additive form, the quintessence is represented by the quincunx ( ) as the center of four. Jung says of the quincunx:

> The four [forms], as it were, a frame for the one, ac-
> centuated as the centre. . . . By unfolding into four it
> acquires distinct characteristics and can therefore be known.
> . . . So long as a thing is in the unconscious it has no
> recognizable qualities and is consequently merged with
> the universal unknown, with the unconscious All and
> Nothing, with what the Gnostics called a "non-existent
> all-being." But as soon as the unconscious content enters
> the sphere of consciousness it has already split into the
> "four," that is to say it can become an object of experience
> only by virtue of the four basic functions of conscious-
> ness. It is *perceived* as something that exists (sensation);
> it is *recognized* as this and *distinguished* from that (think-
> ing); it is *evaluated* as pleasant or unpleasant, etc. (feeling);
> and finally, intuition tells us where it came from and where
> it is going. . . . The splitting into four has the same
> significance as the division of the horizon into four quar-
> ters, or the year into four seasons. That is, through the
> act of becoming conscious the four basic aspects of a
> whole judgment are rendered visible.[28]

Jung goes on to say that it is naturally possible for the intellect to devise additional means of viewing a subject, but
the four mentioned appear to constitute the fundamental
minimum means for subdividing and thus classifying the
circle or wholeness.

Traditionally, the number one has been geometrically

28. C. G. Jung, "Flying Saucers: A Modern Myth," *Civilization in Transition*, CW, Vol. X, ¶ 774.

linked with the point, two with the line, three with the plane surface, and, as we have already seen, four has, since Plato, been equated with the body in Euclidean space. But it seems to me that we should bear another, inverted, retrograde apportionment in mind, in which one as unity *and* wholeness corresponds to the nondimensional point and to the infinite dimensional space. Two would then correspond to Hilbert's space,[29] as well as to all matrices of double sequences and all geometries constructed out of points and straight lines with an incidence relationship (by which means geometry must contain an infinity of elements). Three would correspond to all ordered sets, and four to all finite mathematical structures, such as finite groups, as well as to compact topological spaces.[30]

The difficult step from three to four would, according to this hypothesis, also be the progression from the infinitely conceivable to finite reality, and this agrees with Jung's psychological explanation of the step.[31] The incommensurability of three dimensions to the fourth and the latter's asymmetry are based on the inclusion (no longer avoidable) of the observer in his *wholeness* within the framework of his processes of understanding. These processes are based on individual experience occurring in a particular and distinctive way. But their results are not unalloyed subjectivity, insofar as the realizations taking place are fashioned not only out of the subject's ego but out of his "objective" psychic wholeness, which participates in the surroundings and in the actual moment of time.

29. The vectors of Hilbert's space are an infinite series of real numbers, whose quadratic sums are convergent. (See further W. I. Smirnow, *Lehrgang der höheren Mathematik* [Berlin, 1964], II, 137.) As opposed to an all-dimensional space Hilbert's space possesses *one* limitation.

30. Interestingly enough, the so-called "law of rationality" or "law of zones" in crystallography says that *four* surfaces, or their associated vectors, suffice to derive all other possible surfaces and vectors. See P. Niggli, "Symmetrieprinzip und Naturwissenschaften," *Studium generale*, II, nos. 4–5 (1949), 228–29.

31. But not with Plato's.

The great significance of the quincunx, the centered four, may be reexamined in its primal form in ancient Chinese number theory, where five stands in the *center* of the first number series, 1, 2, 3, 4, 5, 6, 7, 8, 9 (before ten). For this reason it occupies the center position in the Ho-t'u and Lo-

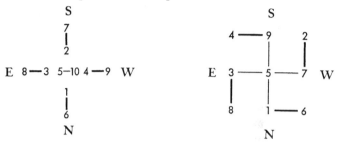

Left, the Ho-t'u model; *right*, the Lo-shu model [Source: Marcel Granet, *La Pensée chinoise*, © Albin Michel 1936, 1968, Collection Evolution de l'humanité, p. 164.]

shu number diagrams already described. In China the number five stands for the element of the earth carrying and centering all things at the center of the foundations of existence. The yellow color ascribed to this earth center characterizes it, nonetheless, as a spiritual principle, not as the concrete soil of the earth. It is the principle of *k'un*, the expanding feminine, which brings the spirit into material and spatial manifestation. It stands at the center of quaternary mandala structures. The primal one made manifest, and its progressive ordering effect on the number hierarchy, is also recognizable in the number fifty as a symbol "de la grande expansion." [32]

Five is the center of four. [33] The rectangle represents the totality of the kingdom and every temple, [34] and was utilized for army encampments as well as town plans. From another

32. Marcel Granet, *La Pensée chinoise* (Paris, 1968), pp. 168 f., 217, 241, 253 f.
33. 1 = water = North, 2 = fire = South, 3 = wood = East, 4 = earth = West, 5 in the center.
34. Granet, *Pensée chinoise*, p. 81.

point of view five represents merely the center of the first decade's uneven numbers: 1, 3, 5, 7, 9, while six stands for the center of the even ones: 2, 4, 6, 8, 10. Because of this eleven is considered to be the number of the Way of Tao; as the sum of five and six it unites the two centers "like a gnomon or a tree raised up in the center of the cosmos." [35] As an image this tree symbol points once again to a "realization," or the coming to consciousness of an individual, which occurs through personality growth.

From this angle the number four constitutes a "field" with an internal closed rhythmical movement that proceeds to fan out from the center one into four and contracts back again to the center. The Chinese Ho-t'u model may be taken as an illustration of this "field." If the starting point and the end point of the field are separately calculated, the result is a series of double pyramids, a structure dealt with in the dream quoted in the last chapter. This form is connected with a mathematical model of the archetype of wholeness, which Jung elaborates in *Aion.* We shall discuss it more fully later on.

The numerical rhythms one, two, three, and four, described in the last chapter, indeed appear to manifest themselves as delineating structures when combined with all sorts of psychic contents, *but they acquire an especially decisive significance when they appear as the structural characteristics of the Self symbol,* in the form of cosmic models and divine symbols. According to the manner in which these images are specifically associated with the numbers one, two, three, and four, they become bound up with specific psychic attitudes toward reality, which correspond to certain levels of consciousness. In his paper on the Trinity, Jung describes the first three of these steps in detail: [36] at the level of one, man still naïvely participates in his surroundings in a state of uncritical unconsciousness, submitting to things as they

35. *Ibid.,* p. 166.
36. *Psychology and Religion,* CW, Vol. XI, ¶¶ 269 ff.

are. At the level of two, on the other hand, a dualistic world-
and God-image gives rise to tension, doubt, and criticism of
God, life, nature, and oneself. The condition of three by
comparison denotes insight, the rise of consciousness, and
the rediscovery of unity on a higher level; in a word, gnosis
and knowledge. But no final goal is reached by this step, for
"trinitarian" thinking lacks a further dimension; it is flat,
intellectual, and consequently encourages intolerant and absolute declarations.[37] The "eternal" character and "absolute
validity" of certain archetypal structures is certainly recognized, but ego consciousness assumes the role of their herald.
From this standpoint one overlooks the fact that although
these structures may well be timeless and eternal in the unconscious, they become modified when they make the transition into the field of individual consciousness. They become
transient contents suffering various personally conditioned
limitations.[38]

By granting absolute validity, within the framework of
trinitarian thought, to a realization, we overlook the fact
that an element shining forth as a "timeless structure" in the
unconscious has been reconstructed through discursive
thought processes, and, in this process, became temporally
conditioned. This is the reason why in number symbolism
three is so often connected with time. The elements of our
understanding become irreversible by entering time. One
cannot, for instance, prove the Pythagorean theorem by
starting with its conclusions. The transition of an unconscious content into our time-bound consciousness involves a
diminution of the primal forms simultaneously comprehended, and precisely because of this it is erroneous to
evaluate our insights by naïvely attributing eternal validity

37. The formalistic direction in mathematical thought corresponds
to this step, for example. So does Platonic philosophy, Descartes's
work, and existential philosophy, to mention a few instances.
38. For instance, Poincaré "saw" in a flash the whole derivation
of the theta-fuchsian functions in his "subconscient," but his description of these functions is a product of his discursive (temporal) conscious thinking.

to them. Though we realize the eternal character of a primal intuition in consciousness, we overlook the fact that this realization is a reconstruction reached by way of time-bound discursive mental processes which have no absolute validity.

When an individual becomes aware of this differentiation a transformation of consciousness results, in which the ego no longer identifies its insights with an "eternal" verity, but distances itself and becomes capable of comprehending the insight as only one of many possible revelations contained within the unknown psychic and universal background of existence. Instead of proclaiming absolute dogmas, a "quaternary" attitude of mind then develops which, more modestly, seeks to describe reality in a manner that will—if it is based on archetypal concepts—be understandable to others. One remains simultaneously aware of the fact that assumptions of the unconscious do indeed reflect outer or inner reality, but also that they are transformed, through their passage into consciousness, into constricted, time-bound language. They surrender their absolute validity and assume the character of approximations. It becomes evident that a psychological problem of considerable importance is constellated between the numbers three and four. Jung has dealt with the significant relationship between these two numbers at length in his writings.

Insofar as three (as we have seen) qualitatively illustrates a dynamic process, its retrograde connection to the primal one in the number four signifies a kind of rupture between the linear quantitative flow of the number series and the "wholeness" aspect of number, grasped strictly in a retrogressive way. The step from three to four acquires a particular significance, which Jung endeavored to portray using numerological and psychological testimonies. A well-known illustration of this step from antiquity can be found in Plato's *Timaeus*. The text runs:

> Hence the god, when he began to put together the body of the universe, set about making it of fire and earth. But

two things alone cannot be satisfactorily united without a third; for there must be some bond between them drawing them together. And of all bonds the best is that which makes itself and the terms it connects a unity in the fullest sense; and it is of the nature of a continued geometrical proportion to effect this most perfectly.[39]

According to Plato, the similarity of the relations of these numbers to one another brings about their unity. Plato follows up this point with a reflection that Jung declares to be of far-reaching psychological consequence:

If a simple pair of opposites, say fire and earth, are bound together by a mean [μέσον], and if this bond is a geometrical proportion, the *one* mean can only connect two plane figures, since two means are required to connect solids. . . . The two-dimensional connection is not yet a physical reality, for a plane without extension in the third dimension is only an abstract thought. If it is to become a physical reality, three dimensions and therefore two means are required.[40]

Two pairs of opposites, a *quaternio*, are therefore required to set up a bodily unity. Jung goes on to comment:

It is interesting to note that Plato begins by representing the union of opposites two-dimensionally, as an intellectual problem to be solved by thinking, but then comes to see that its solution does not add up to reality. In the former case we have to do with a self-subsistent triad, and in the latter with a quaternity. This was the dilemma that perplexed the alchemists for more than a thousand years, and . . . is also found in psychology as the opposition between the functions of consciousness, three of which are fairly well differentiated, while the fourth, undiffer-

39. Secs. 31B–32A. I am quoting from Jung, *Psychology and Religion*, ¶ 182. I assisted Jung in a translation of the text, which differs from Cornford's, and accordingly use our rendering. A geometrical proportion of the type mentioned here would be: 1 : 2 : 4 : 8, since one stands in the same ratio to two as two does to four and four does to eight, etc.
40. *Ibid.*

entiated, "inferior" function is undomesticated, unadapted, uncontrolled, and primitive. Because of its contamination with the collective unconscious, it possesses archaic and mystical qualities, and is the complete opposite of the most differentiated function.[41]

(In Plato's case we are confronted with the opposites of feeling and thinking.)[42]

The psychological and spiritual attitude corresponding to the problem of three and four is depicted by Jung in terms of the progressive development of consciousness from a purely imaginary standpoint on the world to one in which the observer experiences himself as a participant on the level of a thinking and *experiencing* being. From intellectual and theoretical generalizations, thinking proceeds in this manner to mental "realization." Jung describes the problem, as it applies to the thinker Plato, in the following terms:

> He had to content himself with the harmony of airy thought-structures that lacked weight, and with a paper surface that lacked depth. The step from three to four brought him sharply up against something unexpected and alien to his thought, something heavy, inert, and limited, which no μὴ ὄν and no "privatio boni" can conjure away or diminish. Even God's fairest creation is corrupted by it, and idleness, stupidity, malice, discontent, sickness, old age and death fill the glorious body of the "blessed god."[43]

(This is the form in which Plato extolled the cosmos.)

Medieval Christian trinitarian thought had this element in common with Platonic philosophy; it too sought to banish the problem of material reality along with the problem of evil and the sorrowful imperfections of reality.[44] For this reason certain medieval philosophers tried to include matter

41. *Psychology and Religion*, ¶ 184.
42. For more information on the theory of functions, see C. G. Jung, *Psychological Types*, *CW*, Vol. VI, *passim*.
43. *Psychology and Religion*, ¶ 185.
44. I must direct the reader to Jung's explanations in *Psychology and Religion* and in *Aion*, *CW*, Vol. IX, p. 2.

in the Trinity as God's fourth aspect.[45] In the field of personal psychology the problem, already mentioned, of the so-called inferior function provides another parallel. Jung says:

> Three of the four orienting functions are available to consciousness. This is confirmed by the psychological experience that a rational type, for instance, whose superior function is thinking [in the sense of intellect], has at his disposal one, or possibly two, auxiliary functions of an irrational nature, namely sensation (the "fonction du réel") and intuition (perception via the unconscious). His unconscious function will be feeling (evaluation), which remains in a retarded state and is contaminated with the unconscious. It refuses to come along with the others and often goes wildly off on its own. This peculiar dissociation is, it seems, a product of civilization, and it denotes a freeing of consciousness from any excessive attachment to the "spirit of gravity." . . . The connection with the earlier attitude is maintained because part of the personality remains behind in the previous situation; that is to say, it lapses into unconsciousness and starts building up the shadow.

The inferior function thus retains "the 'all or none' character of an instinct. . . . Thus it often happens that people who have an amazing range of consciousness know less about themselves than the veriest infant. . . ."[46]

It is therefore not surprising that the step from three to four involves particular difficulties, for it is bound up with painful insights. The step is portrayed in alchemistic tradition by Maria Prophetissa's famous axiom: "Out of the One comes Two, out of Two comes Three, and from the Third comes the One as the Fourth." Clearly, the four contains a powerful retrograde connection to the primal one. On the

---

45. Cf. Joannes Mennens who added matter to the Trinity, calling it "posteriora Dei" (behind of God), or David of Dinant who equated God with the *prima materia*. Examples in W. Preger, *Geschichte der deutschen Mystik im Mittelalter* (Aalen, 1962), I, 186 ff.

46. *Psychology and Religion*, ¶ 245.

artistic level this four-one relationship is very beautifully illustrated in the drawing of a modern Navajo Indian reproduced below. It is a representation of four goddesses: in counting their heads, four simple units result. But the series actually begins with the skirt of the fourth, so that one and four are identical; they frame and contain the other

Handicraft tile of the Tama Indian settlement [In the possession of the author, gift of Mrs. Marian Bayes.]

three figures. As the result of an inversion process, one simultaneously appears to be the fourth.[47] In other words, the primal one reappears as the fourth, while still retaining its original oneness. Among the natives of the Admiralty

47. Might it not be possible to discover the parallel physical process in so-called "click reactions"?

Islands the words for "four" and "one" are actually identical.[48] This "one" undoubtedly exhibits an asymmetrical quality in its relation to the preceding threeness,[49] as well as a curious *coincidentia oppositorum*.

In a curiously retrograde manner the number four brings us, once again, back to the *unus mundus*. As a consequence of the step to four, our mental processes no longer revolve about intellectual theorizations, but partake of the creative adventure of "realizations in the act of becoming."

Ferdinand Gonseth endeavored to introduce this new quaternary outlook, which he calls "une expérience d'ouverture," into the field of mathematical thought.[50] This *expérience d'ouverture* consists in a deepening of realization[51] which, he says, no longer involves the summary and brutal coercion of one variant over another, but the play of identifications and differentiations, agreements and complements, limitations and expansions, a game which can lead to dialectical synthesis, built up in four rhythms.[52] In geometry, for instance, this new scientific attitude requires four (!) principles for its fulfillment. They run as follows:

1. The principle of openness, which means that one does not begin on the assumption that every (geometrical) realization is incapable of being reformed;
2. The principle of plurality which means that one and the same reality can be approached by different modes of approximation, whose interrelations can be subjected to the dialectical synthesis mentioned above;
3. The principle of engagement, which leads one technically to new discoveries (creative aspects);

48. Cf. E. Fettweis, *Das Rechnen der Naturvölker* (Leipzig, 1927), p. 62.
49. Cf. also "Flying Saucers," ¶¶ 740–42.
50. *La Géometrie et le problème de l'espace* (Neuchâtel, 1955), p. 616.
51. *Ibid.*, p. 527.
52. *Ibid.*, p. 583.

4. The principle of integrability, whereby the entirety of our organized means of understanding contains within itself adequate meaning and cannot be divided into disconnected elements (aspect of wholeness).[53]

In modern physics certain scientists have begun to search for similar quaternary thought models. Thus Eddington suggested using the symbol J for existence solutions. The so-called "idempotency" condition or equation $J^2 - J = 0$ or $J^2 = J$ has the two solutions $J = 1$ (unity, existence), and $J = 0$ (nonexistence). In his view such a fourfold existence symbol plays a role in physical measurement. It is conditioned by four factors: the observer, the relationship between two objects, plus a standard measure. He remarks:

> From the association of measurement with four entities we are led, without further investigation, to expect that the number 4 will in some way make itself evident in the world-picture which embodies the results of our measurements. It is the seed from which arise those oddly assorted pure numbers which we call constants of nature. This conclusion in itself tells us very little, and gives no warrant for numerological speculations. I believe that the number 4 introduced in this way is actually responsible for the four dimensions of space-time, *but only indirectly.* In an actual calculation the number of dimensions of space-time is reached by the route $\dfrac{4 \cdot 3}{1 \cdot 2} - 1 - 1 = 4$ and it is a coincidence that the number we end with is the number we start with. Many threads must be woven together before we make anything out of this small beginning.[54]

In physics we also find the following thermodynamical quaternity ($VESM$) and trinity ($PT\mu$):

53. *Ibid.*, p. 620.
54. *Physical Science*, pp. 168–69.

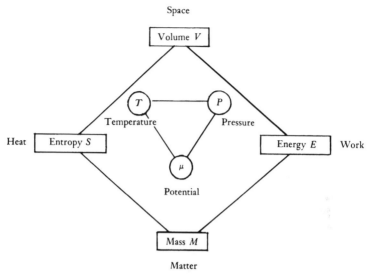

[Diagram by Prof. W. Byers Brown.]

with the relations $dE - TdS + PdV - \mu dM = 0$ and $VdP -$
$SdT - Md\mu = 0$. These relations and their generalizations
govern the vast range of physical and chemical equilibria
in biological, geological, and cosmological phenomena.

The outlook dominating modern physics, which includes
the observer and takes into account such new insights as the
irreversibility of measurement acts, is paralleled in psychology by recognition of the reality of the unconscious and by
the serious consideration given to the shadow as well as to
the psychic reality of dreams and "numina" (signs), through
which synchronistic events manifest themselves.[55] In this
way intellectual formulations take on the character of more
modest attempts at description, and individual moral respon-

55. See *Psychology and Religion,* ¶ 272 (latter half).

sibility plays a far more significant role in psychological understanding. Insight into the unconscious aspects of one's own personality becomes unavoidable, because "the shadow and the opposing will are the necessary conditions for all actualization," and for every achievement of consciousness as well.[56]

In this connection my views diverge from those of Ernst Anrich. In many parts of his book Anrich describes relations in the sense used above, but he does not take into account the problem of synchronicity.[57] Although he postulates an aspect of the archetypes that contains not only psychic but world-shaping factors,[58] he does not seriously take into account Jung's view that a psychoid aspect of the archetypes, which reaches across the psychic into the sphere of matter, becomes perceptible in synchronistic phenomena. Because of this his statements in the second half of the book relapse once again into a "trinitarian" or "idealistic" pattern of thought,[59] and he backs away from the essential problem he so courageously advanced at the beginning of the work.[60] He does indeed speak of a "functional union of object and subject," [61] but he does not consider the only *observable* and actual manifestations we experience of it in the form of synchronistic phenomena. The problem confronting us in parapsychological synchronistic events is undoubtedly a "hot potato" we must have the courage to grasp, because

56. *Ibid.*, ¶ 290.
57. He only mentions it briefly: *Moderne Physik*, pp. 503–4.
58. In the course of which he curiously reproaches Jung for not emphasizing this aspect sufficiently (*ibid.*, pp. 222, 223, 225, 237, 238–39, 244–45, 279, 408). In this way he reproachfully conveys the impression that Jung remained stuck in Cartesian thought. In my opinion this misunderstanding is the result of a typical projection whereby Anrich accuses Jung of the very thing he himself is doing.
59. *Ibid.*, p. 311.
60. Time and again Anrich acknowledges that Jung himself went beyond his own definition of the archetypes as "only" psychic (*ibid.*, pp. 312 f.). Nevertheless Anrich follows up these admissions by accusing Jung once again of "psychologism" (p. 317).
61. *Ibid.*, p. 335.

these experiences throw true light on the problem of the relation of psyche and matter. It is my belief that future scientific and intellectual works will not only recognize the relativity of all individual statements, but will give scrupulous consideration to parapsychological phenomena, the material "numina" representing "signs of the unknown." We need such an *expérience d'ouverture* in the face of these intellectually disagreeable facts. In this setting the advancement of "valid" theories will no longer succeed, but in their place honest descriptions of experienceable events, and the conclusions to be derived from them, will open up.[62]

62. Cf. "Flying Saucers," ¶¶ 740–42.

PART III

The Field of the Collective Unconscious and Its Inner Dynamism

CHAPTER EIGHT

Archetypes and Numbers as "Fields" of Unfolding Rhythmical Sequences

1	2	3	4	5	6
7	8	9	10	11	12
13	14	15	16	17	18
19	20	21	22	23	24
25	26	27	28	29	30
31	32	33	34	35	36
37	38	39	40	41	42
43	44	45	46	47	48
49	50	51	52	53	54
55	56	57	58	59	60
61	62	63	64	65	66
67	68	69	70	71	72
73	74	75	76	77	78
79	80	81	82	83	84
85	86	87	88	89	90
91	92	93	94	95	96
97	98	99	100		

IN MODERN NUMBER THEORY one speaks of integers in their entirety as a field.[1] Particularly in research on the distribution of prime numbers, attempts have been made since early times to arrange numbers in various field or matrix forms, beginning with the famous "sieve of Eratosthenes" (see left), from which the nonprime numbers can be crossed out.

1. See Tobias Dantzig, *Number: The Language of Science* (New York, 1954), p. 92: "To accomplish this with respect to subtractions it is sufficient to adjoin to the sequence of natural numbers zero and the negative integers. The field so created is called *the general integer field*."

Sieve of Eratosthenes [Source: Martin Gardner, "Mathematical Games," *Scientific American* (March, 1964), p. 120, copyright © 1964 by Scientific American, Inc. All rights reserved.]

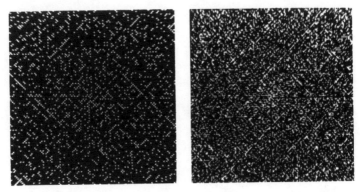

[Photographs courtesy of the Los Alamos Scientific Laboratory, University of California.]

In the illustration above, the numbers have been spirally arranged in lattice formation and calculated, by means of a computer, from 1 to 10,000 and from 1 to 65,000 (the dots represent the prime numbers). The order of numbers was spirally arranged as follows:

etc.

37	36	35	34	33	32	31
38	17	16	15	14	13	30
39	18	5	4	3	12	29
etc.	19	6	1	2	11	28
	20	7	8	9	10	27
	21	22	23	24	25	26

etc.   etc.

etc.

Although it is only since Evariste Galois that the use of such matrices has been systematically developed in the West, constructions of this type have, from the very beginning, been employed in the East for calculation.[2] Nowadays, the field concept holds sway in broad areas of Western number theory. In geometry, too, similar notions have been adopted. Today, for example, space is termed a "manifold whose contiguous relationships may be defined."[3]

In other provinces of science the field concept, a concept of structure, holds slightly different nuances. Lancelot L. Whyte, for instance, defines the concept of structure as "effective patterns of relationships in any situation." Applied to particles, for instance, this means that they "tend to assume regular or ordered spatial arrangement."[4] To this one may add that in the area of elementary particles the coherence factors are conceived to be actively effective.[5]

This concept of a field or structure appears to me to be applicable, in another form, to an aspect of the qualitative one-continuum. The Chinese matrices referred to are obviously taken to be qualitative "fields," not matrices in the occidental sense of the word. They represent, so to speak, the total archetypal order of the *unus mundus* and all its conceivable contents.

Such arrangements also existed in Western ancient number speculation; the Pythagoreans, the aging Plato, as well as the bulk of mythological and qualitative Western number

2. See Joseph Needham, *Science and Civilization in China* (Cambridge, 1959), II, 60 ff.

3. See V. Fritsch, *Links und Rechts in Wissenschaft und Leben* (Stuttgart, 1964), p. 64. Fritsch adds, "According to the theory of relativity local occurrences are placed in significant relation to occurrences or physical conditions in the immediate neighborhood, whose sum constitutes the field."

4. L. L. Whyte, *Accent on Form: World Perspectives* (New York, 1954), p. 28. By "structure" is meant not only a plane, but every spatial extension.

5. For instance, when defective arrangements occur (i.e., in crystals) we can observe how they actively reform themselves. See *ibid.*, pp. 97–102.

theories, all postulated an equation between archetypal images (or ideas) and numbers—seeking to arrange them in hierarchical order.[6] In his paper on synchronicity Jung speaks of various such historical attempts. He mentions the *Dialogus inter naturam et filium philosophiae* of Aegidius de Vadis in which the author associates a set of religious and alchemistic symbolic contents with every number.[7] Similar attempts to regard the relation of archetypal images to number in terms of correspondence, or simply identity,[8] were also made by Agrippa von Nettesheim and certain numerologists who preceded him.[9] Plato's effort to arrange all "ideas" hierarchically in a pyramidic structure culminating in the idea of good was another model of this kind. The exceedingly varied history of these numerical models, which bred like rabbits in the seventeenth-century "Theatra," cannot be detailed here.[10] They consisted, for the most part, of static arrangements in which numbers were equated with "ideas" or "cosmic regions" on the basis of a mystical analogy. Translated into psychological language, this means that they were attempts to outline *the total order of the collective unconscious* (as the sum of the archetypes).[11]

These models were strictly conceived of as a static order of existence. Moreover, the images and numbers in them were, for the most part, simply equated with one another, without any investigation of their more exact relationship. But before we attempt to carry out this latter step, we are confronted with the question: How can we differentiate natural numbers from other archetypal symbols, such as the sun-wheel, the tree of life, and so forth? Although numbers

6. Cf. J. E. Raven, *Pythagoreans and Eleatics* (Amsterdam, 1966).

7. *Theatrum Chemicum*, ed. L. Zetzner (Strasbourg, 1602), II, 103.

8. Aegidius de Vadis, quoted in C. G. Jung, "Synchronicity," *The Structure and Dynamics of the Psyche*, *CW*, Vol. XIII, ¶ 965: "elementa certis numeris ligantur."

9. See Frances Yates, *Giordano Bruno and the Hermetic Tradition* (London, 1964), pp. 130 ff.

10. See P. Rossi, *Clavis universalis: Arti mnemoniche e logica combinatoria da Lullo a Leibniz* (Milan and Naples, 1960), pp. 179 f.

11. In numerological language, the God-image.

have always been considered analogies for such figurative symbols, they definitely possess a more abstract aspect. Jung defined natural number as *the archetype of order which has become conscious.*[12] This would mean that our idea of order possesses a preconscious aspect, or, to put it another way, it is based on an inborn unconscious psychic disposition in man. As a secondary effect this inborn disposition engenders the knowledge and rational formulations of order we experience in consciousness.[13]

In contradistinction to numerical symbols and certain geometrical symbols, all of which bring "pure order" to consciousness, most of the other symbols known to the human mind are images whose "Gestalt" is derived partly from our experience of the outer world. Examples of these, to name but a few, are the "tree of life," the "totem animal," "water of life," the "underworld," and the "spirit-fire." The element of "pure order" is far more predominant in numerical symbols than in other ones. Nevertheless mythological images and numbers have always been associated with one another. "Indeed," Jung once remarked,

> one only subsequently recognizes the relation of number to mythological assertions, although the contents of number undoubtedly adhere in an a priori fashion to these

12. "Synchronicity," ¶ 870. See also his "The Psychology of Eastern Meditation," *Psychology and Religion, CW,* Vol. XI, ¶¶ 942–44.

13. Some mathematicians likewise maintain that it is primarily the idea of an ordered arrangement that lies concealed in the number concept. What is more, Dantzig says (*Number*, p. 210): "The notion of 'equal-greater-less' precedes the number concept." And: "Arithmetic does not begin with numbers; it begins with *criteria.*" Man's next step was to devise models for every type of plurality. "The principle of correspondence generates the integer and through the integer dominates all arithmetic." In my opinion this contention goes a little too far: behind the idea of "equal-greater-less" lurks the *preconscious* notion of one and two. This means that one and two, and the three concepts mentioned above, are preconsciously identical and cannot be separately examined. They form the basis for the most primitive calculation. The common denominator of "similar-more-small-less" and number is *order,* and the maintenance of order is obviously based on a preconscious psychic disposition. *When it becomes conscious it takes on the form of number concepts.*

assertions; they are only later made conscious. [They are
not added on.] In this sense number is a genuine symbol,
not only by virtue of its arithmetical nature, but its contents as well.[14]

This association of archetypal images and numbers is demonstrated clearly in the Mayan religion. There individual gods
and numbers are simply identical. The transcendental primal
god, hovering over all creation, is Hunabku, the "Single
One" (from *hun*, "one"). Great heroes are called "One
Hunter," "Seven Hunter," and so forth. At the same time
these numbers are also "temporal numbers" because a specific day of the Mayan calendar is allotted to each god. Only
the powers of the underworld, the founders of chaos and
meaninglessness, possess no such calendrical assignations. To
them belong the "five nameless days" at the end of the year.[15]

Similarly, in ancient Babylon all numbers from one to
sixty were reserved for special divinities; there was a god
"Eight," a god "Three," and so on.[16] These numerical gods
were likewise related to time in that specific calendar dates
were assigned to them.

The idea of a fieldlike arrangement of the archetypes, or
the collective unconscious, to which William James has already drawn attention,[17] derives from the fact that the archetypes exist in a state of mutual contamination; they overlap

14. Private communication in my possession.
15. See W. Cordan, *Das Buch des Rates: Mythos und Geschichte
der Maya* (Jena, 1962), pp. 166, 181–82.
16. See A. Seidenberg, "The Ritual Origin of Counting," *Archive
for History of Exact Sciences*, II (1962–66), 7, and other examples
there given.
17. Cf. Wolfgang Pauli, "Naturwissenschaftliche und Erkenntnistheoretische Aspekte des Ideen vom Unbewussten," *Aufsätze und
über Physik und Erkenntnistheorie* (Brunswick, 1961), p. 113, and
Pauli's further explanation of the concept of the field in physics and
its applicability to the unconscious. In *An Experiment with Time*
(London, 1927), J. W. Dunne was also trying, even then, to describe
time as a multitude of "time-field series" in order to elucidate the
phenomenon of precognition. His book contains reflections that are still
worth reading, although it seems to me that a single "field of time,"
in addition to the many possible time vectors, suffices; further "fields
of time" are, in my opinion, unnecessary conscious constructions.

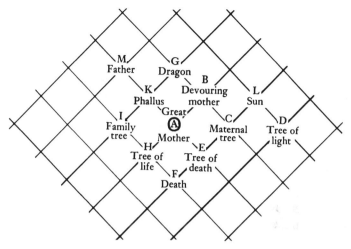

in meaning. We can illustrate this phenomenon by taking the archetype of the "Great Mother" as an example. This figure plays a role in the religions and mythologies of nearly all nations and cultures. Familiar representations in the Mediterranean area include Hathor, Nut, Isis, Cybele, Astarte, and Anat, among others. In Christianity we find the Virgin Mary, in India Shakti, in North America the so-called Spider Woman, and among the Eskimos Sedna, the Lady of the Sea Beasts, to name a few.

One special aspect of this figure takes the form of the "devouring mother" (B). She is personified by the Polynesian Hine-nui-te-po, the Russian fairy-tale witch Baba Jaga, the Indian Kāli Durga, and the Germanic Hel, to mention a few examples.

Another form of the Great Mother consists of the maternal tree (C). This form is depicted in the mythic image of the tree whose leaves provide a dwelling place for the souls of unborn children, as well as in all myths about births from trees. The tree in the grave of King Sethos I, from whose breast the king was nourished, is another example.

For its own part, the tree is closely connected with the sun symbol (L). Indeed, according to many myths the sun was born from a tree or hangs in the form of a fruit from the tree of light (D).

As a coffin, the tree is also connected to death (E). In many parts of the world, dead people were buried in trees. Death itself (F) is likewise personified by the mother, the dark feminine figure (*mors*, fem.!).

Another specific form of the devouring mother is the dragon (G), which itself possesses an affinity to death. This is evident in numerous medieval representations of Limbo, which situate the kingdom of death in the dragon's maw.

The death aspect stands in sharp contrast to the tree of life (H), which plays an important role in most religions. As the "family tree," the same motif acquires a paternal significance (I), and is related to the phallus symbol (K). By itself the father motif links up, once again, with the sun symbol and others, and the phallic motif relates back to the "Great Mother" who often is characterized by a gigantic nose, a broom, or some other phallic attribute.

These examples of the partial aspects and overlapping meanings an archetypal image is endowed with can be multiplied at will. But the examples given suffice to demonstrate the net of interwoven symbolic images in which, on closer investigation, the archetypes are embedded. In other words, they are contained in a field of inner qualitative nuances.[18] This field may be termed a manifold of psychic contents, whose relations are defined by meaning.

In a fashion similar to certain arrangements in the material realm, groupings in the archetypal sphere that become defective spontaneously and actively take on new forms. The presence of existing structures facilitates the formation of similar complementary or identical representations. The fact that complex structures display a tendency to selectively influence one another, in the formation of similar structures, can also easily be demonstrated.[19]

18. See Marie-Louise von Franz, "Bei der schwarzen Frau," *Studien zur analytischen Psychologie C. G. Jungs*, II (1955), 4 ff.

19. Concerning these laws in matter see Whyte, *Accent*, pp. 101–2.

The "nucleus" of the archetypal field (in our case, the arbitrarily chosen archetype of the Great Mother) is its most imperceptible aspect. Its existence can nevertheless be regarded as consisting of the one that holds together all the other ones. Examining the web in our illustration more closely we might just as well place the archetype of the "sun" at the center of our field of observation, and reestablish from this starting point the identical web of amplifications. In this way every archetype forms *the virtual center of a fieldlike realm of representational contents* definable strictly in relative terms, a region overlapping other archetypes.[20] This structure is also characteristic of natural numbers when they are regarded qualitatively. As a result of their observations on this phenomenon, the Chinese actually combined numbers together in matrices which served as rhythmically organized "ensembles," time-conditioned images of the aspects of the cosmic whole.[21] In this sense, the Lo-shu model may be viewed as a qualitative field of one, five, and ten. It portrays, in other words, the primal one's evolution into Tao ($10 + 1 = 11$).

It is possible that the famous Pythagorean *lambdoma* (the system of musical intervals) also was originally a field arrangement in circular form (a mandala). Gertrude Degenring has recently rediscovered this *through a vision* (!) in which she was shown a circular pattern that is a most important ordered structure. Professor Rudolf Haase discovered and proved that it was a circular arrangement of the Pythagorean *lambdoma*, which was identical to an unexplained pattern held by the figure of Pythagoras on a mosaic dating from the second century A.D.[22]

W. Hartner (who also postulates the existence of a pre-

20. We could also arrange such a field as a matrix.
21. In Chinese number theory there are also artificial numerical patterns, but we shall only consider their ancient structures, spontaneously revealed by the unconscious.
22. According to Haase, the original *lambdoma* had a quadratic (!) structure. See R. Haase, "Eine unbekannte Pythagoräische Tafel," *Antaios*, XII, no. 4 (1970), 357 ff.

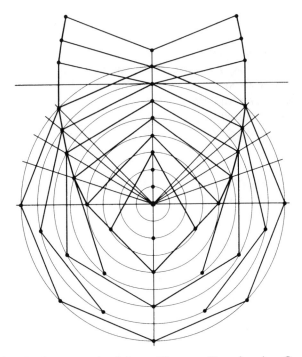

The Pythagorean *lambdoma* [Source: Drawing by Gertrude Degenring for Rudolf Haase, "Eine unbekannte
pythagoräische Tafel," *Antaios*, XII, no. 4 (1970), 358,
reproduced by permission of Ernst Klett Verlag and
Professor Rudolf Haase.]

conscious mathematical instinct in man) points out interestingly enough that in earliest cultures, such as the neolithic
and Bronze Age, two types of mathematically styled orna-
mentation appear. One of them is characterized by a rhythmic arrangement of constant elements and can be mathematically investigated. The other is subject to a "higher
rhythm" consisting of elements in continuous alternation
and can be equated with the curved fields of differential
equations (see the illustration p. 149).[23] The first type is

23. W. Hartner, "Zahlen und Zahlensysteme bei Primitiv- und
Hochkulturvölkern," *Paideuma*, II (1940–44), 269–70.

[Source: W. Hartner, "Zahlen and Zahlensysteme bei Primitiv- und Hochkulturvölkern," *Paideuma*, nos. 6–7 (1940–44), 270.]

arithmetical, in contradistinction to the more fluent second type. It corresponds more to a mathematical pattern of thought, and the second type more to a *mathematical feeling*.[24] These "fields" formed out of oscillating curves with "excited points" (the eyelike elements in our diagram) directly illustrate the idea of the one-continuum, or numerical field, as I attempt to present it. Hartner's notion that this aspect of mathematics is more concerned with the feeling function (the curves produce a musical effect) strikes me as very much to the point. The perception of number's "field" quality is largely a feeling experience. I shall take up this matter again later on.

The question we must first ask about the archetypal field

24. Jung also observed that undulating curves in his patients' pictures indicated feeling.

is whether all its nuclei (see illustration p. 145) possess equal rank and value, or are ruled by a central ordering factor, a central ruler, in other words, over all the archetypes. Throughout the course of his lifework Jung sought to demonstrate the likelihood of the existence of this central structure, namely, a superordinate archetype which he termed the Self.[25] Its structure becomes clear in mandala formations, those spherical or circular patterns[26] which are usually subdivided into four parts and often exhibit a relationship to time.[27] Jung says: "The mandala symbolizes, by its central point, the ultimate unity of all archetypes as well as of the multiplicity of the phenomenal world, and is therefore the empirical equivalent of the metaphysical concept of the *unus mundus*." [28]

Turning back to our illustration on p. 145, I should also mention that the single differentiable partial aspects of a constellated archetype are not manifest in an *arbitrary* time sequence, but in *typical sequences*. Comparative mythology does not only present typical image motifs, but typical phases of narration as well. Individual motifs accordingly tend to arrange themselves in regular recurring temporal phases. The human mind seems to have surmised this from an early stage; the German word *erzählen*, "to tell," contains the idea of counting (*zählen*), just as the French *raconter* is related to *compter*, and the English "recount" to

25. See *Psychology and Alchemy*, CW, Vol. XII; *The Archetypes and the Collective Unconscious*, CW, Vol. IX; p. 1; *Mysterium Coniunctionis*, CW, Vol. XIV, etc.

26. "Synchronicity," ¶ 870.

27. This would also have been the empirical basis on which Leibniz built up his idea of God as a central monad which from moment to moment flashed lightning before the other monads (here too a rhythmic action, not a continual flowing activity): "Ainsi Dieu seul est l'Unité ou la substance simple originaire, dont toutes les Monades crées ou dérivatives sont des productions et naissent pour ainsi dire par les Fulgurations continuelles de la Divinité de moment en moment," etc. (G. W. Leibniz, *Grundwahrheiten der Philosophie* [*Monadologie*], text and commentary by J. C. Horn [Frankfurt a. M., 1962], p. 90).

28. *Mysterium*, ¶ 661; cf. also ¶ 662.

"count." [29] In Chinese, the word for "counting up" is composed of the elements *suan*, "to reckon or count up," and the origins, *chi*, of that which will come to pass, *lai*. [30]

Psychological facts such as these caused the investigator A. Seidenberg to assume that the act of counting had its origins in the rites based on creation myths. According to him, "Serialization is the rite and the 'counting' of the myth," and he suggests that, very possibly, counting began with the attention paid to long processions. [31] I am not entirely convinced of this derivation, although it seems plausible because processions, from their very beginnings, consisted of something in the nature of a transient unfolding or "unrolling" of archetypal symbols in time. Nevertheless, it seems to me that the temporal relations of number and archetypal symbol must possess a more universal common root than merely the tabulation of processional figures.

In the interpretation of mythical narratives it is also advisable to count the characters taking part. Let us take the Russian fairy tale "The Virgin Tsar" to illustrate this. [32] The tsar of a country challenges each of his three sons to "pluck

29. Prof. Gertrud Hess was kind enough to draw my attention to the following remarks of E. Daqué, in *Der Schöpfungsmythus neu erzählt* (Leipzig, 1940). In the whole of paganism primal consciousness remained alert to the fact that the divinity's primal form "was the innermost timeless undivided unity. Because the divinity was aware of himself, both his fundamental poles of being were conscious. He was God and his self-knowing wisdom." In the first origins "lies the deepest foundation of all prototypes; in it lie all quantity and all numbers of things. And when it reveals itself, when it steps forth creatively working, it weighs and recounts the existence of things. This weighing and recounting is at the same time creative reality."

30. I am indebted to Mrs. Nora Mindell for this information.

31. Seidenberg, "Ritual Origin," p. 10, says: "The above hypothesis has a number of aspects and depends for its validity on evidence in myth, ritual, and custom for the existence of the following features: a) the ritual procession, b) the ritual procession in pairs, c) the appearance of the participants in ritual on the ritual scene upon announcement, d) the announcement taking the form of numbers."

32. From *Die Märchen der Weltliteratur*, Vol. VIII: *Russische Märchen*, ed. Friedrich van der Leyen (Jena, 1959).

his flowers and seek his footsteps." One after another they set out on the great quest and come to a crossroads where the signpost reads: "Whoever rides to the right will have food to eat, but his horse will remain hungry. Whoever rides to the left will find food for his horse but will himself remain hungry. Whosoever rides straight ahead will suffer death." The two elder brothers choose right and left and get lost, but the simpleton Ivan chooses the way of death. He comes to three Baba Jaga witches in turn and with their help wins "Marja; the beauty with the golden tresses" in the "kingdom beneath the sun." She bears him twin boys. Ivan's two brothers are later eliminated at the tsar's court, but Ivan moves to the "kingdom beneath the sun" and reigns there for the rest of his life.

The opening situation consists of a *quaternio* of four masculine figures, the tsar and his three sons. This is followed by the appearance of another *quaternio* of four feminine figures, the three witches and Marja, the beautiful. At the end of the story a new "rejuvenated" *quaternio* of three men and one woman is set up. The sequence of archetypal images thus points as well to an interplay of *numbers*, which can be formulated as follows:

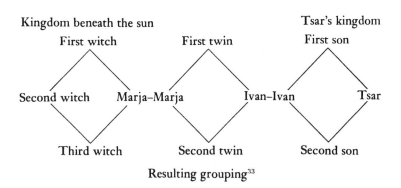

Resulting grouping[33]

33. After the removal of the tsar's two elder sons the four figures left over from the two first *quaternios*, the tsar and the three witches, also form a fourfoldness.

In this way most mythological stories may be described as *temporal number sequences*. (To the best of my knowledge triads and *quaternios* play the central role in their elucidation.) In this phenomenon lies proof, in my opinion, of the isomorphism between archetypes and numbers when they are taken to be qualitative configurations. In his earliest work, *De principio individui* (1663), Leibniz gave expression to this observation when he wrote that the essence of things "behaved" like number.[34] The verb "to behave" points to the dynamic aspect of "essence" (Leibniz' variant of the archetype) and thus brings a temporal aspect into consideration. In present-day depth psychology, we can demonstrate the probability of archetypal manifestations in the human unconscious, in the form of typical image *sequences*. Perhaps, as Pauli once remarked, by this means the phenomenon of precognition may become understandable: the unconscious psyche within us knows that—when a certain constellation is present—certain further developments may be expected.[35]

Perhaps a study of linguistic structures would help to clarify the time-phase aspect of archetypal structures. G. B. Milne made a beginning by showing that the proverbs and traditional sayings of all nations and races tend to display a quadripartite structure.[36]

Peter Hofstätter maintains that the science of human feelings and characteristics displays nothing analogous to the universally binding classificatory system of chemistry.[37] If, however, it should prove feasible to set up such a sys-

---

34. Cf. R. F. Merkel, *Leibniz und China* (Berlin, 1952), p. 19.

35. Private letter in my possession. This hypothesis is in no way surprising when one considers that animal behavior patterns also appear to be built into time phases. See A. Portmann, "Die Zeit im Leben der Organismen," *Eranos Jahrbuch*, XX (1952), 443 ff.

36. G. B. Milne, "What Is a Proverb?," *New Society* (February, 1969). I owe the knowledge of this article to the kindness of Mr. Fowler McCormick.

37. Peter Hofstätter, "Psychologie und Mathematik," *Studium generale*, VI, no. 11 (1953), 653.

tem, it would become possible to formulate individual transformative equations. I believe the field of numbers and archetypes I am endeavoring to outline in this work constitutes just such a system. The difficulty in dealing accurately with it arises from the fact that it lies at the basis of every effort man makes to attain a greater conscious understanding. As a result, it constitutes simultaneously a subjective and an objective reality. Every process of understanding, in terms of both its dynamic preconscious set of motivations and its conscious temporal developments, moves along the latent patterns of this field. At one and the same time, the process of understanding consists of a pattern in this field and mirrors it.

For this very reason, number appears to pertain essentially to the *behavior of archetypal dynamics*. The archetypes are given to manifesting themselves in an "ordered sequence," of which the number series forms, as it were, the most primitive expression.[38] The element connecting the sequence of archetypal images with the series of natural numbers seems to be psychic energy. We shall study this phenomenon more closely in the next chapter.

38. This might be misunderstood as a vicious circle if one objects that the expression "ordered sequence" implies the concept of time. I would rather consider it in this way: ordered sequences exist simultaneously and timelessly (in the sense of formalistic mathematics) in the one-continuum. Only when they are regarded in terms of the progressive, quantitative number series (in a consecutive order of additive units) is a quantitative concept of time implied. All classes or "groups" that can be included in the number series possess, in my opinion, these same characteristics. In other words they constitute eternal timeless forms of order on the one hand, but become "temporal" forms when our consciousness begins to operate with them. (Probably because of this circumstance Hamilton even wished to elevate algebra to a science of time.) See G. J. Whitrow, *The Natural Philosophy of Time* (London and Edinburgh, 1961), p. 121.

CHAPTER NINE

Numbers as Isomorphic Configurations of Motion in Psychic and Physical Energy

Jung has already suggested that the concept of energy applied in present-day physics is in many respects similar to the concept of psychic energy underlying the observations of depth psychology. In fact, they may well designate one and the same factor viewed from two complementary angles.[1] The archetypes primarily represent dynamic units of psychic energy. In preconscious processes they assimilate representational material originating in the phenomenal world to specific images and models, so that they become introspectively perceptible as "psychic" happenings.[2] What they consist of in themselves, prior to our introspective perception of them, we cannot tell; but as regulatory factors they must, on account of the existence of synchronistic phenomena, be endowed with a nonpsychic aspect. (This aspect ceases to manifest itself in synchronistic peripheral phenomena as soon as its ordered contents become conscious.)[3] This psychoid aspect of the archetypes (ordering

1. See *The Structure and Dynamics of the Psyche*, *CW*, Vol. VIII, ¶¶ 438–39.
2. Cf. *ibid.*, ¶¶ 439, 440.
3. Cf. *ibid.*

factors) thus manifests itself as a psychic as well as a physical energetic phenomenon. It therefore seems advisable to conclude, in the final analysis, that we are dealing with one and the same energy which we designate as physical energy when it is physically measurable, or as psychic energy when it becomes psychically and introspectively perceptible.[4] We experience the latter as "intensity" or as varying gradations of feeling and of the emotional impact that psychic experiences have on us. "The psychologist," says Jung,

> talks of energy although he has nothing measurable to manipulate, besides which the concept of energy is a strictly defined mathematical quantity which cannot be applied as such to anything psychic. . . . If psychology nevertheless insists on employing its own concept of energy for the purpose of expressing the dynamism [ἐνέργεια] of the psyche, it is not of course being used as a mathematical formula, but only as its analogy. But note: the analogy is itself an older intuitive idea from which the concept of physical energy originally developed. The latter rests on an earlier application of an ἐνέργεια not mathematically defined, which can be traced back to the primitive or archaic idea of the "extraordinarily potent." This is the concept of mana. . . . The use of the term libido in the newer medical psychology has surprising affinities with the primitive mana. This archetypal idea is therefore far from being only primitive, but differs from the physicist's conception of energy by the fact that it is *essentially qualitative and not quantitative*. In psychology the exact measurement of quantities is replaced by an approximate

4. One of the best-verified empirical conclusions of physics, says Wolfgang Pauli ("Naturwissenschaftliche und erkenntnistheoretische Aspekte der Ideen vom Unbewussten," *Aufsätze und Vorträge über Physik und Erkenntnistheorie* [Brunswick, 1961], p. 101), is the structure of the electrical charge. The values of the charge are integral multiples of a basic number of the electrical quantum element e, energy quantum $\hbar$, and speed of light c from which a dimensionless number $\hbar c/e^2 = 137{,}034 \ldots$ can be formed, but we can neither explain nor understand the said number.

determination of intensities, for which purpose . . . we enlist the function of feeling (valuation).[5]

However, these intensities are more or less graduated, as Jung notes, thus pointing to "a sort of latent physical energy" in psychic phenomena.[6]

According to this viewpoint, the psyche should also be capable of appearing in the form of mass in motion;[7] and insofar as psychological interaction takes place, matter should possess a latent psychic aspect. If we apply these reflections of Jung's to number, this would mean that number is bound up with the latent material aspect of the psyche and with the latent psychic aspect of matter. Up to the present time, however, no means of measuring psychic intensities numerically has been envisaged, although I believe such a possibility exists because of the fact—to which Jung had already called attention in his earlier work, *Symbols of Transformation*—that *all emotional, and therefore energy-laden, psychic processes evince a striking tendency to become rhythmical.* "Any kind of excitement . . . displays a tendency to rhythmical expression, perseveration, and repetition. . . ."[8] This fact presumably also explains the basis of various rhythmical and ritual activities practiced by primitives. Through them, psychic energy and the ideas and activities bound up with it are imprinted and firmly organized in consciousness. It also explains the dependence of work-achievement on music, dancing, singing, drumming, and rhythm in general; through such means a restraint on uncoordinated instinctuality is achieved.[9] The application

5. *Structure and Dynamics,* ¶ 441. (my italics).
6. *Ibid.*
7. *Ibid.* "While psychological data are essentially qualitative, they also have a sort of latent physical energy, since psychic phenomena exhibit a certain quantitative aspect. . . . In this connection I would remind the reader of the existence of parapsychic phenomena."
8. *CW,* Vol. V, ¶¶ 219–20.
9. *Ibid.,* ¶¶ 218–19.

of rhythm to psychic energy was probably the first step toward its cultural formation, and hence toward its spiritualization.

Before such higher rhythmical formations of psychic energy take place, they are often preceded by simple movements which behavioral psychology interprets in animals as a "displaced reaction." The energy striving toward a pattern of behavior, but blocked by obstacles, manifests itself in such motions as scratching and rubbing, as well as in such human gestures as finger-drumming and foot-tapping, all *rhythmical* movements. For instance, Koch-Grünberg describes how the Indians sit on rocks and scratch lines on them with sharp stones, while waiting for their canoes to be transported round the rapids.[10] In the course of time, sharp lines have come into being from this repeated activity. The networks of lines which cover entire walls in certain mid–Stone Age caves in France are probably of similar origin.[11] Interestingly enough, regular, well-proportioned, and ordered geometrical and mathematical patterns are found to be interspersed among them. These (appear to) indicate a higher, *ordered* rhythmical activity, to which we shall return for discussion later.

The Chinese conception of number is based on association with this type of rhythmical activity in man. Moreover, from the beginning, the Chinese *also* utilized number to assess feeling-intensities of all things that had a psychic effect on man (psychic energy). In this way, number was even envisioned to be the regulator of ethics, the feeling-value par excellence, in other words. For the Chinese, ethics is based on feeling-determined "restraints" or measures. Their word for this *dsië* (or *chiëh*), originally referred to the joints into which bamboo stems are divided, and in an I Ching chapter with this word as the title, it is said: "thus

10. South American rock drawings, referred to by Jung, *ibid.*, ¶ 217.
11. Cf. M. E. P. König, "Die Symbolik des urgeschichtlichen Menschen," *Symbolon*, V (1966), 121–22.

the superior man creates number and measure and examines the nature of virtue and correct conduct." [12] *Dsië* also signifies "morality" and "loyalty," and the "measuring rod" of the highest ruler, with which he orders the world. The ruler maintains the virtue and order of his realm by receiving through inspiration from above "the [right] numbers of the heavenly calendar." Similarly, a decadent virtue can draw the cosmos into disorder by bringing the numbers of the calendar "out of their order." Here too, in the final analysis, these numbers represent all the rhythmical configurations of the universe in its wholeness.[13]

The Lo-shu matrix and the Ho-t'u linear cross are both fundamental (cosmic) rhythmical configurations of this kind. Exactly the same patterns are to be found, in the West, among the ancient artifacts of man's mental and spiritual activity, such as the prehistoric rock scratchings in the Grotte des Fées near Milly-la-Fôret in France, the Villetard cave on the Essonne, and the arrangement of small round cavities in the Jean Angelier cave near Noisy-sur-Ecole, to mention only a few. In the latter motif, we again come across the number nine, in addition to the familiar arrangement of the Lo-shu model in nine fields.[14] Marie E. P. König, the investigator of these caves, surmises that these drawings must refer to an attempt at ordering time and space: "The world was delineated in the form of geometrical figures and

12. Richard Wilhelm, trans., *I Ching or Book of Changes*, English trans. C. F. Baynes, 2 vols. (London, 1960), I, 247. Cf. also Marcel Granet, *La Pensée chinoise* (Paris, 1968), pp. 176 ff. The length of bamboo flutes was also specified by the number of joints (*ibid.*). Still further important connections may be found in M. von Hornbostel, "Die Massnormen als kulturgeschichtliches Forschungsmittel," *Festschrift für Pater W. Schmidt*, ed. W. Koppers (Vienna, 1928), pp. 303 ff. The same standard measurements were also to be found in ancient Egypt (*ibid.*, pp. 322 ff.).

13. Granet, *Pensée chinoise*, pp. 143 ff., 132 ff.

14. Moreover, the numerical arrangement of the Lo-Shu model is still in use today among the Hausa of northwest Africa as a magical means of calculation, as well as in the Mayan culture. Cf. P. G. Höltker, "Zeit und Zahl in Nordwestafrika," *Festschrift für Pater W. Schmidt*, ed. W. Koppers (Vienna, 1928), p. 298.

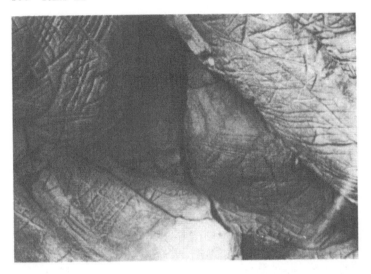

Above, Grotte des Fées, near Milly-la-Forêt (Seine et Oise); *below,* detail from the Villetard cave on the Essonne [Source: M. König, "Die Symbolik des urgeschichtlichen Menschen," *Symbolon,* V (1966), 135, 136, reproduced by permission of Schwabe & Co.]

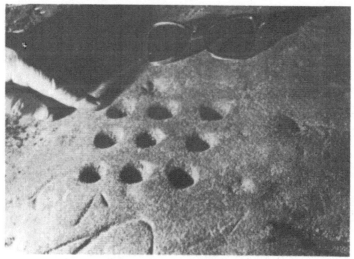

Above, detail from the cave at the Dame Jeanne iñ Larch-mont (Seine et Marne); *below,* detail from the Jean Angelier cave near Noisy-sur-Ecole [Source: König, "Die Symbolik," pp. 137, 132, reproduced by permission of Schwabe & Co.]

numbers." (We also find the well-known triplets here, probably as the principle of ordering time.)[15] The Ho-t'u linear cross, later developed into a "wheel" by the addition of a circle, also plays an extremely important role in these cave drawings and is reminiscent of the Ho-t'u model.

Among these samples there is also a mandala, which is reminiscent of the divisions of the Mühlebrett (at Milly-la-Forêt, and also in "Höll" Totes Gebirge, Warscheueck).[16]

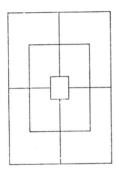

The Mühlebrett, from Milly-la-Forêt and "Höll" Totes Gebirge, Warscheueck [Source: M. Riemschneider, "Glasberg and Mühlebrett," *Symbolon*, VI (1968), 137, reproduced by permission of Schwabe & Co.]

Margarete Riemschneider is of the opinion this may have to do with an oracular game serving cult purposes;[17] it may also signify an ordering arrangement of the Beyond, the land of the dead[18]—or in more modern language, the unconscious. As well as this "board," we find also various streak and scratch patterns of a kind similar to those already described.

Such patterns obviously serve as general orientation models; they contain an *aspect of order* which can still today be detected in such products of the unconscious as dreams. The dream of a theologian who, at the time, was struggling with

15. König, "Symbolik," pp. 121 ff., 148–49.
16. Cf. Margarete Riemschneider, "Glasberg und Mühlebrett," *Symbolon*, VI (1968), 137–38. (The *Mühlebrett* is the board of a game played with checkers.)
17. *Ibid.*, p. 141.
18. That there is a connection with the motif of the Glass Mountain seems to me in no way obvious. It is far more likely that it refers to the geography of the "Beyond" in general, i.e., the unconscious.

the problem of differentiating his feeling-function, may serve here as an example: In a park he encounters a rough man who threatens him, but he finally succeeds in getting rid of him. Half sitting, half lying, he then moves down to a slow-flowing stream. Glancing up, he spies a wonderfully beautiful, distinguished woman sitting on a seat. He approaches her and gradually slips into half-sexual love-play. Next he suddenly finds himself at a psychological lecture and is invited to recite a prayer, whereupon he is exhorted by the woman lecturer not to forget his "daughter" in the prayer. The scene changes again and he is at a psychological seminar. He recounts a dream of his own, in which he sees five white stripes broken off from four black ones. The woman speaker says: "Stripes are equivalent to the number nine." Then he sees an old man cringing on a bed; beside him stands a boy of whom the old man appears to be very proud.

The first part of the dream pictures the overcoming of a coarse attitude, standing in the way of the differentiation of Eros. As a result, the dreamer is able to approach his feminine side (anima) and establish contact with her. The following scene shows how he should also include feeling and the feminine principle in its religious aspect (the prayer for his "daughter"). Then follows an explanation of the motif of stripes, which illustrates a differentiated nuance of the feeling-problem and its spiritual dynamism,[19] and should help to guide him in the chaos of as yet undifferentiated eroticism.[20] Considered from this point of view, number might also signify gradations of feeling-intensity values. I believe that, like light and other energy phenomena, psychic energy also has a spectrum which can be "measured," but expresses itself in *value* numbers.

19. In number symbolism nine stands for the number of the Holy Ghost (V. F. Hopper, *Medieval Number Symbolism* [New York, 1939], pp. 122–23), and for all particularly potent dynamisms.
20. The old man and the boy symbolize a possibility of renewal of consciousness.

In China, says Granet, number is generally used to estimate worth, not quantity.[21]

> It is an emblem through which the—more or less noble—
> aspects of wholeness, as those of effective energy and
> power, are given expression. . . . Only the number one,
> as the united wholeness comprising two, the pair, forms
> a complete expression of the Whole and All-embracing,
> and of the universal animating power proper to the prince
> and the superior man.[22]

Subjectively we experience this aspect of number, retrogressively brought back into relation with the primal unity,
as meaning, for the uniting characteristic of meaning can
draw the broadest categories of phenomena together into a
Gestalt. In the spiritual and mental realms of the psyche,
quantitative universal numbers are, as it were, "demultiplied"
and drawn back again into their unified forms. In his
Memories, Jung writes a short but very significant passage
concerning the problem of meaning which well repays closer
study. He raises the question as to whether, in the world in
which we must live, meaning or meaninglessness predomi-
nates, and expresses the "anxious hope" that meaning will
prevail over its opposite. As the basis for this hope, he suggests: "If meaninglessness were absolutely preponderant,
the meaningfulness of life would vanish to an increasing
degree with each step of our development. But that is—it
seems to me—not the case." [23]

Why, one asks oneself, should meaning vanish with
higher development? The answer seems to be that greater
numerical conglomerates are generated in the process (multi-

---

21. Granet, *Pensée chinoise,* p. 153. "In ancient China, when one
was not sure what course to follow one had to take a yarrow stalk
in one's hand as a guiding rod. The written character for this rod
was the class sign 'bamboo,' with below it a complex of strokes which
represent 'the tracks left in the ground by a cart.'" Number in this
case obviously provides a means of psychic orientation within the
chaos of the world.

22. *Ibid.,* p. 247.

23. *Memories, Dreams, Reflections* (London, 1963), p. 330.

billion-celled organisms in place of single-celled ones, for instance). If, in a multiplication such as this, the comprehensive, "retrogressive," form-creating connections to the one-continuum were not continually reestablished, every multiplication of discontinuities would lead to an agglomeration of formless and meaningless chaos. In themselves, however, "order" and "meaning" are not, as Jung points out, automatically the same thing. "An organism is not, in spite of its inherent, meaningful arrangement, necessarily meaningful in the total context." In the context of this statement, Jung uses the word "meaning" solely in the sense of cosmic cohesion. He continues:

> Without man's reflecting consciousness the world is monstrously meaningless; for according to our experience man is the only creature that can determine "meaning" at all. . . . Since a creation without the reflecting consciousness of man has no *recognizable* meaning, the hypothesis of a latent meaning invests man with a cosmogonic significance, a veritable *raison d'être.*[24]

In our present context, this point is illustrated by the fact that the *Gestalt* numbers of divination techniques possess no significance unless someone, acting individually, intervenes in the latent order of existence and takes the trouble to read a "meaning" into the number he obtains. At the same time, it is only because the qualitative aspect of number continuously hearkens back in a retrogressive way to the one, that such a total meaning can be read from it. It was precisely for this reason that in the I Ching the Chinese made a bold attempt to seek, through a retrograde counting system,[25] an approach to the meaning of seemingly chaotic situations. Number thereby was considered to be the mediator between psychic situations and "outer" ones. Just as the steps of

24. *Erinnerungen, Träume, Gedanken* (Zurich, 1962), p. 360. (This passage, an Appendix, is not included in the English translation.)
25. Forty-nine stalks are counted off *backwards*, until the remainder of one or two is obtained! Counting in geomancy is done the same way.

qualitative numerical counting are, as I have tried to demonstrate, retrograde, the values of feeling-toned numbers also exhibit a mirror-symmetrical relationship to quantitative number. This means that, in qualitative terms, one and two-one embody the highest value, and succeeding numbers gradually lose their energic value as numerical symbols. Thus psychic energy must be reckoned in an inverse way in comparison with the manner in which physical energy is read off through quantitative numbers.

In spite of this antithesis, natural number remains the common ordering factor of both physical and psychic manifestations of energy, and is consequently the element that draws psyche and matter together. In other words, amorphous energy probably does not exist at all; when energy manifests itself in either psychic or physical dimensions, it is always "numerically" structured, e.g., as "waves" or as (psychic) rhythm.[26] Natural numbers appear to represent the typical, universally recurring, common motion patterns of both psychic *and* physical energy.[27] Because these motion patterns (numbers) are identical for both forms of energy, the human mind can, on the whole, grasp the phenomena of the outer world. This means that the motion patterns engender "thought and structure models" in man's psyche, which can be applied to physical phenomena and achieve

26. Sir Arthur Eddington formulates it in *The Philosophy of Physical Science* (Cambridge, 1939), p. 110, as follows: "Energy which, since it is conserved, might be looked upon as the modern successor of substance, is in relativity-theory a curvature of space-time and in quantum-theory a periodicity of waves. . . . The two great theories, in their efforts to reduce what is known about energy to a comprehensible picture, both find that they require a conception of 'form'."
27. When one tries to understand these patterns consciously, one makes use of the abstractions of higher mathematics for the observation of quantitative manifestations of energy (physics). For the observation of qualitative forms of energy, however, one must first develop a qualitative view of number, as has been attempted in the foregoing passages. L. L. Whyte has demanded that "a new branch of mathematics" be developed which would make structures comprehensible (*Accent on Form: World Perspectives* [New York, 1954]).

relative congruence. The existence of such numerical nature constants in the outer world, on the one hand, and in the preconscious psyche, on the other (e.g., in the quaternary structures of the "psychic center," the triadic structure of dynamic processes, the dualistic structure of threshold phenomena, and so forth) is probably what finally makes all conscious knowledge of nature possible.

PART IV

Historical and Mathematical Models of the *Unus Mundus*

CHAPTER TEN

Historical Mandala Models as Inner Psychic Equivalents of the *Unus Mundus*

JUNG USED THE EXPRESSION *unus mundus* to designate the transcendental unitary reality underlying the dualism of psyche and matter. The idea of such a unity behind all existence is itself based on an archetypal foundation. The expression *unus mundus* originated in medieval natural philosophy, where it denoted the timeless, preexistent, cosmic plan or antecedent world model, potential in God's mind, according to which he realized actual creation. Joannes Scotus Erigena, for instance, describes the process of creation (in imitation of Dionysius the Areopagite) as a transition of the excellence of God's seminal power[1] from a "nothingness which lies beyond all being and nonbeing, into forms innumerable."[2] This God accomplishes by means of his

---

1. *De divisione naturae*, Migne, Patrologia Latina, Vol. CXXII, 1.5: "Virtus enim seminum eo tempore quo in secretis naturae silet, quia nondum apparet, dicitur non esse."

2. *Ibid.*, 3.19: "Divina igitur bonitas, quae propterea nihilum dicitur quoniam ultra omnia quae sunt et non sunt, in nulla essentia invenitur, ex negatione omnium essentiarum in affirmationem totius universitatis a se ipsa in se ipsam descendit, veluti ex nihilo in aliquid, ex inessentialitate in essentialitatem ex informitate in formas innumerabiles et species."

Wisdom (through the Son "through whom he knows himself").[3] In Wisdom God creates the universe,[4] i.e., "the primal original forms which not only lie in God, but constitute God Himself."[5] These "causae primordiales" know themselves, for they were created in Wisdom and remain eternally in her.[6] The Sapientia Dei or Sophia is a kind of primal unity, a uni-form image which reproduces herself, yielding a multitude of primal forms, which abide simultaneously in the unity.[7] These "primal forms" possess self-consciousness;[8] Joannes Scotus Erigena also calls them the "rationes rerum," "ideae," or "prototypa" of all existent things.[9] Hugo de St. Victor likewise termed the Sapientia Dei the "exemplar" of the universe, or the "archetypus mundus" in God's mind, in whose pattern the visible world was created.[10] Since God created the world (*vide* Wisdom of Solomon 11:21) "in conformity with mass, number, and weight," the Sapientia Dei, or *archetypus mundus*, was also equated by many theologians with a mathematical ordering of nature; number, in terms of the Trinity, was especially

3. *Ibid.*, 2.31: "Ad similitudinem Dei et Patris qui de se ipso Filium qui est sapientia sua gignit, qua se ipsum sapit."

4. *Ibid.*, 2.20.

5. Ibid., 3.8: "In primordialibus rerum causis quae non solum in deo verum etiam deus sunt."

6. *Ibid.*, 2.18: "Primordiales causae se ipsas sapiunt, in sapientia creatae sunt aeternaliterque in ea subsistunt."

7. See W. Preger, *Geschichte der deutschen Mystik im Mittelalter* (Aalen, 1962), I, 161.

8. *Divisione naturae*, 2.18: "Sicut ipsa sapientia se ipsam cognoscit et quae in ipsa facta sunt, non solum se ipsam cognoscere sed et rerum quarum principia sunt notitia non carere."

9. Preger, *Geschichte*, I, 161.

10. *Annotationes elucidariae in Evangelium Joannis*, quoted in Preger, *ibid.*, I, 328: "Unde et a Sapientia Dei omnia et vitam et esse habent . . . quia juxta Sapientiam Dei, quae vita omnium est, factum est omne quod factum est. Hoc enim exemplar Dei fuit ad cuius exemplaris similitudinem totus mundus factus est, et est hic ille archetypus mundus, ad cuius similitudinem mundus iste sensibilis factus est." According to Saint Thomas (*Summa* pars I, quaest. 56, art. 2) the Sapientia Dei consists of the "rationes omnium spiritualium creaturarum."

equated with the Son, mass with God the Father, and weight with the Holy Ghost.[11] Even Leibniz much later on says: "Cum Deus calculat et cogitationem exercet fit mundus." [12]

A notion similar to that of medieval theologians is also to be found in the works of certain alchemists. But they did not only conceive of the *unus mundus* as the initial plan of the universe existing in God's mind; for them it was also identical with the goal they were seeking, the *lapis*. It, like the *res simplex* or the philosophers' stone, was the *one* world. According to Paracelsus' pupil, Gerhard Dorn, the highest grade of the alchemical *coniunctio* consisted in the union of the total man with the *unus mundus*.[13]

The medieval philosophers merely ascribed potential reality to this "one world" (i.e., as a "nothingness" lying on the far side of being and nonbeing); Jung also stresses the fact that he views the unitary reality underlying synchronistic phenomena as a "potential" reality "in so far as all those conditions which determine the form of empirical phenomena are inherent to it." [14] The phenomena of synchronicity, however, represent sporadic actualizations of this unitary

11. See Ps.(?) Albertus Magnus, *Biblia mariana*, in *Opera* (ed. Borgnet), 37. 466. The basic explanations can be found in Saint Augustine, *De genesi ad litt.*, Migne, Patrologia Latina, Vol. XXXIV, col. 229, 1. 4. c3 and c8. Cf. also Marie-Louise von Franz, *Aurora consurgens*, trans. R. F. C. Hull and A. S. B. Glover (New York, 1966), pp. 278 ff.

12. *Dialogus de connexione inter res et verba*, ed. W. W. Erdmann (Berlin, 1840), p. 44, quoted by G. Martin in "Methodische Probleme der Metaphysik der Zahl," *Studium generale*, VI, no. 10 (1953), 611.

13. *Mysterium Coniunctionis, CW*, Vol. XIV, ¶ 759. See also Marie-Louise von Franz, "The Idea of the Macro- and Microcosmos in the Light of Jungian Psychology," *Ambix. Journal of the Society for the Study of Alchemy and Early Chemistry*, Vol. XIII, no. 1 (February, 1965).

14. See *Mysterium*, ¶ 769. "All that *is* is not encompassed by our knowledge, so that we are not in a position to make any statements about its total nature. Microphysics is feeling its way into the unknown side of matter, just as complex psychology is pushing forward into the unknown side of the psyche. Both lines of investigation have yielded findings which can be conceived only by means of antinomies, and both have developed concepts which display remarkable analogies" (*ibid.*, ¶ 768).

world.[15] In contradistinction to the medieval speculations, synchronistic phenomena provide us, as Jung emphasizes, with *empirical* evidence of the existence of such a *unus mundus*.[16]

According to Jung, the symbolic structure of the mandala forms our psychic equivalent of the *unus mundus*. At the same time, it represents an attempt to describe the archetype of the Self as the regulating center of archetypal and numerical fields. The rhythmical configurations of the number four play an especially outstanding role in the mandala. In *Aion*, Jung geometrically reconstructed the internal rhythm of the Self archetype in terms of a ring of four double pyramids, a construction to which the dream mentioned at the end of chapter six also alludes.[17]

Remarkably, the internal rhythm of the Chinese Ho-t'u model is similarly constituted. This structure, which represents the basic order of the archetypal field, can also be detected in certain cabalistic representations of the *sephiroth*. As primal numbers, the *sephiroth* are, it is known, supposed to symbolize the "potencies" "of which the creative divinity is formed," and through which—in the language of the cabalists—he "acquires a visible form." [18] At the top of the

15. Strictly speaking, the experience of synchronistic events is not based on the coincidence of inner and outer events but, as Jung says, "on the *simultaneous occurrence of two different psychic states*." (More precisely, it is by no means the case that we comprehend an event of the outer world "in itself," since it is also, in the final analysis, perceived via the filter of our psyche.) The two conditions are 1) the normal, probable (i.e., causally explainable), and 2) another which is not causally deducible from the first state, namely, the critical occurrence which, as it were, "breaks into" the first state. In the latter case "an unexpected content which is directly or indirectly connected with some external objective event coincides with the ordinary psychic state" ("Synchronicity," *The Structure and Dynamics of the Psyche, CW*, Vol. VIII, ¶ 855).

16. *Mysterium*, ¶¶ 767–68.

17. *Aion, CW*, Vol. IX, pt. 2, ¶¶ 390–91.

18. See G. Scholem, *Von der mystischen Gestalt der Gottheit* (Zurich, 1962), p. 32. The word s-f-r, *sephira* in place of the ordinary word *mispar* for number "appears to indicate that this is not simply a question of the ordinary numbers, but of numbers as metaphysical

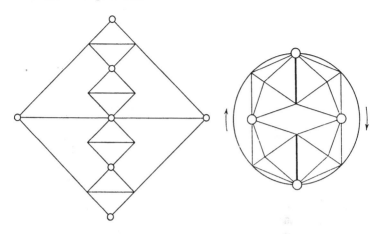

Jung made these schemata in *Aion* by reconstructing certain evolutions of the symbol of the Self in Gnostic and alchemical texts. They seem to prove that within the archetype of the Self there are circular transformative energetic processes taking place. [Source: C. G. Jung, *Aion*, *CW*, IX, pt. 2, 248, 249, copyright © 1959 and 1968 by the Bollingen Foundation, reproduced by permission of Princeton University Press and Routledge & Kegan Paul Ltd.]

sephiroth-tree (p. 176) stands the unknowable Primal One (En-Soph); then follows an unfolding into four (Bina, Chokhma, etc.); then again a central one, followed by a second unfolding which does not, however, appear to be further amplified in the official diagrams. This situation was

universal principles or steps of creation" (quoted from Scholem, *Ursprünge und Anfänge der Kabbala* [Berlin, 1962], p. 22). I am indebted to Dr. S. Hurwitz for this information. Dr. Hurwitz describes the *sephira* as "numerus archetypus." "The God Image in the Cabbala," *Spring* (1954), p. 46.

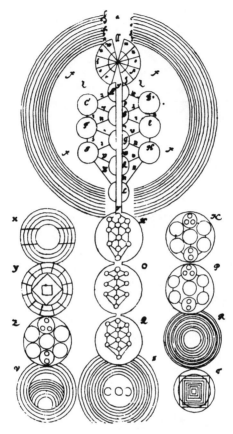

Numerical configurations of the cabalistic *sephiroth* tree
[Source: Knorr von Rosenroth, *Kabbala denudata* (Sulzbach, 1677), I, 243.]

probably considered unsatisfactory by certain cabalists, because many of them sought to construct whole "chains"
or numerical fields of this kind, which would illustrate the
effective emanations of the Primal One throughout the
various realms of nature. They resemble the Gnostic thought
patterns with which Jung illustrates his diagrammatic structure. The preponderant numbers in them are always four
(also the centered four **:•:**) and six, the double triplet.
Giordano Bruno's *Sigilla* and other Renaissance models of
the universe (to which we will return later) were probably
also influenced by these cabalistic models. All the rhythms
here referred to are mandala structures, therefore circular,
and divided by four or one of its multiples.

On the whole, the most ancient thought patterns concerning the totality of existence were usually mandalas, and
were very frequently models of an infinite sphere. The
source of these conceptions in the West is considered to be
older Orphic pantheism. An ancient hymn extols Zeus as
the first and the last, "the depths of the earth and the star-
sown heavens," and the "great body of the king, in which
all that exists rotates." [19]

Xenophanes of Colophon then expressly described his
cosmic god as ἴσον ἀπάντῃ, similar on all sides, and possibly
also spherical.[20] His successor Parmenides defined absolute
being as something merely bodiless and spaceless, but this
was also interpreted by his followers as a spherical continuum in which "a movement takes place in fullness." [21]
And in Empedocles' view, the cosmos in its state of φιλία,
harmony, is unequivocally an infinite, limitless sphere continually impregnated with matter.[22]

19. See Dietrich Mahnke, *Unendliche Sphäre und Allmittelpunkt*
(Stuttgart, 1966), p. 243.
20. See C. Bäumker, *Das Problem der Materie in der griechischen
Philosophie*, repr. ed. (Frankfurt a. M., 1963), *passim*.
21. Mahnke, *Unendliche Sphäre*, p. 58.
22. See *ibid.*, p. 68. Anaxagoras, on the other hand, attributed circular motion only to the spirit (nous), while matter was considered to
be formless and chaotic.

These first attempts to draw up a cosmic mandala already demonstrate that it was thought to exist beyond material space and time, or entirely corporeally, or within cosmic matter in a separate, distinct form. In Plato's work this problem led to the construction of a double cosmic mandala, one aspect of which was considered to be timeless and non-material, and the other to be cyclically moving in space and time. The latter belongs to the models which we will consider in the following chapter more closely in connection with the problem of time. For the former type, one should refer to Dietrich Mahnke's outstanding study, *Unendliche Sphäre und Allmittelpunkt*. Mahnke has made a special study of the history of the famous sentence "Deus (vel mundus) est sphaera infinita, cuius centrum est ubique et circumferentia nusquam," thus providing a vivid and perceptive survey of the mandala as the thought model of the totality of existence.

A double mandala of special interest to us is described in Plato's *Timaeus*.[23] There Plato assumes the existence of an eternal extracosmic realm in which ideal geometric solid forms, latent within themselves, timelessly coexist. Since the Creator of the universe could not transfer all these figures *simultaneously* into his cosmic creation, he decided to create a moving image of the eternal unity and its timeless coexistent order, actually isomorphic to the sequence of natural numbers.[24] In this way, time came into being and formed a bridge between the two models, one of which was a timeless continuum, and the other a rotating and, as such, time-bound mandala. The next significant step in the development of this idea occurs in Plotinus' work, from which it was carried into medieval tradition.[25]

In the writings of Neoplatonic philosophers, attempts

---

23. *Timaeus* (ed. Burnet [Oxford, 1905]), 37c–38a. See also 30a–c.
24. Cf. with this G. J. Whitrow, *The Natural Philosophy of Time* (London and Edinburgh, 1961), pp. 28–29, 35.
25. Concerning this see Mahnke's detailed exposition, *Unendliche Sphäre, passim*.

were also made to investigate the empirical aspects of synchronicity and to integrate them into their world-picture. These developments were probably connected with the great contemporary flowering of astrology, during which the time-bound mandala of the horoscope increasingly became an object of study. At the same time, the projection of this mandala image (the horoscope) onto the heavens began to be withdrawn, only to be projected anew onto another unknown region: the mystery of matter. Thus, in the earliest chemistry we find extremely interesting models of the *unus mundus,* which all represent efforts to probe not only the ultimate unity of existence, but also its circumstantial "temporal" manifestations.[26]

In the earliest alchemistic texts, we find mandala-shaped models of matter and of the Opus. In manuscript 2325 in the Bibliotheca Marciana in Venice there appears the picture of the so-called Chrysopoiea of Cleopatra (p. 180).[27] In the inmost circle stand the signs for the sun, moon, and Mercurius. The second ring contains the words: "The serpent is the One which possesses the poison according to the two symbols." And the outermost circle bears the words: "One is the Whole and by its means the Whole [exists] and toward it the Whole [tends] and if the Whole should not comprise the Whole [everything] it would be nothing." Here the circle of the zodiac is identical with the *ouroboros,* the serpent in matter, a symbol of the all-encompassing unity of the cosmos.

In one of the earliest texts, the celebrated instructions of Komarios to Cleopatra (1st–3d centuries A.D.), the transformation of matter into gold is described as a death

26. See Marie-Louise von Franz, "The Idea of the Macro- and Microcosmos in the Light of Jungian Psychology," *Ambix. Journal of the Society for the Study of Alchemy and Early Chemistry,* XIII, no. 1 (February, 1965).

27. M. Berthelot, *Collection des anciens alchemistes grecs* (Paris, 1887–88), I, 132. See also the same circle as the so-called "Labyrinth of Salomo" (pp. 163 and 157).

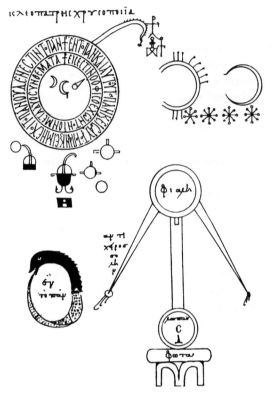

The Chrysopoiea of Cleopatra: the structure of matter
(*left, top and bottom*) and the retort (*bottom right*), according to Komarios (top right is as yet unexplained)
[Source: M. Berthelot, *Collection des anciens alchimistes
grecs* (Paris, 1887–88), I, 132.]

mystery, a voyage into Hades, and a resurrection; and just as in Egypt the dead, at the end of the underworld journey, reached the never-setting circumpolar stars and circled with them in their round dance, so equally, at the conclusion of the alchemical work, there arises a rotating eternal structure, the "one nature" which, like a deadly poison, permeates all other substances.[28] In this context, one of the philosophers quotes an "ancient word": "The Art is the body of the Whirlwind, and is like unto the wheel on high above it, like unto the mystery and the orbit and the pole above, with its houses, degrees, and famous divisions." According to this, the *prima materia* is, in Komarios' view, a rotating heavenly order come down into matter "which God, not man, has transferred there." [29]

Since matter itself appeared to possess a mandala structure, the alchemists claimed time and again that the Opus must follow a cyclic course.[30] It wanders through the four elements[31] until they come together in a "pearl," merging in the "center between the opposites." Then "nature conquers nature and is completed and becomes vortex-shaped" (*illingiosa*).[32]

This "whirlwind" in matter moves analogously to the course of the stars in the firmament, but it also represents the mystery of the soul (personified by Cleopatra) and is a *substance*, namely, the all-permeating Mercurius which is simultaneously described as a murderous poison and a re-vivifying *pharmakon*. It is thus an *all-permeating world-spirit* which gathers the cosmos and all that is contained in

28. It is a kind of subtle body. See *ibid.*, I, 298–99. Komarios comes from the Syrian *komar*, "priest."

29. See *ibid.*, pp. 298, 299.

30. *Ibid.*, p. 191: The Opus contains four stages (*tetrameria* of the Work): *melanōsis*, *leucosis*, *xanthosis*, and *josis* (*rubedo*), as well as four intermediary steps: mummification, ablution, liquefaction of the gold, and division into two. See also pp. 219–20.

31. *Ibid.*, pp. 143 f., 290–91.

32. *Ibid.*, p. 112. This is one of Zosimos' ideas.

it together into a unity. Man unites with it at death and thereby achieves eternity himself, because he then circles in the course of the never-setting circumpolar stars.[33]

In the writings of the Gnostic alchemist Zosimos, especially, an interesting attempt at differentiating this horoscope transferred to matter can be found. He distinguishes between the so-called *kairikai baphai, kairos*-conditioned transformations of matter, and his own individual, more profound, and more "genuine" alchemistic transformations. The "*kairos*-determined" transformations are dependent on astrological constellations and on the demons or star divinities that operate through them. "Genuine" transformations, on the other hand, are brought about by a union of the alchemist's soul with the divine spirit (nous), which permeates and orders the universe. When, by meditation, the alchemist unites with the nous, he is himself redeemed and can simultaneously effect "true" alchemical transformations.[34]

In particular, Zosimos presents the substantially new idea that there are two ordering powers that influence matter: the astrological gods of the cyclical time mandala (the zodiac circle), and the spontaneous manifestations issuing from a center above them, the divine nous, which alone can bring about synchronistic events of positive and lasting value. Although this differentiated conception is not worked out, the fundamental idea of a circular or spherical basic structure to matter and the Opus was, like all the other intuitive, scientific perceptions of antiquity, preserved by the Arabs and transmitted, via their traditions, back to the West. In the Middle Ages, the circular form of the Opus was, for the most part, summarized by the Pseudo-Aristotelian saying: "When thou shalt have obtained water from

33. In my opinion this complex of ideas infiltrated alchemy by way of Egyptian rituals of embalming and burial. For the details of the embalming liturgy see G. Roeder, *Urkunden zur Religion des alten Ägypten* (Jena, 1923), pp. 297–98.
34. See Berthelot, *Collection*, I, 228.

earth, air from water, fire from air, and earth from fire, then possessest thou our Art fully and completely." [35]

The circular movement of the four elements forms a parallel to the same motion common to the soul, logos, and the cosmos.[36] By means of this circulation, a "spiritual earth" is built up, a mystical body which was identified both with man's resurrection body and with the world-spirit.[37]

A bias toward mandala-shaped models of the *unus mundus* can likewise be found in medieval speculations concerning the Sapientia Dei and the Holy Ghost, though once again the timeless and eternal aspect is more emphasized. The problem of time is rarely worked out explicitly. Nevertheless, we find exceptional cases of double mandalas dating back to this period, which touch on the problem of time. The heavenly clock mandala of Guillaume de Digulleville, abbot of Châlis, which was rediscovered by Jung, offers an interesting parallel to the dual systems mentioned above.[38] Guillaume describes a vision of paradise in which he perceived that heaven consisted of forty-nine rotating spheres. These spheres represent the *saecula* composing eternity. They are encompassed by *one* golden circle. The latter is intersected by a second orbit on which a three-foot wide blue circle rolls, standing for the calendar of the church year. Here again we have two systems, one relatively eternal and one cyclically time-bound. Above the blue circle we find the mysterious sentence: "Il sortait du ciel d'or en un point et y rentrait d'autre part, et il en faisait tout le tour." On its orbit the blue circle somehow passes through the

35. "De regimine principum," quoted in the *Rosarium philosophorum*, ed. J. J. Mangetus, Bibliotheca chemica curiosa, 3. 101C. See von Franz, *Aurora consurgens*, pp. 307–8, 346.
36. See von Franz, *Aurora consurgens*, p. 347.
37. See C. G. Jung, *Psychology and Alchemy*, CW, Vol. XII. The *Aurora consurgens* centers almost exclusively on these ideas. Reference is therefore made to my commentary on the text.
38. *Psychology and Religion: West and East*, CW, Vol. XI, ¶¶ 115–18.

gold-encompassed sphere. As Jung explained, the threefold structure of Guillaume's mandala is bound up with medieval trinitarian thought, which excluded matter and the feminine principle from its God-image.

In *Psychology and Alchemy*, Jung compares this medieval vision with a modern parallel, the vision of a "world clock" from the dream series of a modern scientist. The dreamer describes his vision thus:

> [I see] a vertical and a horizontal circle, having a common centre. This is the world clock. . . . The vertical circle is a blue disc with a white border divided into $4 \times 8 = 32$ partitions. A pointer rotates upon it. The horizontal circle consists of four colours. On it stand four little men with pendulums, and round about it is laid a ring . . . now golden. . . . The "clock" has three rhythms or pulses:
>   1. The small pulse: the pointer on the blue vertical disc advances by 1/32.
>   2. The middle pulse: one complete revolution of the pointer. At the same time the horizontal circle advances by 1/32.
>   3. The great pulse: 32 middle pulses are equal to one revolution of the golden ring.[39]

Jung comments:

> Circle and quaternity on one side and the threefold rhythm on the other interpenetrate so that each is contained in the other. . . . Such interpenetrations of qualities and contents are typical not only of symbols in general, but also of the essential similarity of the contents symbolized.[40]

Continuing his commentary, Jung stresses the fact that the Self here appears to *consist of two heterogeneous systems* which stand in a functional relationship to each other,

39. *Psychology and Alchemy*, ¶¶ 307–8.
40. *Psychology and Religion*, ¶¶ 125–26.

regulated by three rhythms and lawfully ordered—perhaps analogously to the three *regimina* of alchemy. He continues:

> Since the figure has a cosmic aspect—world clock—we must suppose it to be a small-scale model *or perhaps even a source of space-time,* or at any rate an abstract of it and therefore, mathematically speaking, four-dimensional in nature although only visible in a three-dimensional projection.[41]

In this mandala vision, all the principal opposites are reconciled. If we apply here the ancient Pythagorean concept that the soul consists of a tetrad, the mandala would then express the Godhead through its threefold rhythm, and the soul through its static quaternity (the circle divided into four colors). The innermost meaning of the vision would thus signify nothing less than a union of the soul with God.

In her outstanding book, *Giordano Bruno and the Hermetic Tradition,* Frances Yates has recently shown how the type of mandala structure described by Guillaume was revived intensely in Renaissance philosophy and led to the most curious theoretical developments. Strongly influenced by the then rediscovered *Corpus hermeticum,* Marsilio Ficino was the first, in his work *De vita coelitus comparanda,* to take up the old practice of magic again.[42] His theory was based on the idea that the entire universe is composed of *one* single being (the *unus mundus*), consisting of the substance of the cosmos, the world-soul, and the nous as the divine world-spirit. The last named contains the *ideae;* the world-soul contains the *rationes seminales;* and the sphere of the world comprises the *species* of all things. Among these three (*ideae, rationes, species*) exist magical connections (*concatenationes*), so that by bringing the "correct" earthly substances together, the *ideae* can be magically

41. *Psychology and Alchemy,* ¶ 312 (my italics).
42. See Frances Yates, *Giordano Bruno and the Hermetic Tradition* (London, 1964), for this and the following. This writing of Ficino forms the third part of a work, *De vita,* which came out in 1489.

captured and constellated.[43] In this way, portions of the world-soul can also be pulled down into the lower world and captured, thereby even "deconstellating" adverse physical and psychic conditions.[44] For this reason, Ficino believed, it would be particularly beneficial to fashion a likeness of the whole universe (a *mundi figura*).[45] This figure should consist of bronze combined with gold and silver (= Jupiter, Sol, Venus). The work should be begun when the sun enters Aries, and completed when it stands in the sign of Venus. It must contain three lines and three colors: green, gold, and blue.[46] The sum total is envisaged to be a kind of talismanic object, in the form of a mandala,[47] which can either be worn like a medallion or a jewel, or hung on the wall to be contemplated. One must, he continues, meditate on this figure in one's soul and then it can exert a positive influence on the world. Whoever contemplates such an image and impresses its lines and colors on his memory can, when he goes forth from his house and is overwhelmed by the many impressions of the outer world, transform their chaotic appearance into a unity through the image of higher reality carried within himself.

43. Yates, *Giordano Bruno*, p. 65; Campanella, a later magician working along the same lines, actually performed a rite of this kind to protect Pope Urban VII from a dangerous eclipse (see *ibid.*, p. 375).

44. *Ibid.*, pp. 64, 65. See her commentary, p. 65: "There is further in Ficino's words the notion that the material forms in the world of sense can be, as it were, reformed when they have degenerated, by manipulation of the higher images, on which they depend. In his analysis of this passage E. Garin has defined this process as imitation or reconstruction of the higher images in such a way that the divine influences are recaptured and reconducted into the deteriorated sensible forms."

45. *Ibid.*, pp. 73–74.

46. For Venus, Sol, and Jupiter. Blue designates the world, and green represents the earth or Vesta-Ceres.

47. Since Ficino refers to Lorenzo della Volpiaia's construction of an astronomical world clock as a parallel, he was clearly thinking in terms of a spherical form.

Significantly, this world mandala is triadic (three metals, three colors), Ficino's outlook having remained strictly Christian. In contradistinction to him and to Pico della Mirandola, Giordano Bruno was converted to a pagan Egyptian attitude while at the same time retaining Ficino's propensity to deepen and intensify introverted reality. In Bruno's view, too, every man bears the image of the universe in his soul. He therefore constructed various models, and, in accordance with his paganism, his cosmic mandala was quaternary.[48] According to him, when one restructures and reconstellates the inner world in a positive sense, a superior inner personality is engendered.[49] The inner individual imagination is so reconstituted that spiritual and demonic powers are drawn to the personality and become bound to it. At the same time, Bruno's mandala forms a mnemotechnical system[50] through which the inner personality can be specifically influenced by means of memory; but the final aim of this magical memory-imprinting is the formation of an inner religious personality.[51]

In his work *De umbris idearum* (by which he means magical shadow facsimiles of the heavenly archetypes),[52] Bruno arranges the thirty-six images of the decanates, the forty-nine planetary images (seven per planet), and finally the thirty-six representations said to pertain to the circle of the twelve zodiac signs, into a circular system. The complete structure, however, is not meant to represent a horoscope, but a cosmic "memory system";[53] it functions, simultaneously, as a means of becoming identical with God. Through it, the imagination becomes imprinted with the

48. Yates, *Giordano Bruno*, pp. 265, 272 n.
49. *Ibid.*, p. 220.
50. *Ibid.*, p. 266. See also P. Rossi, *Clavis universalis: Arti mnemoniche e logica combinatoria da Lullo a Leibniz* (Milan and Naples, 1960), *passim.*
51. Yates, *Giordano Bruno*, p. 271.
52. See *ibid.*, p. 197.
53. *Ibid.*, pp. 198–99.

proper inner images.[54] The infinite number of worlds, whose existence Bruno assumed, were all divine centers of the boundless universe, for God is "omnia infinitus ubique totus." He embodies the "soul of the world-soul," not just the soul itself.[55]

In another of Bruno's books, *Articuli centum et sexaginta adversus mathematicos atque philosophos* (1588), he presents a collection of the most curious and original mandala drawings, which he describes variously as "figura mentis," "figura intellectus," "figura amoris," and "Zoemetra." Some of these are slightly asymmetrical.[56] These structures were obviously images meant to impress the memory in such a way that it would become structurally unified and the soul would thereby attain direct contact with higher reality.[57] "For the soul," says Bruno, "is the light of God." [58]

Giordano Bruno was so profoundly moved by his mandala model of the universe that he also interpreted Copernicus' heliocentric theory and Mordente's invention of the compass in the same way, maintaining that these discoverers insufficiently grasped the meaning of their own theories (or discoveries) because they merely comprehended them scientifically. For himself they held a deeper, *magical* significance.

54. *Ibid.*, p. 201. In another work, *Sigillus sigillorum*, or *Explicatio triginta sigillorum* (published ca. 1583), Bruno explains that in every human being there reposes an image of the universe, which should be reformed in order for the individual personality to be transformed (See Yates, *Giordano Bruno*, p. 205).

55. Yates, *Giordano Bruno*, pp. 246–47, 269.

56. Cf. *ibid.*, pp. 306–7. Some are not named. The only complete copy is in the Bibliothèque Nationale Res. D² 5278.

57. *Ibid.*, pp. 308, 313. In Bruno's view the spiritual and mental life of man is based on four principles: love, art, mathesis, and magic. Love is the life force in all things, which the magician draws up from a lower to a higher level. Art is the knowledge whereby one can unite with the world-soul. Mathesis is the art of learning how, while relinquishing visible matter in space and time, to understand the intelligible. Magic is that which unites the soul with God through love.

58. *Ibid.*, pp. 271–72, 282. For this elevation of the soul to God certain *contractiones* ("exercises in introversion") and a specific *furor* ("ecstasy") are necessary.

Top left, Figura mentis; *top right,* Figura intellectus; *bottom left,* Figura amoris; *bottom right,* Zoemetra [Source: Frances Yates, *Giordano Bruno and the Hermetic Tradition* (London, 1964), p. 307, reproduced by permission of the Bibliothèque Nationale, Paris.]

These various examples of mandala structures, representing a psychophysical *unus mundus,* were predominantly transsubjective. In fact, their purpose was primarily an inner psychic one, namely, to protect the individual soul from distintegrating influences, and to reconstellate it positively. They served as objects of meditation leading the personality toward inner concentration and unification. They stood for a higher order, contemplation of which also led man to attain an ordered state of mind. In the speculations of the Gnostic Zosimos, and again later in Giordano Bruno, another still more far-reaching concept about such structures became discernible: namely, the idea that a "magical" influence could emanate from their centers or, in more modern language, that synchronistic and therefore parapsychological phenomena could be connected with them. *At the same time, such synchronistic events appear to be linked up with an individual's inner development and in some way dependent on it.*

Mutatis mutandis, this cosmic mandala concept once again enters into the speculations of some modern physicists. It appears again in the cosmic model of the relativists, in their concept of a "world-body" describable in terms of three space coordinates and one time coordinate. In itself, this four-dimensional world is conceived as being timeless. It is transcendental. Man's consciousness merely moves along the world-lines of his body and his immediate surroundings and thus subjectively experiences the world as a temporal factor.[59] In a timeless world such as this, everything is strictly determined. Because this point of view conflicts with Heisenberg's uncertainty principle,[60] the Munich physicist

59. Aloys Wenzl, in *Die philosophischen Grenzfragen der modernen Naturwissenschaft* (Stuttgart, 1960), pp. 43–44, formulates this as follows: "The universe is a construction, an order of systems which appear equally to be independent of each other, but which, for this very reason, can only represent for one another perspectives of a supraordinate reality. In this 'world' there is true temporality, namely, the actualization of preformed, prestabilized, predestined possibilities in causal processes; but for the actualizations which are independent of each other temporal coincidence is only an ideal state, an intuitive idea realized by no one. There is a vague relationship, with regard to time. For those remote occurrences which have not yet manifested themselves to us there is an uncertainty about time." See also pp. 33, 39.

60. The determinism of general relativity theory stands in a certain (complementary) antithesis to quantum theory which, as a result of Heisenberg's uncertainty principle, admits of a certain freedom. The

Aloys Wenzl suggests that the four-dimensional geometrical continuum of the Einsteinian world-model possesses merely a potential existence. He considers it to be a "pattern of space-time reality, insofar as this can be determined, and strictly the potential scope of possibilities, insofar as a free actualization can take place in them." [61]

In this sense, the world-model of the relativists closely approximates the Jungian concept of the *unus mundus*. Everything appearing to us in space and time, then, strictly speaking represents merely the realization of the essential characteristics of a mathematical structure, in which not only space and time, but also substance and dynamism, are translated into mathematical values.[62] This structure is a four-dimensional continuum of constant measuring values, a "world" or "world-plane" on which material events are

----

question is whether this represents only a practical limitation of determinism or an objective indeterminism. In other words, does the expression "probability wave" mean something real, or is it only an ideal methodological concept? If this indeterminism is real then a certain ultimate indeterminism adheres in the final analysis to material events, i.e., an objective randomness. "A not unequivocally calculable universe concretizes its possibilities with a certain contingency." "The world that was being realized would then," as formulated by Wenzl, "not be a hundred per cent rational, but would also be a voluntative world, as a result of which it would at the same time be both arational and final or evaluating" (*ibid.*, p. 56). Thus from the viewpoint of relativity theory the time factor is problematic, while in contradistinction the standpoint of quantum physics calls the principle of causality into question. Viewed psychologically, the theory of relativity embodies a more introverted attitude, and that of quantum theory a more extraverted one.

61. *Ibid.*, pp. 128–29. The mathematician Riemann has already raised the question as to whether the reality underlying space forms a discrete diversity, or whether the basis of dimension must be sought externally in the binding forces operating upon it (space); the latter thesis was interpreted by Hermann Weyl (*Raum, Zeit, Materie* [Darmstadt, 1961], p. 101) to the effect that space is a formless, three-dimensional manifold whose material contents first shape it and determine its measurable dimensions. See also p. 139.

62. See Wenzl, *Philosophische Grenzfragen*, p. 127: "In this sense the laws of nature simply represent realized mathematical laws."

visualized by means of a purely mathematical formalism.[63] "On the basis of a coordinate system for space and time," says Hermann Weyl, "physical reality in the world can also be determined according to all its definitions by means of numbers." [64]

Inspired by his studies of information theory and the problem of entropy, the French physicist Olivier Costa de Beauregard recently attributed an additional psychic aspect to the relativistic world model. He emphasizes that "the Universe explored by physicists is not the entirety . . . from it the existence of another, far more primordial *psychic* universe may be surmised, of which the material Universe only represents a passive and partial double." [65] This psychic universe is imagined to be only a formal, potential, and timeless frame for events, and simultaneously an undivided, homogeneous, universal background. In addition, de Beauregard suggests that we regard the psychic unconscious to be timelessly coextensive with the Minkowski-Einsteinian "world";[66] this means that the timeless extension of the

63. Within this "continuum" there is no absolute space, objective synchronism, or objective system-independent mass quantity, but all phenomena are relational in the sense of reciprocity (*ibid.*, p. 25). Space, time, and substance are only modes of manifestation which, when they are surveyed from different systems, appear different (p. 26). Nevertheless natural laws take on the same form in all systems when the mass-values of space and time are correspondingly amended (p. 29). Every field of gravity can therefore be expressed by the metric system for space-time (p. 30). In other words, the curvature of space and its metrics are shaped by the nature of material existence. Space is formed by matter and the distribution of energy, and what we call matter becomes describable through the mathematical shaping of the continuum (p. 32).

64. Weyl, *Raum, Zeit, Materie*, p. 9.

65. Translated from *Le Second Principe de la science du temps* (Paris, 1963), p. 14.

66. *Ibid.*, pp. 115–16, 124: "Similarly, it belongs to the very essence of consciousness to explore closely and always in the same direction, without interruption, the time dimension of the cosmos, trailing behind it the memory traces which form the reward of acquired information; the unconscious, on the contrary, has no reason to be subject to the same law. Could it not, therefore, be the unconscious about

relativistic Einsteinian "world" would be coexistent with the timeless extension of the unconscious psyche.

I do not intend to criticize in any way the validity of these modern theories in physics.[67] The remarkable fact about them, in our context, is that they illustrate the way in which modern physicists also grope toward a model of the *unus mundus* resembling Jung's concept to some extent. De Beauregard's hypothesis strikes me, moreover, as being particularly noteworthy because, instead of merely introducing arbitrary symmetries and "hidden" parameters in the wrong place, he has had the courage to postulate the reality of a psychic dimension which he considers to be the "mirror-image" of the material world.[68]

---

which we could say that it is coextensive with the time dimension of the cosmos?"

67. *Second Principe*, ch. 22. De Beauregard's proposition has innumerable less scientific parallels which have been collected by R. Weitzenböck in his book *Der vierdimensionale Raum* (Basel and Stuttgart, 1956). After a demonstration of the purely mathematical construction of a four- and more-dimensional space and of the idea of a fourth dimension in the relativistic sense, he describes with amusement and scorn a survey of the many fantastic, romantic and semiserious, pseudoscientific, and spiritualistic fantasies about a fourth dimension. In the light of Jungian psychology, it becomes quite clear that a projection of the collective unconscious has fallen heavily on the idea of a fourth dimension.

68. In this sense the introduction of "hidden parameters" in physics has always seemed to me somewhat questionable because it offers too much scope for possible projections. In addition, many of the constant laws of symmetry have recently proved to be pure projections. T. D. Lee therefore quite rightly concludes his article "Space Inversion, Time Reversal, Particle-Antiparticle Conjugation," *Physics Today*, XIX, no. 3 (March, 1966), with the words: "The progress of science has always been the result of a close interplay between our concepts of the universe and our observations of nature. The former can only evolve out of the latter, and yet the latter are also conditioned to a remarkable degree by the former. As we expand our fields of observations, naturally, we also extend our basic concepts. At times, these two factors, the concept and the observation, may become so interlocked that even some of the fundamental principles used in an entire domain of familiar phenomena may, to our chagrin, turn out to have no actual experimental basis. The history of these discrete symmetries has been a particularly rich one, full of such surprises" (p. 31).

From this standpoint, however, the question of time "in itself" remains problematic, and one excludes the problem of "chance," both in the ordinary sense of the word and in its connotation of "meaningful chance"—the phenomenon of synchronicity. In this respect the Minkowski-Einsteinian universe resembles Platonic and Neoplatonic models of the cosmos, which either did not take the problem of time into consideration, or considered it only as a cyclic process, intellectually excluding the concept of a *creatio* in the sense of undetermined "new creations."

CHAPTER ELEVEN

Divinatory, Mnemotechnical, and Cybernetic Mandalas

I₎ MYSTERIUM CONIUNCTIONIS, Jung made the important statement that the mandala is the inner psychic counterpart, and synchronistic phenomena the parapsychological equivalent, of the *unus mundus*.[1] Small wonder if, on that account, numerous attempts have been made in the past to combine these two equivalents into a unitary reality and to construct mandalas through which one hoped, by virtue of the principle of synchronicity, to acquire parapsychological "knowledge." As we have already seen, such ideas played an undeniable role in the works of both the Gnostic Zosimos and Giordano Bruno.

To those models of the universe in which the problems of time and synchronicity have, from time immemorial, been brought together belong above all the horoscopes, and especially the transit horoscope, known since earliest times. By means of them, an effort was made to investigate the quality of a specific moment in time and the possible events contained within it. In antiquity we also find other mandalas, derived from these astrological instruments of divination,

---

1. *Mysterium Coniunctionis, CW*, Vol. XIV, ¶ 662.

Sphere of Petosiris [Source: M. Berthelot, *Collection des anciens alchimistes grecs* (Paris, 1887–88), I, 88.]

which were no longer exclusively associated with real constellations of stars. In antique medicine, for instance, certain magical circles were employed in order to discover the prognosis of life or death for a patient. These circles formed a kind of horoscope encompassing the critical days of the illness, and were supposed to function similarly to the transit horoscope. Examples are the so-called "sphere of Democritus" and the "spheres of Petosiris." [2] The text on the sphere of Democritus runs:

> Prognosis concerning life and death. Acquaint thyself with the moon under which the patient became ill, and with the number of his birth name, add the calculation for the moon, observe how many times 30 days have passed since then, take the remainder and look in the circle: if the number falls in the upper half the patient will live, if in the lower he will die. [3]

2. M. Berthelot, *Collection des anciens alchimistes grecs* (Paris, 1887–88), I, 88, text 86.

3. The number of the birth name was reckoned in accordance with the technique of gematria, in which every letter possesses a numerical value.

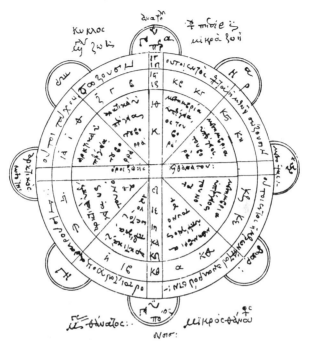

Another sphere of Petosiris [Source: Berthelot, *Collection des anciens alchimistes grecs*, I, 90.]

We are here concerned with a horoscope that is relatively independent of the stars, being based instead on the time qualities occurring in the course of an illness and on the momentary individual "fate" of a patient. These structural models were thus more individual than the alchemistic world-models and more related to a specific time moment in the life of a single person. Such instruments, which were also often based on other principles of calculation (the sphere of Petosiris, for example),[4] came originally from Egypt and remained in use throughout the entire medieval tradition.

4. Berthelot, *Collection*, I, 87 f. There were also circular divinatory figures for discovering the whereabouts of a runaway slave, etc.

They served as tools for magically acquiring information about the rationally unknowable.[5] This use of the mandala reappears in Giordano Bruno's work, for he applied it not only to the technique of inner concentration but also to parapsychological ends.

These examples of mandalas were not supposed to mirror the static and eternal fundamental structure of the universe and the human soul, but to function as instruments of divination, suppliers of information, or pointers to the constellations, which served specific purposes in the immediate present. In the first instance, an ordered timeless structure of the universe or the human mind and spirit was kept in mind, while in the latter case either allusion was made to the correct understanding of synchronistic phenomena as uniquely happening "miracles," or a magical attempt was made to acquire knowledge concerning an individual "just-so" experience.[6] A time-bound, individual factor had therefore to be introduced into these later mandala structures.[7] In this connection, it is particularly striking that the crucial time moment and the act of personal intervention were observed to somehow belong together,[8] which implies

5. An analogous example is provided by an ancient Chinese text on arithmetic, the Sun-Tzu: a pregnant woman is due to give birth in nine months. Will it be a boy or a girl? Take forty-nine, add the number of the time moment of her pregnancy and subtract her age. From the remainder subtract 1 for heaven, 2 for earth, 3 for man, 4 for the four seasons, 6 for the six hours, 7 for the seven stars, 8 for the eight winds and 9 for the nine provinces. If the remainder is uneven the child will be a boy; if even, a girl. (J. Mikami, *The Development of Mathematics in China and Japan* [Leipzig: 1913], p. 34.) I am indebted to Mr. Arnold Mindell for bringing this text to my attention.

6. Cosmic models probably represent an effort to seize hold of the "acausal orderedness" of the universe, in contradistinction to divinatory mandalas which sought to comprehend the synchronistic event.

7. In the horoscope, the moment of birth; in divination about illness, the day of contracting the disease; in the geoscope, the individually effected accumulation of points; in the I Ching, the throw of coins in the querent's own hand, etc.

8. A complementary relation probably exists between that aspect of the *unus mundus* which constitutes acausal orderedness and its parapsychological manifestations in the phenomena of synchronicity; the

that qualitative, specific time moments only emerge out of a latent, undifferentiable continuum when an individual confronts the continuum. Giordano Bruno, who was more of a highly gifted but naïve thinker than a rational one, sought especially to discover these empirical means of experiencing the unity of the world. He tried through his mandala to build a kind of cybernetic machine which he hoped would establish connections with the "light" of the unconscious, just as the ancients endeavored to achieve such connections by means of their "spheres" and geomantic geoscopes.

These attempts, absurd as they may seem to us today, were directed toward solving a problem which is still unsolved, namely, the fact that the unconscious actually appears to contain a kind of "knowledge" which is not identical with ego consciousness. In his paper "On the Nature of the Psyche," [9] Jung took great pains to demonstrate that the archetypes of the unconscious possess a kind of "quasi intelligence" which is not the same as our ego consciousness. [10] Jung applied the term "luminosity" to this quasi consciousness of the archetypes, in order to differentiate it from the "light" of ego consciousness. The same phenomenon can be observed from another angle when a synchronistic occurrence takes place. Inner and outer facts then behave as if their meaningful relation were in some way known, but not to our personal consciousness. Differently expressed, a "meaning" manifests itself in synchronistic phenomena which appears to be independent of conscious-

---

two facets can only be expressed by the antinomies of timeless-eternal and sporadic-temporal.

9. *The Structure and Dynamics of the Psyche*, CW, Vol. VIII, ¶ 388.

10. This can perhaps best be made clear to the psychological layman by the fact that we are at times motivated by an unconscious urge to do something life-saving and meaningful, something very "intelligent," whose positive value we only subsequently recognize. Its "intelligence" we can therefore in no way ascribe to an achievement of our ego.

ness and to be completely transcendental.[11] It consists of representational images (*simulacra*), and its appearance seems to be connected with the momentary activation of an archetype manifesting itself simultaneously in physical and psychic realms[12] in the form of acausal orderedness.[13] The meaning that unites these inner and outer happenings consists of knowledge unmediated by the sense organs. This quality of knowledge is what Jung calls "absolute knowledge," since it seems to be detached from our consciousness.[14] In other words, although the initial significance of a synchronistic event can only be experienced subjectively, the fact of a meaningful coincidence on psychic and physical levels suggests that the meaning may also have been originally present in the objective event itself; something rational or similar to meaning may inhere in the event itself.[15] Surprisingly enough, certain representatives of modern theoretical physics have arrived at similar conjectures. Aloys Wenzl, for instance, says that "on account of its mathematical expressibility" the concrete individual material event within the Einsteinian continuum expresses a logos ordering of existence.[16]

The idea that meaning lies concealed in events themselves

11. When such an image arises spontaneously out of the unconscious and breaks into the normal course of consciousness, the categories of space, time, and causality seem to become relativized. The "meaning" that shines through synchronistic phenomena thus seems to exist in a relative psychic space-time continuum which is not directly accessible to our perception. ("Synchronicity," *Structure and Dynamics of the Psyche*, ¶ 948.)

12. *Ibid.*; this means that absolute knowledge is a form of cognition not mediated by any sense organ.

13. *Ibid.*, ¶ 965: "The meaningful coincidence or equivalence of a psychic and a physical state . . . means, in general terms, that it is a modality without a cause, an 'acausal orderedness.' "

14. *Ibid.*, ¶ 148.

15. Cf. *ibid.*, ¶¶ 921–23.

16. *Die philosophischen Grenzfragen der modernen Naturwissenschaft* (Stuttgart, 1960), p. 95. It is also pertinent that certain relativists construct an "absolute observer" which, in contradistinction to a real observer, can simultaneously survey all the world-systems.

was, as Richard Wilhelm has shown, predominant in earliest Chinese culture. We also come across it in the West, in Heraclitus' conception of logos, to mention one example. Another version of this view is to be found in the Aristotelian idea of the *nous poietikos*, an active intelligence inherent in the physical universe which is secondarily manifest in the human soul as the "natural light" and is capable of influencing man's thinking.[17]

In his work on synchronicity, Jung cites a number of other thinkers, both ancient and medieval, who believed in an *oulomelia*, a *correspondentia* or sympathy of all things, whose "meaning" lay hidden in objective phenomena of the outer world and could be investigated with the help of mantic procedures. These are the residue of a primitive magical type of thinking which has been more or less eliminated in the development of our more exact modern sciences. In the course of the development of these sciences, however, the baby has, as so often before, been thrown out with the bathwater, so that the directly observable manifestations of "absolute knowledge" in the collective unconscious have also been thrown away.

Yet another form of man's endeavor to establish contact with the "absolute knowledge" is to be found in certain mnemotechnical arts of antiquity.[18] Some ancient orators (Cicero among them) sought to bolster their memories by associating specific oratory themes with specific positions (*loci*) in the halls where they were to speak. As their gaze then wandered around the hall during an address, they

17. See Marie-Louise von Franz, *Aurora consurgens*, trans. R. F. C. Hull and A. S. B. Glover (New York, 1966), pp. 166 ff. The suprapersonal aspect of the "nous" was equated by Thomas Aquinas with the Sapientia Dei; the latter brings about greater mysteries than does faith. See E. Gilson, "Pourquoi St. Thomas a critiqué St. Augustin," *Archives d'histoire doctrinale et littéraire du moyen-age*, I (1926–27), 5–9, especially 7.

18. For further details see P. Rossi, *Clavis universalis: Arti Mnemoniche e logica combinatoria da Lullo a Leibniz* (Milan and Naples, 1960), *passim*.

recalled the themes in their correct sequence. The orator Metrodorus of Scepsis then substituted the twelve houses of the horoscope for these *loci*, thus making use of the zodiac pattern as a sort of mnemotic mandala.[19] He was probably inspired to this innovation by the notion that connecting a generally known pattern of ideas up with the themes of one's discourse would make them "stick" extremely well.[20]

The basic idea underlying these techniques is that our mental processes are based on a *numerical structure* in the final analysis, which harmonizes with the structure of the universe. In his description of the acausal orderedness in nature which appears to underlie synchronistic experiences, Jung emphasized the fact that such a structural correspondence may be entirely possible. This correspondence should not be sought, however, in human brain processes. Rather, he stresses, the "intelligent" behavior of lower brainless organisms more closely approaches this "formal factor."[21] We now know that the giant four-component molecules of ribonucleic acid can produce a memorylike accumulation of information in every living cell, by a kind of mathematical Morse code.[22] With such discoveries we arrive at the psychoid frontier of the psyche, where its ordering principle

19. See Frances Yates, *Giordano Bruno and the Hermetic Tradition* (London, 1964), p. 191.

20. This is actually the case, for it is well known that all impressions are more firmly fixed in the memory if they are accompanied by positive or negative affects. To this the psychologist can add that all impressions resembling, however obliquely, archetypal contents are bound up with particularly violent emotions. The archetype accordingly produces affect-laden ideas, and it is precisely these which "stick" better than nonarchetypal ideas. See G. J. Whitrow, *The Natural Philosophy of Time* (London and Edinburgh, 1961), pp. 107–8, with his references to authors who rely on preconscious representational patterns to explain the phenomenon of memory.

21. "Synchronicity," ¶ 947. McConnell's experiments with flatworms are still, alas, too controversial to permit of further inferences.

22. The same is valid for the genetic code of the DNA. See Wolfgang Pauli, "Naturwissenschaftliche und erkenntnistheoretische Aspekte der Ideen vom Unbewussten," *Aufsätze und Vorträge über Physik und Erkenntnistheorie* (Brunswick, 1961), p. 128, n. 22.

appears to be transgressively manifest in matter. Jung's conjecture thereby becomes a good deal more probable, namely, that the archetypes, as psychophysical formal structures, are in the final analysis a world-forming principle, a common transcendental ordering factor of existence.

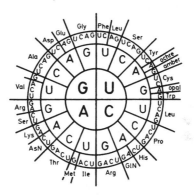

The so-called sun-code of the genetic substances (the codones should be read from the inside outwards) [Source: C. Bresch and R. Hausmann, *Klassische und molekulare Genetik*, 2d ed. (Berlin, 1970), p. 193, reproduced by permission of Springer Verlag.]

Considered in this light, the naïve mnemotechnical mandalas of antiquity discussed above are not quite as ridiculous as they might first appear. They are the first attempts to express, in a hunch, the numerically ordered foundation of our mental processes.[23] They signal the first beginnings of an *ars combinatoria* like the one that engages the attention of many logicians once again today.

23. It must be emphasized, however, that these ordering principles which underlie memory in the cell cannot be identical with what Jung termed "absolute knowledge," but can only be an approximate form of it. This is because these arrangements in the material substratum can only, as far as I see, store up what is regular and recurring, whereas absolute knowledge appears to contain foreknowledge of unique events, like the case quoted by Jung where a printer's error was dreamt in advance.

It is probable that these memory mandalas, like the alchemical "spheres" of Petosiris already discussed, exerted an influence on one of the most curious inventions of the Middle Ages, the idea of a magical idea-computer, celebrated in the *ars magna* of Raimon Lull of Majorca (ca. 1235–1315). He invented a mandala-shaped cybernetic machine which he

One of the main designs in Raimon Lull's *ars magna*. A signifies God; B to K signify attributes of God, such as goodness, truth, and wisdom. Thus one can relate God's characteristics to each other by mathematical equations. [Source: E.-W. Platzeck, *Raimund Lull*, 2 vols. (Dusseldorf, 1962), I, 195, reproduced by permission of Dr. E.-W. Platzeck.]

hoped would answer all the questions put to it. Significantly, this idea came to him in a sudden inspiration from the unconscious, which earned him the title of *doctor illuminatus*.[24] His *ars magna* consisted of a mandala composed of various circular discs, some static, some rotary, arranged concentrically above one another.[25] In order to answer theological questions, for instance, the bottom circle was inscribed with the word "God" at its center and separated on its circumference into sixteen divisions, distributed with such attributes

24. See F. Yates, "Ramon Lull and John Scotus Erigena," *Journal of the Warburg and Courtauld Institute*, XXIII (1960), 1 ff. See further E.-W. Platzeck, *Raimund Lull* (Düsseldorf, 1962), Vol. II.

25. L. Thorndike, *History of Magic and Experimental Science* (New York, 1923), II, 862 ff.

as good, great, and so on. At the center of another circle stood the *anima rationalis*, which was represented by four squares and divided on its circumference into sixteen parts each containing a suitable characteristic. By turning the discs it was mechanically possible to obtain a "logical" answer to all questions concerning these matters.[26] This magical machine naturally failed, just as I am quite sure the modern wish-fulfilling dreams of replacing the human brain by a giant computer will also fail.

What differentiates Lull's model from those we mentioned earlier (he exerted an enormous influence on Giordano Bruno, by the way) is the fact that he did not hope to produce magical effects, or impress the imagination, or even uplift the personality, but wished, by a purely *mechanical* arrangement, to produce *logical* answers to specific questions.[27] For Lull, the numerical structure of a mandala model was associated not with qualitative symbols, but with the necessity for rational thought. He believed that with a mathematical thinking machine the questions posed by an individual would elicit correct replies. In this way Lull made far more rational use of his mandala than the thinkers discussed above (such as Ficino, Pico della Mirandola, and Giordano Bruno) made of their mnemotechnical ones. *Mutatis mutandis*, this more rational attitude ultimately triumphed in the form of Johannes Kepler's model of the planetary system, which he himself defended against Robert Fludd's more symbolic and Pythagorean model in terms of its "pure and mathematically logical" character.

Finally, we must mention the famous Cartesian coordinate system which, it seems to me, as a thought pattern, can also

26. *Ibid.*, p. 865.
27. Penetrating the spirit of Arab culture, Raimon Lull became impressed by their mathematical gifts and somehow hoped, with the help of his geometrical-mathematical idea-machine, to convert the Arabs "logically" to Christianity, where theological arguments had failed. But the Arabs—perhaps with reason—stoned him for his efforts.

be traced back to the same archetype.[28] It is on Descartes's system that all the calculations of classical physics are based; the limited, relative nature of its applicability was not grasped until this century. His discovery of this system was originally connected with an illumination he experienced which represented a breakthrough of the unconscious.[29] On November 10, 1619, the night before his famous great dream occurred, he was filled with great enthusiasm because he believed himself to have discovered the fundamentals of a "wonderful science" (*scientia mirabilis*). The conjectures of savants as to what this *scientia mirabilis* consisted of differ. Some writers suggest it was the discovery that mathematics, geometry, arithmetic, astronomy, and music could all be reduced to a *mathématique universelle* whose basic principles consist of the seriality of number and its proportional relations. Others say it dealt with the creation of algebraic and cossic signs. Still others maintain it was the discovery of analytical geometry. Actually, G. Milhaud puts forward the most likely suggestion, that these various discoveries were only later elaborated.[30] Initially, he surmises, Descartes experienced a general mathematical enlightenment, a sort of intuitive insight into the immanent orderedness of thought processes induced and structured by the archetypes (and especially by numbers). It was therefore an experience of "absolute knowledge." [31] Everything that is accessible to true understanding, in Descartes's later view, is also susceptible to

28. Rossi, in *Clavis universalis*, also correctly perceived this connection.

29. For further details, see Marie-Louise von Franz, "The Dream of Descartes," *Timeless Documents of the Soul* (Evanston, Ill., 1968), pp. 65–67. See further Rossi, *Clavis universalis*, pp. 153 ff. Rossi says that in his youth, at the time of his "great dream," Descartes was influenced by Lullian and Cinquecento fantasies of the *ars universalis* and by then prevalent cosmic constructions of unity, which he later turned away from.

30. G. Milhaud, *Descartes savant* (Paris, 1921), and also L. Maritain, *Le Songe de Descartes* (Paris, 1932), p. 255.

31. Further details in von Franz, "Dream of Descartes," p. 72.

the mathematical method.[32] Possibly this assumption is due to the fact that he was granted a mathematical "revelation" of the structure of the unconscious. When he subsequently elaborated his coordinate system, it was, in my opinion, an attempt to dovetail this original vision of the mathematical structure of existence into a homogeneous formalism. Significantly, however, his system is only three-dimensional. It is psychologically in keeping with this triadic system that Descartes repudiated "images" and the "imagination" in his later development, and would only admit mathematical abstractions for the description of existence,[33] although he originally recognized the equal value of poetic imagery and philosophy. As I have tried to show elsewhere, this shift in attitude was paralleled in Descartes's development by a gradual repression of the feeling-function and by the growth of a rationalistic outlook.[34]

The problem of dealing with the rational recognizability of the whole of existence through mathematical procedures finds its counterpart in modern physics in certain questions raised by cybernetical research.[35] A purely positivistic attitude does indeed try to ignore the psychological aspects and implications which have inevitably seeped into this branch of science, but theorists like Léon Brillouin, M. Ruyer, and Olivier Costa de Beauregard have come to the conclusion that "psychic resonance" cannot be excluded.[36] Brillouin, Gabor, and Rothstein have therefore admitted the results and problems posed by cybernetics into the scope of their

32. See E. Gilson, *René Descartes' Discours de la méthode* (Paris, 1947), p. 60.
33. Cf. Rossi, *Clavis universalis*, p. 153.
34. Von Franz, "Dream of Descartes."
35. Cybernetics is the science of technical "information," registering, encoding, telecommunication, computers, etc., and their mathematical foundations. See J. R. Pierce, *Symbols, Signals and Noise: The Nature and Process of Communication* (New York, 1961), and also L. Brillouin, *Scientific Uncertainty and Information* (New York and London, 1964).
36. M. Ruyer, *La Cybernétique et l'origine de l'information* (Paris, 1954).

reflections concerning physics.[37] Brillouin and de Beauregard
have now advanced the following theory: the predictions of
physics are based on probability theory, while the real state
of affairs permits only prediction and not retrodiction.[38] In
physical reality, entropy (and the retardation of waves) engenders a time arrow of natural happenings which is irreversible.[39] Going further, John von Neumann has demonstrated that every physical act of measurement is also
irreversible.[40] In other words, every piece of acquired information concerning a physical state is bound up with an in-
evitable and irreversible increase of entropy in the universe.[41]
At this point, cybernetics introduces still another new idea:
every increase of information is equivalent to the possibility
of a system's entropic state being reduced by an ordering
intervention.[42] At all events, Brillouin expressly emphasizes
that the word "information" in the sense used by physics
must not be confused with its normal connotation. In physics, it deals with "latent information" and experimentally
reached insights into a specific quantity of a system's micro-
structures.[43] But even in this limited form it concerns "insights" that human consciousness has about the structure of
material reality. *The information consists of a representa-*

37. Brillouin, *Scientific Uncertainty, passim;* J. Rothstein, *Communication, Organization and Science* (New York, 1958).
38. Mathematical calculation itself unequivocally permits the latter,
of course. This has even led to the purely mathematical construction
of an "antiphysical" world (in which a confusion, i.e., syntropy, of
waves is computed, instead of a diffusion). Cf. Olivier Costa de Beauregard, *Le Second Principe de la science du temps* (Paris, 1963), p. 30.
According to this author a retrodiction of this sort is also practically
possible as soon as we deal with an individual happening and special
facts, whereas a prediction "des futurs contingents" in theoretical
physics is excluded in principle from the scope of their deliberations
(*ibid.,* p. 45).
39. Entropy, causality, and their subjective equivalent, the principle
of sufficient cause, are thus inseparably bound up with one another.
40. De Beauregard, *Second Principe,* p. 30.
41. *Ibid.,* p. 65.
42. *Ibid.,* pp. 66–67; "by an ordering intervention" is my addition.
43. Brillouin, *Scientific Uncertainty,* p. 14.

tional idea which becomes realized in consciousness:[44] it is, as de Beauregard says, registered by a "psychisme incarné." [45]

In order to realize the ordering intervention in a system, the observing psyche must, of course, transform its merely passive, contemplative attitude into an active and voluntatively intervening one.[46] The possibility of counteracting the law of entropy by a law of negentropy which exists in the psyche, not in the sphere of individual consciousness but in what de Beauregard, viewing it as a cosmic actuality, terms the *infrapsychisme*.[47] While the regulating power opposing entropy increasingly disappears from the universe, it circulates in a potential form in an "elsewhere" (*ailleurs*) in the shape of information, i.e., as a psychic representation.[48] What de Beauregard calls *infrapsychisme*[49] corresponds to the psychoid aspect of the collective unconscious in Jung's terminology. According to de Beauregard, this *infrapsychisme* also includes a *supraconscience*, analogous to Jung's "absolute knowledge." [50] The existence of energy as negentropy outside the material universe constitutes, in this case, a psychic factor which is representational without being identical to human ego consciousness.[51]

44. De Beauregard, *Second Principe*, p. 69: "Cyberneticians admit that acquiring a piece of information enables us to restore a system into a more ordered state than that in which we had first encountered it."

45. *Ibid.*, p. 65.

46. *Ibid.*, p. 69. In the first state the information subsists by an acquisition of knowledge, in the second by the possibility of organization (*ibid.*, p. 76).

47. *Ibid.*, pp. 79–80.

48. *Ibid.*, pp. 101–2.

49. *Ibid.*, pp. 89–90.

50. The "survol absolu" of Ruyer (*Cybernétique*, p. 91); de Beauregard, *Second Principe*, pp. 90, 120.

51. De Beauregard, *Second Principe*, pp. 101–2: "The enormous loss of blood by universal negentropy in the cosmos might have a hidden opposite principle, since scientists assume that they can see certain restoring processes at work. And the astonishing discovery of Cybernetics is the fact that when negentropy disappears from the cosmic world, it can do so only to the profit of its potential form as informa-

The knowledge contained in this *infrapsychisme* is diffused among individual souls in a form superior to (i.e., faster than) the speed of light, and "synchronizes" them, because they all originate from the same cosmic "réseau de télécommunication."[52] De Beauregard names this reservoir the "origin and objective" of all information;[53] in it everything is already known. The material universe, on the other hand, is somewhat like a gigantic cybernetic machine which serves an individual's coming to consciousness[54] and strives for his return to the extracosmic source of information.

In many aspects, de Beauregard's conceptions coincide with Jungian ideas.[55] They present a remarkable parallel—independently derived from physical considerations—to Jung's concept of the *unus mundus* and the "absolute knowledge" contained within it.[56] They also demonstrate the fact that the problem of the relationship of outer material structures to the psyche is not yet solved today. Some physicists like de Beauregard are searching for the answer in a third

---

tion, which participates in the [psychic] nature of representation." The latter would be an immaterial world with final, not causal laws (*ibid.*, pp. 108–9). It is universally coexistent with matter and is crystallized in the individual psychisms of men and beasts (*ibid.*, pp. 120–21). In it exist "les futurs contigents en acte" but we are unconscious of them (*ibid.*, p. 131).

52. *Ibid.*, pp. 135–36.
53. *Ibid.*, p. 137.
54. *Ibid.*, p. 141.
55. But de Beauregard views the *infrapsychisme* as an exclusively positive source and postulates that it contains only meaning, not its opposite, meaninglessness. In other words he is here bound to the scholastic tradition.
56. Sir Arthur Eddington also says (*The Philosophy of Physical Science* [Cambridge, 1939], pp. 150–51): "The recognition that physical knowledge is structural knowledge abolishes all dualism of consciousness and matter . . . all that physical science reveals to us in the external world is group structure and group structures are also to be found in consciousness. . . ." And: "Although the statement that the universe is of the nature of 'a Thought or sensation in a universal Mind' is open to criticisms, it does at least avoid this logical confusion. It is, I think, true in the sense that it is a logical consequence of the form of the thought which formulates our knowledge as a description of a universe" (*ibid.*, p. 151).

factor which may unite the subjective psyche and the material outer world. Obviously all these thought patterns originate from an archetypal foundation, manifest in varied forms, everywhere and always, whenever a question about the unity of existence is raised.

CHAPTER TWELVE

The Archetype
of the Number-Game
as the Basis
of Probability Theory
and Number Oracles

J UNG HAS DESCRIBED the phenomena of synchronicity as parapsychological manifestations, and it is not by chance that certain physicists turn to this marginal field of science for insight into the relationship between psyche and matter.[1] It therefore seems appropriate to include a few reflections on this field here. As already mentioned, Jung termed *number the most primitive form of the spirit*. But this statement requires a more exact definition of the meaning intended by the word "spirit" in this context. In his paper "The Phenomenology of the Spirit in Fairytales," Jung first of all enumerates various turns of speech in which the concept "spirit" is used to designate a "nonmaterial substance," or the opposite of matter.[2] In this context, "spirit" refers to a general cosmic principle. But we also use the word "spirit" to describe the psychic capacities and attributes of man, analogous to "reason," "intellect," and "capacity for thought." Moreover, in the expression "spirit of the age," "spirit" designates the col-

---

1. P. Jordan, F. Karger, and others, for example.
2. "The Phenomenology of the Spirit in Fairytales," *The Archetypes and the Collective Unconscious*, CW, Vol. IX, pt. 1 ¶¶ 384 ff.

lective fund of judgments and ideas common to groups of people. Consequently, a certain antithesis arises between the "spirit" ascribed to objective extrahuman existence and the "spirit" experienced as a conscious activity of the human ego. Concerning this antithesis, Jung writes: "When . . . something psychic happens in the individual which he feels as belonging to himself, that something is his own spirit. But if anything psychic happens which seems strange, then it is somebody else's spirit, and it may be causing a possession."[3] In the latter case, we are dealing with a disposition not yet human, representing a projected aspect of the still unconscious psyche,[4] which is often experienced as a parapsychological phenomenon.

That aspect of the soul that we call "spirit" comprises above all the active, winged, animating, stimulating, inspiring components of the unconscious, i.e., its *dynamics*. When the spirit is experienced as being a subjective component of an individual it is also experienced as that factor which creates images in the inner field of vision and organizes them into a meaningful order.[5] "The hallmarks of spirit," says Jung,

> are, firstly, the principle of spontaneous movement and activity; secondly, the spontaneous capacity to produce images independently of sense perception; and thirdly, the autonomous and sovereign manipulation of these images.

3. *Ibid.*
4. "As linguistic usage shows, spirit in the sense of an attitude has unmistakable leanings towards personification: . . . for spirit still has the spookish meaning. . . . The 'cold breath of the spirits' points on the one hand to the ancient affinity of ψυχή with ψυχρός and ψῦχος, which both mean 'cold,' and, on the other, to the original meaning of πνεῦμα, which simply denoted 'air in motion.' In the same way animus and anima were connected with ἄνεμος, 'wind.' The German word *Geist* probably has more to do with something frothing, effervescing, or fermenting; hence affinities with *Gischt* (foam), *Gäscht* (yeast), *ghost*, and also with the emotional *ghastly* and *aghast*, are not to be rejected" (*ibid.*, ¶ 387).
5. *Ibid.*, ¶¶ 389–90.

This spiritual entity approaches primitive man from outside; but with increasing development it gets lodged in man's consciousness and becomes a subordinate function.[6]

A large portion of spiritual phenomena persists untouched, however, in a natural state of autonomy, and can therefore still manifest itself as a "breathlike presence," i.e., a parapsychological phenomenon.[7]

The history of the development of mathematics demonstrates this gradual "subjectivization" of the spirit particularly clearly. Whereas the Pythagoreans considered numbers to be spiritual/material cosmic principles, and even Leopold Kronecker continued to ascribe their origins to a creative act of God,[8] they are now viewed to be pure "constructions" of human consciousness by many contemporary mathematicians. They are evaluated as the signs with which consciousness "plays," according to specific rules laid down by itself.[9] There arises on this basis

> a purely intellectual mathematics, dissociated from all intuition, a pure theory of forms, which has as its object not the combination of quanta or their images, the numbers, but intellectual objects, to which there may (but need not) correspond actual objects or relations.[10]

By this means modern, and especially formalistic, mathematics has turned its back on the concern for individual natural numbers. The latter, as Hermann Weyl says, "are not individually exhibited as they actually occur, but their symbols are projected onto the background of an ordered mani-

6. *Ibid.*, ¶ 393.

7. *Ibid.*, ¶¶ 393–95. Parapsychological phenomena also have an ordering aspect, which is often illustrated in dreams—when it is wholly unconscious—by lattice and stripe motifs, since they point to the most primitive signs of differentiating the chaos of appearances.

8. "The integers were created by God; all else is man-made" (quoted by Hermann Weyl, *Philosophy of Mathematics and Natural Science* [Princeton, N.J., 1949], p. 33).

9. See *ibid.*, p. 17.

10. Hankel, quoted *ibid.*, pp. 27–28. See also D. Hilbert, quoted *ibid.*, p. 35.

fold of possibilities which can be generated by a fixed process and is open to infinity."[11] The number series itself suggests this basic internal antithesis between conformity, obliterating all individual characteristics, and unique actuality, embodying every individual number.

A parallel development may also be observed in modern physics, as it makes increasing use of the probability concept, which ignores all exceptional unique facts as much as possible. Pauli formulated this antithesis most aptly: "As a consequence of the indeterminate character of natural law postulated by quantum physics, physical observation also acquires the character of an irrational unique actuality with nonpredictable results." Opposed to this stands "the rational aspect of an abstract order of possible evidence with the help of the mathematical concept of probability and the ψ-function."[12]

The greatest possible repetition of experiments reflects an effort on the part of man to forcibly channel events within the scope of probability theory, because the latter can only attain precision through the greatest possible number of repetitions. Only under this condition do significant trends become observable.[13] Modern scientific experimentation is built up entirely on this assumption that only very extensive repetition of experiments yields significant results. This modern scientific faith in the "law of large numbers" and the generalizing approximations of mathematics is, nevertheless, not merely a product of consciousness, but itself is based on the fascination of an archetypal idea. The concept of an "ordered manifold of [abstract] possibilities . . . open to infinity" is deduced from observing the natural integer series:

11. *Ibid.,* pp. 37–38.
12. "Naturwissenschaftliche und erkenntnistheoretische Aspekte der Ideen vom Unbewussten," *Aufsätze und Vorträge über Physik und Erkenntnistheorie* (Brunswick, 1961), p. 21. This remains true even in the face of newer developments in probability theory in physics (Kolmogoroffs, for instance). See C. Fr. von Weizsäcker, *Die Einheit der Natur* (Munich, 1971), especially pp. 242 ff.
13. See W. Strombach, *Natur und Ordnung* (Munich, 1968), p. 92.

among primitives, who possess words for only the first few numbers of the series, it crops up when the conscious ability to count comes to an end and the remainder is designated by some variation of the word for "many." In the world of primitives, the only powers that can "always count further" are gods and demons, i.e., archetypal personifications of the unconscious. Even in the New Testament, God is said to have counted the hairs on our heads and the fallen sparrows. The negative aspect of this "ability to count into infinity" (negative because it threatens to blot out the individual) is also embodied in archetypal powers. A prayer of the West African Yoruba, for instance, runs as follows:

> Death counting continually, counting continually,
> does not count me!
> Fire counting continually, counting continually,
> does not count me!
> Emptiness counting continually, counting continually,
> does not count me!
> Wealth counting continually, counting continually,
> does not count me!
> Day counting continually, counting continually,
> does not count me!
> The spider's web is round the cornbin.[14]

Death, fire, emptiness (= meaninglessness), wealth, and day are all symbols illustrating psychic energy (in its function as the source of consciousness).[15] This energy "counts continually," which probably means that it pulsates in numerically organized rhythms, and in this universal form of operating it can also obliterate the individual and his unique creative foundations. A trace of this notion of "counting" death has been preserved in the saying "his number was up," to which

14. See B. Maupoil, *La Géomancie à l'ancienne Côte des Esclaves* (Paris, 1943), p. 529. The last line can read "There is soot around the cornbin" (to prevent theft?).

15. Fire and day = emotion and latent consciousness, wealth = libido, emptiness and death = the opposite of the above-mentioned powers.

we resort when we feel that a death was intended by God. The individual corresponds, in this context, to a single individual number which expresses his transcendental being. The "continual counting" of death sooner or later envelops this single number and extinguishes the individual's life.[16] The colloquial expression "I don't have his number," which means that one does not understand a person, also implies the equation of individual human qualities with specific numbers. The extent to which statistics, in its applied and dogmatic form, has become a destructive, deadly tool in the hands of sociologists and politicians today need not be emphasized. The modern man who still wishes to preserve his individuality in the midst of our collective civilization, might well pray, like the Yoruba: death, fire, emptiness, day (= rational consciousness) and wealth, do not count me. In the rich night of meaning and spiritual poverty, let me live!

The contemporary overvaluation of statistics and probability originates in an inflated identification with the archetypal power "which can count all things." [17] What has happened to us can best be illustrated by a Navajo Indian story on the origins of gambling. The Navajos once built a house

16. In the Vedas it says of the Goddess Uṣas (I. 92, 10), according to H. Güntert, *Der arische Weltkönig und Heiland* (Halle a. S., 1923), p. 233, "She approaches veiled in lively colors and leads man's life to old age. As a gambler cunningly slips the dice away, so she takes the human generations away."

17. This is clearly recognized by Sir Arthur Eddington when he makes the point that the mathematics of quantum physics can no longer be equated with ordinary mathematics. The "cosmical number" N is not an uncountable infinity but a construction of consciousness and therefore logically limited (*The Philosophy of Physical Science* [Cambridge, 1939], p. 175). He also says: "I think it will be clear that in claiming to determine a priori the number of elementary particles in the universe we are not usurping a prerogative which has usually been ascribed to the Creator of the universe" (p. 175). And (p. 176), "From this it appears that the cosmical number must be the total number of independent quadruple wave functions, which is found to be $2 \times 136 \times 2^{256}$. The number 136 is characteristic of the group structure of the quadruple existence symbols." "From this point of view the 'highest integer' in quantum arithmetic is 2^{256}. To form N we add together 2×136 such numbers by ordinary arithmetic" (p. 177).

for one of their important chiefs, where he lived concealed, because he possessed all the jewels of the tribe. The Sun God became jealous of this chief's "great turquoise," although he himself possessed the "perfect turquoise." So he secretly begot a son by a woman called the "rock woman," and trained him to become such an accomplished gambler that he invariably won all games of chance. He then caused him to win all the chief's treasures in gambling, including the "great turquoise" which he coveted. But when the gambler won it he refused to hand it over to the Sun God. The latter became infuriated and begot a second "gambler" who looked exactly like the first, and also learned to gamble. With the help of numerous animals, he learned to cheat so cleverly that he beat the first gambler and relieved him of all his previous winnings. Thereupon the first player withdrew into the heavenly Beyond. But the second player sacrificed the great turquoise he had won to the Sun God, who in return helped him acquire a new country.[18]

The Sun God personifies the suprapersonal principle of consciousness in the psyche, the "light of nature," and he accordingly possesses the core of all secret knowledge about gambling. He corresponds to the powers capable of counting, like "death," "day," "wealth," and so on, according to the Yoruba. Human consciousness, the first "gambler," acquires some of the God's tricks, and thereby succumbs to an inflation. In contradistinction, the second gambler returns the turquoise, "the highest value," to the Sun God; he does not presume to possess more than befits him. He thus embodies the true hero, a model of the correct conscious attitude, which is supported by different animals symbolizing the instincts.

When we today believe we have uncovered nature's secrets through probability theory or statistics, we too have

---

18. "The Story of Naqoilpi the Great Gambler," *The Diné-Origin Myths of the Navahos*, ed. A. O'Bryan, Smithsonian Institution, Bureau of American Ethnology, Bulletin no. 163 (Washington, D.C., 1956), pp. 48 ff.

fallen victim to an inflation like that of the first gambler in the Navajo myth. For "faith in large numbers" causes an inflated identification of consciousness with what is merely one aspect of the archetypal pattern of the infinite number series, set up in opposition to unique events. More precisely stated, this antithesis poses a far more subtle paradox: as Georg Cantor was the first to note, every series open to infinity can be handled as an individual quantity (as Cantor does), but, conversely, every single quantity can also be dealt with as a time-bound aspect of the one-continuum, as I have tried to show.

The opposition of "scientific experiment" and "oracle of divination" in modern thought has led to a split in the paradoxical dual nature of the number archetype. In experiments, an effort is made, by repetition, to thrust aside number's individual aspect under the heading of "chance." [19] In oracles, on the other hand, chance is accorded a central position and used to interpret conditioning factors. This antithesis is familiar to everyone who has ever passionately played a game of chance: the question invariably arises as to whether one is more likely to win chance games by employing a "system" of repeated throws or by depending on a single stroke of luck, since the latter requires us to find the psychically fortunate *kairos* or "right" number. How many people trust to winning a lottery by a system of repetitions, and how often one reads in the papers of some old cook who dreamt the lucky number and so triumphed in a single coup! She, like the second gambler of the Navajo story, was helped by animals, the instincts.

In the light of this, it is certainly not by chance—or if it is, then "chance" signifies a "meaningful coincidence"—that probability theory itself was discovered in the course of Pascal and Fermat's correspondence on the prospects of chance games. Interestingly enough, Dmitri Mendelev was

19. Eddington indeed says: "Without an appeal to the law of chance physics is unable to make any prediction for the future" (*Physical Science*, p. 61).

inspired to discover his famous system of chemical elements while playing patience. He had tried several times to map out a system without obtaining satisfactory results. He then fell into depression and began to play patience. Suddenly he decided to make little cards of the sixty-three elements and play with them instead of ordinary cards, noting down all the steps. After a few hours of hard concentration he formed a system that satisfied him. Then he went to sleep and saw the system in reversed order in a dream; he wrote it down (correcting only one fact) and thus arrived at his famous system.[20]

In more recent discussions about the applicability of mathematical probability to physics, the comparison to gambling is often used as a simile. Olivier Costa de Beauregard goes so far as to say that the physicist finds himself in nearly the same position vis-à-vis the universe as a gambler sitting down to play.[21] All experimentally obtained information, in the final analysis, proceeds from data revealed in successive throws of dice about a universe whose laws are, ultimately, random (i.e., contingent).

D. Rivier goes so far as to state that according to quantum mechanics two kinds of change take place: the first is classical and is subject to the Schrödinger equation, the second is essentially random (*aléatoire*) and is external to time, if not actually reversible.[22] This particular form of change completely evades theory, rather like "the circumstances which induce an honest fortune-teller to draw one card rather than

20. See J. Sergejew, "Psychologische Hintergründe grosser Entdeckungen," *Bild der Wissenschaft*, no. 6 (1970), pp. 546 ff.

21. *Le Second Principe de la science du temps* (Paris, 1963), p. 74. De Beauregard adds in a footnote (3): "According to this hypothesis all sorts of chance in the macroscopic realm would have their remote (and often deeply hidden) causes in the chance events of the microcosmic realm."

22. D. Rivier, "La Physique et le temps," *Verhandlungen der schweizerischen naturforschenden Gesellschaft* (Bern and Geneva, 1965), p. 225. I am indebted to Dr. Dieter Baumann for drawing my attention to this article. See also Eddington, *Physical Science*, p. 50.

another from the pack, evading probability theory, whose rules apply only to the totality of all card draws." [23]

In this way some physicists at least have become truly conscious of the fact that probability theory no longer deals with the objective facts of a case but only with our own knowledge about them; "probability" is not an attribute of an occurrence, either taking place or not taking place: "probability can only be an attribute of our knowledge of an event." What lies objectively behind our observations is "life," "consciousness," or "spirit." [24] This formulation by Eddington displays the subjective and mental character of probability theory in the proper light.

In a certain sense, man also seeks to fathom subjective and psychological probability by means of numerical techniques of oracles. What differentiates probability theory in quantum physics (and experiments coordinated with it) from that in "oracles" is the frequent repetition of "throws," in order to reduce the factor of chance to a minimum. In divinatory oracles (the I Ching, for instance), on the other hand, single chance throws become *the* center of attention and form the starting point for all deliberations. Experiments are repeated frequently in time and serve to fix an isolated sector of the universe, while oracles occur only once and serve more to understand as extensively as possible the unity of all contingents. According to the modern standpoint in physics, isolated unique facts are regarded as boundary conditions, and Eddington rightly suggests that if we discovered their conformity the underlying principle would deserve to be called a "natural law," which up to now remains unformulated.[25] In my opinion, the I Ching represents just such an attempt to grasp the psychological probability involved in man's observation of these boundary conditions, by means of

23. Eddington, *Physical Science*, p. 69.
24. *Ibid.*, pp. 63, 66.
25. One start in measuring psychological probability is to be found in the predicator developed by K. Steinbuch. See Strombach, *Natur*, p. 118.

number. Its working seems to outline the probable psychic situations underlying our observation of such conditions.[26]

Experimental repetition in the realm of physics has in fact succeeded in giving us exceedingly productive information about systems in nature. It yields information whose probability at any given time lies between zero and one (i.e., it must be mathematically formulated by a fraction). The tacit assumption persists, of course, that actual and possible repetitions of an experiment do not essentially modify the resulting data. (This does not quite work, however, because of entropy.) But this hypothesis does *not* prove valid for the realm of the psyche, since it is well known that repetition very quickly reduces the "charge" of psychic energy—in other words, affective participation is reduced. *The application of probability theory to psychological phenomena is, therefore (on account of these assumptions about it), inappropriate both logically and empirically.* In the realm of psychological experimentation there are no "fractions," but only zero or one, the existence or nonexistence of just-so facts.

How then is it possible that oracular techniques exist based on repeated "throws" in time? And how is it that the Chinese tried to predict synchronistic phenomena when, by definition, these are creative acts? Clearly a certain "probability" also exists in the psychological realm; it is based on the collective substratum of the individual psyche, on archetypal structural dispositions which remain largely unchanged in the depths reaching beyond all personal variations. As a result, in certain general human situations, typical reactions may be expected. But these reactions only come to light synchronistically with affective, tension-charged conditions. Whereas the precision of probability theory in the quantitative realm is increased through repetition, psychological

26. See de Beauregard, *Second Principe*, p. 45: "The exact prediction of 'future contingencies' is thus radically excluded from the realm of physics." It is precisely these excluded areas that the oracle strives to grasp.

probability theory must draw archetypal situations into the center of the field of observation, as most oracular and divinatory techniques do. In order to meet this specification, the latter do not make use of fractions and limits in their calculations, but (as already explained) rely instead on the qualitatively greatest intensities of the significant natural integers: one, two, three, and four. The isomorphism of these numbers to the archetypal field makes them particularly suitable instruments for comprehending archetypal situations. In experimentation the observer's conscious ego cuts a particular system out of the realm of wholeness. But in the oracle one allows chance to make the cut and only subsequently tries to read a result from it.

The approach of oracle techniques to stating a principle of psychic probability presupposes an indeterminism, an objective contingency which has been denied recognition in modern times. Eddington does emphasize that anomalies can occur in the sphere of objective chance phenomena when consciousness willfully intervenes. He attributes the origin of these manifestations of the will to a bit of "brain-matter" which he calls "conscious matter," in contradistinction to "ordinary matter." [27] Ordinary matter is subject to the laws of probability, which assume that no correlations exist in the undetermined behavior of different single elementary particles. If, on the other hand, such correlations exist, it becomes necessary to speak of the physical aspect of an act of will, and this aspect no longer belongs to the world of physics. One factor nevertheless overlooked here is that we normally attribute acts of will strictly to the conscious ego, but depth psychology has recently demonstrated that unconscious contents can display similar tendencies. It might perhaps be better to describe these unconscious tendencies as goal-oriented trends in order to avoid a confusion of terms.[28] Just such "dynamically excited" *unconscious* contents seem to be

27. See Eddington, *Physical Science*, pp. 48–49, 61, 180–84.
28. See *The Structure and Dynamics of the Psyche, CW,* Vol. VIII, ¶ 440.

bound up with the appearance of synchronistic events. *Logically they invalidate the law of (meaningless) chance.*[29] Jung therefore describes genuine synchronistic phenomena as "parapsychological," marginal phenomena which are only observable when our ego consciousness becomes "dimmed." This would mean that the luminosity of a constellated archetype, which shines forth in the "meaning" of a synchronistic event, increases its energetic charge in proportion to the degree that the light concentration of ego consciousness diminishes; natural number appears to be qualitatively connected with their reciprocal relationship.

It is a curious fact, however, that the same archetypal idea lies behind the thought models of physical experimentation and divinatory oracles, namely the concept of the game of chance. When Einstein defiantly told Niels Bohr that "God does not play with dice," he must have had the God of law in the Old Testament in mind.[30] For dice-throwing is a very ancient symbol, used in earlier times to illustrate the creative activities of the deity. In the Bhagavad-Gita (x. 42), for instance, the god Krishna says of himself: "I am the game of dice. I am the self seated in the heart of beings. I am the beginning and the middle and the end of all beings. I am Vishnu, the beaming sun among shining bodies." In the Satapatha-Brāhmana of the Yajur-Veda (IV Brāhmana 23), Agni, the fire god, says the same of himself: "He, the priest, throws down the dice with 'Hallowed by Svāhā—strive ye with Sūrya's rays for the middlemost place among brethren!' For that gaming ground is the same as 'ample Agni' and those dice are his coals. . . ." Of these texts, which I quote from his exposition, Jung comments:

> Both texts relate light, sun, and fire, as well as the god, the game of dice. Similarly the Atharva-Veda VI, 38 speaks of the "brilliancy that is in the chariot, in the dice, in the

29. On this problem of the relation of brain and psyche, compare also Jung, *Alchemical Studies, CW*, Vol. XIII, ¶ 341.
30. See J. Holton, "The Roots of Complementarity," *Eranos Jahrbuch*, XXXVII (1970), 50.

strength of the bull, in the wind. . . ." The "brilliancy" corresponds to what is known in primitive psychology as "mana," and in the psychology of the unconscious as "libido investment" or "emotional value" or "feeling tone." In point of emotional intensity, which is a factor of decisive importance for the primitive consciousness, the most heterogeneous things—rain, storm, fire, the strength of the bull, and the passionate game of dice—can be identical. In emotional intensity, game and gambler coincide.[31]

A saying of Heraclitus belongs in the same context: "The Aion [eternal duration], is a boy who plays, placing the counters here and there. To a child belongs the cosmic mastery."[32] Here again we find a connection between psychic energy and the game of dice. Indeed, when "God," the spirit of the unconscious, plays, he creates fate, a unique fate occurring but once, namely, the *creatio* of a synchronistic phenomenon. When, on the other hand, man, imitating God, plays, *his* individual mind reconstructs rational possibilities which inspire him with the feeling that he is tracking down the mystery of the objectively unknown, since the numerical laws of his gambling seem identical with the numerical laws of God's game.

When a modern quantum physicist approaches a system with quantitatively formulated matrices and searches, by experimental repetition, for "probable" numerical results, he is unconsciously making use of an ancient pattern of orientation originally revealed by the "spirit" (in the original sense of the word). Gradually, however, this bit of "spirit" has come into possession of his subjective consciousness. By contrast, the use of a divinatory oracle represents an attempt to induce a spontaneous manifestation of the remaining autonomous spirit by offering him "his" speech, in terms of certain archaic numerical sequences, as a medium of expression. By

31. See Jung, *Alchemical Studies*, ¶ 341.
32. See K. Deichgräber, "Rhythmische Elemente im Logos des Heraklit," *Akademie der Wissenschaften und Literatur in Mainz*, no. 9 (1962), p. 513.

means of the chance throw of coins or twigs, a "hole" is introduced into the field of consciousness through which the autonomous dynamism of the collective unconscious can break in. This setup can only lead to results if an archetype and its accompanying high charge of psychic energy are already constellated in the unconscious. For this reason, all divinatory techniques operate with the warning they are only to be used in "serious situations," and the question is never to be repeated in a spirit of frivolity.[33] The greater the psychic tension the more probable and to the point the result. This state of affairs represents in certain ways an inverse picture of certain physical facts, for instance, that in a high intensity field the concept of length becomes blurred.[34]

In order to clarify the functioning of the I Ching oracle, Richard Wilhelm makes use, significantly enough, of the following image:

> The way in which the Book of Changes works can best be compared to an electrical circuit reaching into all situations. The circuit only affords the potentiality of lighting; it does not give light. But when contact with a definite situation is established through the questioner, the "current" is activated, and the given situation is illuminated.[35]

In this passage, Wilhelm also makes use of the same basic "field" image in order to portray an all-pervasive continuum emerging upon stimulation from its latent state to make its dynamic phases of transformation comprehensible through the agency of number.

In China the original connection between "play," "gambling," and arithmetic was well established. The two linguis-

33. See Richard Wilhelm, trans., *I Ching or Book of Changes*, English trans. C. F. Baynes (London, 1960), I, 20 ff.

34. See Eddington, *Physical Science*, p. 79.

35. Wilhelm, *I Ching*, I, 339, n. 2. See also H. Wilhelm, *Change: Eight Lectures on the I Ching* (London, 1960), p. 15: "This designation Ching for the classic texts did not come into use until the 4th century B.C. when we first find it used by Chuang-tzu. The word actually means the warp of a fabric."

tic roots contained in the Chinese word for "calculation" consist, first, of the basis of the word *suan-shu*, "calculation," 𝄐 which also means "lung," "to play or to gamble with bamboo stems," (to be considered in greater detail later on) and, second, of *shih*, a word whose radical was originally, in the Shang period, written 示 and is now rendered 示 . It consists of the character for heaven (the upper cross strokes) and three lower strokes representing the sun, moon, and stars. This character *shih* signifies heaven, the divine, and its influence on the world. At a later date the character meant to show, reveal, announce, or make known.[36]

示 or 示

Joseph Needham stresses the fact that the significance of the character *shih* standing for arithmetic is based on the connection between the two activities, prediction and arithmetic. The association of these two expressions went so far in China that they were used synonymously in ancient texts.[37] In Japan, too, the word *sai*, "gambling with dice," also means to search for a divinity or Buddha, in order to render him honor, or to celebrate the fulfillment of a vow.[38] The heavenly constellations were prototypes of divination, so to speak, which the human mind imitated by arithmetical means. The divining panel of the Chinese *shih*[39] therefore contains at its center a replica of the heavenly constellation of Wain (Great Bear) which was also frequently represented by a magnetized spoon rotating on a board. This instrument of divination led to the invention of the compass (see illustration p. 229).

The concept of a spiritual order was projected onto the firmament by archaic man, and subsequently imitated in gambling. In the process, man gradually became aware of some of the rational laws of this projected spiritual order and devel-

36. I am indebted to Mr. G. Griffin and to Mr. Tang of the Gest Oriental Library for kindly giving me this information.
37. Joseph Needham, *Science and Civilization in China* (Cambridge, 1959), III, 4.
38. I am indebted to Dr. Mokusen Miyuki for this information.
39. Not the same word as *shih* mentioned above. See Needham, *Science and Civilization*, IV, 262 ff.

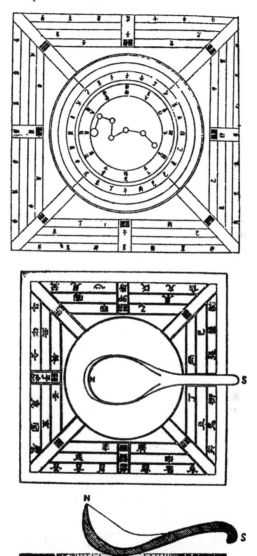

Above, the divination board *shih* with the pattern of the Wain (Great Bear); *center and below,* its earthly likeness, the first compass, on which the Bear appears as a magnetic spoon [Source: Joseph Needham, *Science and Civilization in China* (Cambridge, 1959), IV, pt. 1, 263 and 266, reproduced by permission of Cambridge University Press.]

oped through it his conscious mathematical knowledge. In contrast to Western man, however, the Chinese retained an awareness of the original condition, namely, that mathematics was derived from the spiritual order projected onto the stars and has a close relationship to "chance hits" as indicators of still-unconscious contents. The fact that all these divinatory instruments are mandala-shaped and exhibit a quaternary structure (or a multiple of four) as their basic rhythm can only be mentioned in passing.

Mathematics, which was originally the aspect of order in the collective unconscious, has partly become Western man's subjective conscious possession, and this is nowadays so much taken for granted that Laplace could display surprise at learning that the most important object of human cognition had grown out of the contemplation of games of chance.[40] Whatever cannot be consciously systematized nowadays is termed "chance," with the implication that it is not worthy of further investigation. But it is just in such "chance" occurrences that startling new ideas erupt. It is being more and more firmly established that parapsychological phenomena occur mainly in the surroundings of an individual *whom the unconscious wants to take a step in the development of consciousness*, as, for instance, adolescents who must take the "leap" into adulthood. Creative personalities who must fulfill a new creative task intended by the unconscious also attract such phenomena, as do all people before the outbreak of a psychosis or in a state of severe conflict which can only be overcome by an increase of consciousness. This means that whenever a creative intention is present in the unconscious, parapsychological

40. Cf. E. Kramer, *The Main Stream of Mathematics* (New York, 1951), p. 154. Kramer continues: "We come now to what may be the most curious chapter in the whole of mathematics . . . on the one hand it will help to arrange insurance schemes, improve manufacturing, develop atomic theory, predict genetic phenomena and crystallize hypotheses. On the other hand it is meat for the professional gambler, whether his game be dice, or poker, whether he play a local pinball machine or the Monte Carlo roulette wheel . . . the vital and the trivial have something in common in the element of chance."

and particularly synchronistic phenomena, which Jung calls "acts of creation," may be expected. Oracular techniques of the past actually represented efforts to grasp, by means of games of chance, the general psychological quality of the content constellated in the unconscious.

PART V

Number and the Parapsychological Aspects of the Principle of Synchronicity

CHAPTER THIRTEEN

Number, Time,
and Synchronicity

I‍T WAS NOT my original intention to include the exceedingly complex question of time in this book. Detailed investigation revealed, however, *that number, understood as a psychophysical motion-pattern, is intimately connected with the problem of time.* This link was initially substantiated by the fact that historically number has always been used in divinatory techniques as an indicator of synchronicity. Consequently, in China from earliest times numbers were regarded as being patterns of time sequences. The cosmic numerical models of the Lo-shu and the Ho-t'u, described in chapter two, clearly possess a temporal aspect, which is maintained in their correlation with the order of trigrams in the I Ching. This correlation consists of the combination, already mentioned in the second chapter, of the Ho-t'u with the "Sequence of Earlier Heaven" or "Primal Arrangement," illustrated in the accompanying figure.

Ch'ien and *k'un*, heaven and earth, condition the north-south axis and form a pair of opposites. But "in the primal relations . . . their effects do not conflict. . . ." In this order, all the powers (*pa-kua*) take effect as paired opposites. Furthermore the whole possesses, within this framework, the

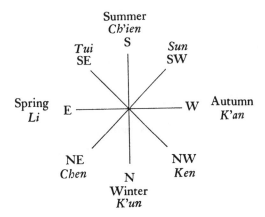

[Sketch by the author following Marcel Granet, *La Pensée chinoise*, © Albin Michel 1936, 1968, Collection Evolution de l'humanité.]

possibility of an internal double movement. An ancient text comments on it as follows:

> Heaven and earth determine the direction. The forces of mountain and lake are united. Thunder and wind arouse each other. Water and fire do not combat each other. Thus the eight trigrams are intermingled. Counting that which is going into the past depends on the forward movement. Knowing that which is to come depends on the backward movement. This is why the Book of Changes has backward-moving numbers.[1]

Wilhelm explains this text by stating:

> When the trigrams intermingle, that is, when they are in motion, a double movement is observable: first, the usual clockwise movement, cumulative and expanding as time goes on, and determining the events that are passing; second, an opposite, backward movement, folding up and contracting as time goes by, through which the seeds of the future take form. To know this movement is to know

1. Quoted from Richard Wilhelm, trans., *I Ching or Book of Changes*, English trans. C. F. Baynes (London, 1960), I, 285.

the future. In figurative terms, if we understand how a tree is contracted into a seed, we understand the future unfolding of the seed into a tree.[2]

We can elucidate these remarks by saying that the Ho-t'u numerical mandala has no cyclical or linear forms of movement, but rather comprises a kind of ordering of powers or directions that stands as a whole, in a timeless equilibrium. It forms the static image of a greatly intensified inner dynamism; to use a simile, it is like a dragonfly stationary in one single spot in the air, yet held in continuous inner motion through the innumerable vibrations of its wings. It requires "intervention" (or "interpermeation") to instigate the cyclical motion of this image. The world-model of the Ho-t'u thus forms *the primal image of a relatively timeless state of universal orderedness.* If we count its numbers sequentially, the same

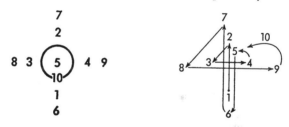

The Ho-t'u movement [Sketch by the author following Granet, *Pensée chinoise,* © Albin Michel 1936, 1968.]

movement invariably results, as shown in the diagram. Contact with the four outer points is always followed by a return to the center. This center is composed of the numbers 0, 5, 10, and so on. If we represent this movement in glide dilatation, it yields the structure shown in the second diagram (top p. 238), which pictures the same string of double pyramids that Jung uses to describe the archetype of the Self in *Aion.*

If the I Ching "Sequence of Earlier Heaven" is "interper-

2. *Ibid.,* pp. 285–86.

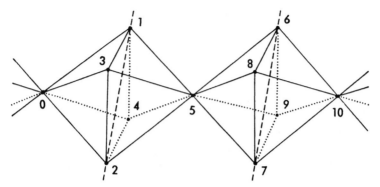

Glide dilatation of the Ho-t'u movement

4	9	2
3	5	7
8	1	6

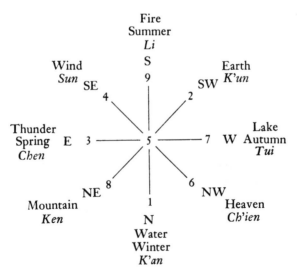

[Source: Granet, *Pensée chinoise*, © Albin Michel 1936, 1968, p. 149.]

meated," the so-called "Arrangement of King Wen" results. It forms the second trigram-sequence underlying the book, and was known as the "Sequence of Later Heaven." This sequence corresponds to the Lo-shu numerical model and operates as shown (bottom p. 238); it is also called the "Inner-World Arrangement." "The trigrams," says Wilhelm, "are taken out of their grouping in pairs of opposites and shown in temporal progression in which they manifest themselves in the phenomenal world in the cycles of the year." [3] In other words, the extraworldly timeless order of the "Earlier Heaven" is transformed into a temporal one (time being regarded cyclically in China) and is thereby specifically altered. Its internal movement develops as shown below. To the

[Source: Granet, *Pensée chinoise*, © Albin Michel 1936, 1968, p. 149.]

right, above the 4–6 axis, the feminine signs are ordered together (*sun, li, k'un, tui*); below to the left stand the masculine ones (*ch'ien, k'an, ken, chen*). This numerical mandala is therefore polarized into pairs of opposites. In the accompanying Lo-shu model all odd numbers are also arranged on the central cross and even ones in the corners. Consequently, odd and even numbers are more separated than in the Ho-t'u. In this way, *nonequilibrium situations* arise which stimulate the whole into motion. (Recall the scientist's dream of the chess game or dance, p. 108).

The magic square of the Lo-shu is also found in North Africa, where it forms the basis of extensive number speculations. It is accounted a great mystery. Whereas in China it was supposed to mirror the order of the universe, in Islamic

3. *Ibid.*, p. 288.

nations it was taken to be Allah's divine energy circulating throughout the world and returning to him. Since Allah forms the source and ultimate unity of all things, he emanates into the world through the numbers of the magic square.[4]

The Chinese did not regard their two world models as a pair of opposites, but as complementary images of one another.[5] If the numerical equivalents of the two patterns are combined, heaven and earth exchange their numerical sequences (even, uneven); this operation represents an interchange of attributes which was interpreted as a *hieros gamos*.[6] To carry it out we must take, for instance, a square of numbers from the Lo-shu:

	9				2	
3	5	7	or	8	6	4
	1				10	

[Source: Granet, *Pensée chinoise*, © Albin Michel 1936, 1968, p. 166.]

When we replace every number of the first (left-hand) square by the number bringing it up to eleven, the number of Tao, the second square results. Furthermore, when we insert the numbers present at a given moment in the second square into the corners of the first square, two swastikas result. If we combine these two swastikas, nine pairs of numbers totaling eleven, the number of Tao, result.[7] In itself the swastika for-

4. See C. Schuyler, "Islamic and Indian Magic Squares," *Part 1: History of Religions, International Journal for Comparative Historical Studies*, Vol. VIII, no. 3 (February, 1969).

5. Marcel Granet, *La Pensée chinoise* (Paris, 1968), p. 166. Re the inversion of the number values of Yin and Yang as "échange hierogamique," see *ibid.*, p. 217.

6. For details see *ibid.*, p. 167.

7. *Ibid.*, p. 166.

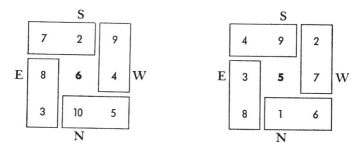

[Source: Granet, *Pensée chinoise,* © Albin Michel 1936, 1968, p. 167.]

mation suggests both a circular motion and the right angle of a set square. Both these numerical squares were also identified with the "Earlier" and the "Inner-World" heavenly orders.[8]

In this connection one of the oldest Chinese shamanistic, divinatory instruments seems to me of peculiar interest. The priests of ancient China made use of two small boards or plates, one round (Yang, "heaven"), one square (Yin, "earth"). These rotated independently around a center (post). "King Wen's Inner-World" numerical model was drawn on the earth board and the "Sequence of Earlier Heaven" on the other. To obtain answers to specific questions the shaman set the two boards spinning in contrary directions. Wherever they came to rest they formed a numerical relationship from which the "circumstantial" forms of the whole could be symbolically deduced. The interplay of the two boards signified a *hieros gamos* of heaven and earth, Yang and Yin, in which these two principles exchanged their attributes.[9] As Joseph Needham has shown, this divinatory instrument lay behind the Chinese invention of the compass.[10]

The unification of the two arrangements signifies the com-

8. *Ibid.,* p. 171. See also pp. 166 f.
9. *Ibid.,* p. 217.
10. See Joseph Needham, *Science and Civilization in China* (Cambridge, 1959), IV, pt. 1, 262–64. The constellation of the Great Bear or Wain was always shown in the center (see *ibid.,* pp. 268–69). Re the geomantic compass, see *ibid.,* pp. 293 ff.

ing together of an eternal order (ideas, heaven, and so on) with the just-so-ness of reality. But when the shaman himself sets the numerical boards rotating against each other he intervenes in the event, as an individual partaking of a specific time moment.[11] According to the Chinese view, the divinatory arrays then appear to indicate certain "fields of probability" within which synchronistic events are likely to occur.[12]

Magicians with the divinatory board (tomb of Wu Liang) [Source: Joseph Needham, *Science and Civilization in China* (Cambridge, 1959), III, 304, reproduced by permission of Cambridge University Press.]

The Chinese board of heaven, with its "Pre-World Sequence," clearly representing a timeless world structure, presumably illustrates what Jung calls "acausal orderedness," [13] whereas the "Inner-World Order" deals more with the time factor. The two orders appear to be complementary to each other; one is temporally invariable, the other seems to be time-bound. This situation accords with Jung's description

11. *Ibid.,* III, 304.
12. Even then an element of unpredictability remains. For example if an I Ching oracle prophesies that "the wagon breaks," a breakdown of one's outlook and behavior in life must certainly be expected. But whether this symbolic image will also be manifest concretely (in an automobile accident, for instance) is *not* predictable with this type of divinatory instrument.
13. "Synchronicity," *The Structure and Dynamics of the Psyche,* CW, Vol. VIII, ¶ 965.

of the archetypal realm. On the one hand, the archetypes possess a timeless, eternal character and, on the other, they are able, through synchronistic phenomena, to break into ordinary time, appearing to individuals as meaningful arrangements of inner and outer factors. Naturally the second, time-bound order does not signify a pattern for reading off actual synchronistic phenomena, because synchronicities are "creative acts" remaining by definition unpredictable; it is merely a model the Chinese created in hopes of determining the quality of temporal conditions which characterize the *quality of possible synchronistic events*. Of the two sequences, the first is a numerical square or array in which all the numbers are simultaneously presented as individuals "organized" into groups of four, while the second forms a numerical array in which the temporal cyclical succession of numbers is more emphasized.

Between the "Pre-World" and "Inner-World" numerical heavenly orders there is another considerable difference. The latter is cyclically time-bound, while the former comprises a latent double internal pattern of motion, which is described in the following passage: "Thunder brings about movement, wind brings about dispersion, rain brings about moisture, the sun brings about warmth." [14] (Images of four forces in nature are described here; their actions are called the "rising lines" by which they take effect.) The text continues: "Keeping Still brings about standstill, the Joyous brings about pleasure, the Creative brings about rulership, the Receptive brings about shelter." As Wilhelm points out, this passage describes a *retrograde* movement. [15] In it, the forces of the coming year are unrolled. Pursuance of this line, says Wilhelm, leads to knowledge of the future, the effect of which is prepared in advance by its causes (i.e., seeds) which take shape by contracting. [16] This "retrograde" movement is

14. Wilhelm, trans., *I Ching*, I, 286.
15. From li = East, to ken = Northwest.
16. In the Chinese "Sequence of Earlier Heaven" the energy gradient is not linear but consists of a rhythmical exchange of powers. The

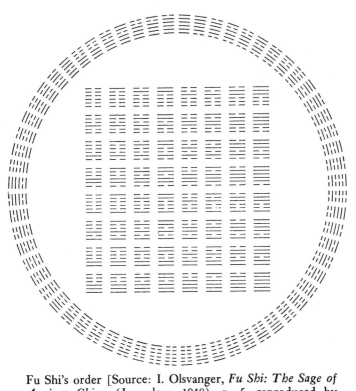

Fu Shi's order [Source: I. Olsvanger, *Fu Shi: The Sage of Ancient China* (Jerusalem, 1948), p. 5, reproduced by permission of Massada Press Ltd. and the family of Dr. Olsvanger.]

analogous to the retrograde number steps which, I have postulated, lie behind the qualitative number series.

Not only did the Chinese possess a twofold model of the universe in the sense of an inner-temporal order (King Wen's) and an extratemporal one (Fu Shi's), but the latter is characterized by a double rhythm of *four* physical and *four* psychic influences. Obviously the inner-temporal model is

---

first four inner rhythms are physical (movement, dissolution, moistening, heating) and the second four are psychic (maintenance, rejoicing, mastery, recovery).

King Wen's order [Source: Olsvanger, *Fu Shi*, p. 6, modified by Robert Dürr, reproduced by permission of Massada Press Ltd. and the family of Dr. Olsvanger.]

more related to actual reality and the extratemporal one represents an attempt to visualize the whole of psychological and physical existence, the *unus mundus*, by antithetical time movements and internal rhythms. (The second model recalls Jung's distinction between a timeless acausal orderedness manifest in the physical discontinuities of physics and the a priori qualities of the concept of number in the psyche.)

In other words, in China number, like the stars, was a "circumstantial time indicator" from which to read off the "will of heaven," and arithmetic was the art of dealing with this kind of temporal number in order to predict the future, i.e., the probabilities or "lists of expectations" concerning the quality of synchronistic happenings. This was all made possible by the fact that numbers always signified the world-totality whose different nuances were qualitatively manifest in the sequence of temporal situations. The fact that divination based on the synchronicity principle was mainly effected by double mandalas could also be the reason that dualistic motifs in the dreams of modern individuals seem to a great extent to allude directly to the *unus mundus*, the primal oneness of all existence which is manifest in synchronistic events.

The latter are parapsychological phenomena, and as such threshold phenomena. It is a known fact that parapsychological events are more prone to take place in the life of an individual when a gradient of energy exists between the unconscious and the conscious, or, to put it another way, when an archetypal content is in an excited state. In the fifth chapter, I described how contents on the threshold between consciousness and the unconscious appear in identical dual motifs. Among other things, they are both timeless and temporal and are consequently possessed of a sort of double nature with regard to time. In his paper on synchronicity Jung himself relates several dreams which allude to this phenomenon: in one of them the woman dreamer finds layers of rock with black squares on them, so exactly formed as to give the impression of being drawn by a human hand. In two other dreams a man likewise comes across a rock face with a low relief with human heads on it and rock pillars with capitals of carved human heads. They are also found in places where they could not have been created by human hands. Jung comments: "The dreams describe not just a *lusus naturae*, but the meaningful coincidence of an absolutely natural product with a human idea . . . apparently independent of it." Another dream quoted by Jung describes how the dreamer finds a long sought-after creature in the Siberian tundra:

> It was a more than life-size cock, made out of what looked like thin, colourless glass. But it was alive and had just sprung by chance from a microscopic unicellular organism which had the power to turn into all sorts of animals (not otherwise found in the tundra) or even into objects of human use, of whatever size. The next moment each of these chance forms had vanished without trace.[17]

17. "Synchronicity," ¶¶ 945–46.

A dream motif of this type would seem to indicate that *there is a formal principle in nature, capable of uniting structures* not ordinarily classified together *into total archetypal images.* This is the "formal factor in nature" revealed by the principle of sychronicity, according to Jung's view. The very word "coincidence" presupposes that two different elements, not commonly appearing together, nevertheless unexpectedly "fall" together. They consist of a representational psychic occurrence and one or more physical events. In this sense, synchronistic phenomena are spontaneous two-manifestations of the primal unity, and this particular aspect lends them their numinosity. In other words, synchronicity requires two essentially heterogeneous world-systems, whose sporadic interlocking causes certain aspects of wholeness to manifest themselves. For this very reason, the term *unus mundus* emphasizes more the oneness of existence, while the visible aspects of reality lead us to posit the duality of psyche and matter, of observer and object. The coincidence of the two realms in synchronistic phenomena is our only *empirical* indication of unified existence to date. For this reason the symbol of dual identity is used by the unconscious as an image for the *empirical* manifestations of the *unus mundus.*

A unitary dualism of this kind has now also been postulated by the mathematician Albert Lautmann in relation to the concept of time.[18] He distinguishes between a geometric vector time, suitable for representing the irreversibility of physical processes, and a time factor which determines the dynamic qualities of bodies, which he calls "cosmogonic" time. It is fieldlike and discontinuous (in contradistinction to the continuum of a vector line). For Lautmann both aspects of time are observable realizations of a structure manifest in the mathematical sphere as well. He also terms the two aspects "parameter time" and "dimension time." The latter he

18. "Le problème du Temps," in *Symétrie et dissymétrie en mathématiques et physique* (Paris, 1946), pp. 26–27, 35–36.

takes to be a field in which "des accidents topologiques" take place.[19] I am not in agreement with his one-sided relegation of the continuum concept to parameter time and the discontinuum concept to dimension time, since in my view both temporal aspects exhibit the attributes of a continuum and of discontinuity. Nevertheless I agree with him as to the importance of describing time by a complementary double model, picturing both irreversible linear time and a time "field" in which creative single acts occur, in order to grasp the full significance of time. In my opinion, this double model also accords with the reality of natural numbers.

Historically, the intuitive recognition of number's connection with the principle of time has been maintained in the West down to recent times. Ludwig von Eckhartshausen, whom we mentioned earlier, called special attention, for instance, to the fact that a universal power representing the unity of all things and residing "in the behavior of time" appears in "his" number series progression.[20] His qualitatively understood natural numbers thus possess a relationship to time. Von Eckhartshausen's idea includes conceptions dating back to antiquity. Aristotle went so far as to define time as the factor "which determines motion because it is number," or, stated differently, "the time marks the movement, since it is number." [21] Thomas Aquinas actu-

19. *Ibid.*, p. 41. Another double model of time has been proposed by Gonseth in *Les Fondements des mathématiques* (Paris, 1926), p. 120. He distinguishes "le temps chronométrique" and "le temps intuitif," which are both experimental from "le temps scientifique," which is an abstract concept based on mathematical assumptions. Mrs. Hedwig Conrad Martius distinguishes our ordinary "quantified" time from an "aeonic time" which lies between ordinary time and eternity (see *Die Zeit* [Munich, 1954]). The "aeonic time" is the sphere of the "world-imagination" (in the sense of the Sapientia Dei mentioned above).

20. *Zahlenlehre der Natur* (Leipzig, 1794), p. 14.

21. *Physics* IV.219a. Cf. G. J. Whitrow, *The Natural Philosophy of Time* (London and Edinburgh, 1961), p. 29. Archytas of Tarentum early on defined time as the number of a determined movement (*ibid.*, p. 30).

ally defined time simply as "numerus movens." [22] Immanuel Kant was another who stressed the close relation of number and time.

Although such early formulations were too inexact to satisfy modern views, the relation of number to time has consistently remained a much discussed topic. In classical physics time was usually expressed by a parameter comparable to the space coordinates. Whereas Newton still looked on time as an independent continually flowing dimension *sui generis*, this hypothesis nowadays is considered to be outdated. Instead moments in time are defined relationally as "classes of events defined by the concept of simultaneity." [23] This concept of relational time goes back to Leibniz. In his view things and events cannot exist in any time or place other than just this one. If they also did so in some other moment, this latter situation would not be discernible from the first one, because "what is indiscernible is identical"; one cannot differentiate two things *sole numero*. Thus "space is the order of coexistence, and time is the order of the succession of phenomena." [24] And indeed this order is identical for all phenomena of the universe. This view certainly overlooks the problem of *time measurement* completely. (An outstanding survey of the various views on the relation of number to time is provided by G. J. Whitrow in *The Natural Philosophy of Time*.)

Until recently, time was almost exclusively analyzed in terms of spatial analogies,[25] but nowadays efforts are being

22. Whitrow, *Philosophy of Time*, p. 30. This connection between the concept of a time sequence and a rhythmical number sequence in terms of the natural number series is disputed by modern mathematics (*ibid.*, p. 120). Nowadays the number series, the functions, etc., are defined by the limit concept as being timelessly existent (*ibid.*, pp. 134–35).

23. *Ibid.*, pp. 35–36.

24. *Ibid.*, pp. 37, 38.

25. The concept of time has primarily been compared with the concept of a continuous stream in the manner of the geometrical line. See Tobias Dantzig, *Number: The Language of Science* (New York, 1954), pp. 170–77. The Cantorian continuum definition is a dynamic

made to grasp it metrically in terms of atomic motion,[26] since the latter yields more exact measurements than the motion of heavenly bodies. According to this method, one assumes that the energy rhythms of atoms remain constant. This postulate has led to the widely accepted hypothesis that *the universe possesses one single fundamental rhythm*, on which our whole concept of physical time might possibly have to be based.[27] According to Eddington, our measurement of time is founded on the temporal periodicity of a quantum-specified structure, and if we consider this structure in four dimensions, periodicity becomes a lattice structure in time.[28] Periodicity, however, is nothing but a rhythm.

This modern rhythmical view of time also seems to have a biological foundation, for it has recently been discovered that all higher organisms possess one or more internal "clocks," relatively independent of their surroundings, which appear to function in the manner of an electromagnetic oscillator. These clocks are possibly situated in every cell, and represent the physiological basis for our sense of time.[29]

Introspective observations on the flow of thought also lead to findings of a similar nature. E. R. Clay, for instance, points out that we cannot arbitrarily divide up our concept of the present moment into compartments of our own choosing; the moment we experience as present retains its own specific character and length. Clay therefore terms it the "specious present" or "mental present." [30] As Whitrow

---

staccato, while the Dedekindian one is static and *apparently* frees the number concept from the yoke of the time concept. Nevertheless it implies a connection between them (p. 177). In fact, it competently paraphrases the characteristics we ascribe to time (p. 178).

26. Whitrow, *Philosophy of Time*, pp. 44–45.

27. *Ibid.*, p. 46.

28. *Ibid.*, pp. 75–76.

29. See *ibid.*, pp. 59–69.

30. Cited *ibid.*, pp. 78–79.

formulates it, the "mental present" comes into being through a certain "perspective unification," with the result that subjectively experienced time is only divisible beyond a certain degree. Paul Fraisse actually goes so far as to assume that we possess no sense of time at all independent of events, *but only a sense of rhythms and sequences. According to this viewpoint time is based on rhythms, instead of rhythms being based on time.*[31]

As Whitrow explains, two opposing tendencies are at play in present-day conceptions of time. One is the Kantian view that time belongs to an a priori category of our mental functioning, and the other is based on Pierre Janet's view that the concept of time is an intellectual construction.[32] According to Whitrow, such an intellectual construction of our time concept is implicitly preceded by an idea of succession and is related to a simultaneous knowledge of distinct "perception phases"—so that we are actually dealing with the coincidence of simultaneity and succession.[33]

"Bundled" realizations of the present overlap and thereby form a kind of continuum. Whitrow calls this "a certain perspective unification," although he cannot explain how it comes about.[34] Precisely in this area our psychological research can make a contribution by pointing out that in its experience this "perspective unification" is caused by the archetypes. Because the archetypes also overlap in the collective unconscious, or, stated differently, are contaminated with one another (as Jung has shown), such curious double representations or "bundled" present moments

31. See *ibid.*, pp. 77, 82, and Paul Fraisse and G. Oléron, "La Structuration intensive du rhythme," *L'Année psychologique*, LII (1954), 39–46.

32. Whitrow, *Philosophy of Time*, p. 77. This actually refers to E. R. Clay's concept of a "specious present" or a "mental present" which is not pointlike but resembles a line segment, or as I prefer to put it, it appears to be "bundled."

33. *Ibid.*, p. 78.

34. *Ibid.*, p. 79; see also p. 95.

form on the threshold of consciousness, imbedded in our underlying intuitive concept of a continuum.[35]

Insofar as we usually associate the concept of time with our discursive stream of thought, viewing it as a linear sequence of clearly differentiable acts of attention, time, in Whitrow's view, is comparable not so much to the continuum of a geometric line as to the simplest fundamental rhythm of the number series.[36] It is not by chance that the Greek word *arithmos*, "number," is etymologically related to *rhythmos*, "rhythm." [37]

On the basis of these considerations, Whitrow tries to formulate a mathematical definition of time, which relates it (in a purely quantitative manner, of course) to the natural number series.[38] But he thereby develops a construction which he himself admits "is not yet capable of yielding the . . . continuum postulated by physics." [39] Though he introduces the concept of a temporal series, this does not include a metrical concept of a temporal series. As a result, as Whitrow himself points out, "the association of specific instants with particular real numbers remains arbitrary." [40] To this critique I must add that, by such means in particular, one produces no relationship whatsoever between time instants and natural numbers. To my way of thinking the isomorphism of time and the number series constructed in this

35. This bundling element also underlies Bartlett's concept of a "memory scheme," which he characterizes as the active organization (or setting) of our past reactions (in contradistinction to the old theory of physiologically converted engrams).
36. Whitrow, *Philosophy of Time*, p. 115.
37. Both come from ῥεῖν "to flow."
38. Whitrow, *Philosophy of Time*, pp. 151 ff.
39. *Ibid.*, p. 165. In my opinion the hypothesis of "overlapping instants" is an artificial concept used to bridge the gap caused by the incompatibility of continuity and discontinuity. In opposition to this I believe that a clarification of the number concept by means of the idea of complementary quantitative and qualitative time aspects would be conducive to greater clarity. The qualitative aspect of number signifies "form" and in my view this is *the* aspect which, when united with the rhythms of time flow, produces the concept of the "instant."
40. *Ibid.*, pp. 295–96.

manner remains purely collective. The same holds true for the relation of the modern concept of causality to time,[41] because the probability theory used to clarify relatively valid causal connections in nature is likewise based on an algebraic and thus a purely collective view of number. Another instance of lack of clarity in our present mathematical approach to the time concept is the unobservability of temporal coincidence at great distances.[42] This fact adds an additional factor of uncertainty in our modern concept of time.

Quantum mechanics has proved, moreover, that the past history of a system does not absolutely determine its future, but merely determines the probability distribution of possible future states. "There is indeed," as Whitrow stresses,

> a profound connection between the reality of time and the existence of an incalculable element in the universe. . . . The fact of transition and "becoming" compels us to recognize the existence of an element of indeterminism and irreducible contingency in the universe. The future is hidden from us—not in the present, but in the future. *Time is the mediator between the possible and the actual.*[43]

But how can time exercise this mediating role when it is not substantially associated with a qualitative and dynamic element? Perhaps it would be better to assume that time exhibits an isomorphism more with the one-continuum and its qualitatively characterized numerical aspects than with the number series in its quantitative sense. In this case rhythm would represent the primary element for quantitative *and* qualitative manifestations of number. It is manifest quantitatively through the element of repetition inherent in

41. See Whitrow's discussion of views, *ibid.*, pp. 294–95.
42. See Sir Arthur Eddington, *The Philosophy of Physical Science* (Cambridge, 1939), p. 42.
43. Whitrow, *Philosophy of Time*, pp. 295–96 (my italics). According to Eddington this mediating role of time is based on the fact that every fresh observation represents a discontinuity in the "world" of probability waves; the probability becomes "concentrated" anew. In so doing this "world" portrays our knowledge of electrons, not the electrons themselves (*Physical Science*, p. 51).

rhythm and qualitatively through the form and content of the numerical rhythms found in nature. "For the Sage," as an ancient I Ching commentary remarks, "time is only of significance in that within it the steps of becoming can unfold in clearer sequence." By these steps are meant the trigrams (i.e., numbers).[44]

This point of view makes it easier to understand why, according to Jung, the manifestation of an archetype in synchronistic phenomena can appear both as an "act of creation in time" and as the "eternal presence of this single act"; the numerically formulated flow of time produces a sense of temporality, while the "bundled" pattern aspect produces a timeless constancy of meaning.[45] Just as the quantitative aspect of the number series is isomorphic with a causal linear time sequence, so too the qualitative aspect of number, because of its retrograde connection to the one-continuum, produces an isomorphism with the timeless primal unity of existence and its synchronistic manifestations.[46]

The relation of number to time is thus ultimately based

44. The steps are also depicted by "dragons," which stresses their dynamic aspect, since in China the dragon personified the principle of cosmic energy.

45. In this way Bartlett's observations concerning the phenomena of meaning constancy in human memory can be explained. See Whitrow, *Philosophy of Time*, pp. 107–8.

46. As Mircea Eliade has explained (in "The Origin of Religion," *Hibbert Journal*, LVII [1959], 349 ff.), the imagination of primitive peoples in general was dominated far more by the aspect of rhythm than by that of continuous succession. Rhythm divides up time in the same way that musical notes do. In earlier times, therefore, the concepts of repetition and simultaneity did not hold sway (Whitrow, *Philosophy of Time*, p. 55). Every ritual performance reproduced a primal performance taking place *in illo tempore*. As a result of such perennial repetitions of an archetypal primal event, the primitive lived, so to speak, in the timeless present rather than in a linear time sequence (*ibid.*, p. 56). Such an "*illud tempus* time" corresponds to the "Sequence of Earlier Heaven" of the Chinese world-system, whereas the "Inner-World Arrangement" corresponds to the rhythmical activities of man through which he rejuvenates archetypal instants of the "earlier" sequence.

on the phenomenon of energy, which we have already discussed. This fundamental relation of number—energy—time is also illustrated in Jean Piaget's demonstration that a sense of "vitesse-mouvement" of a rhythmical "vitesse-fréquence" appears in children before they develop a more abstract time sense.[47]

An important indication of the primacy of the energy concept (over time) also emerges when we investigate the time concept historically. It is a well-known psychological fact that archetypal personifications of time in the most varied religions were gods functioning mainly as symbols of psychic energy. In Hinduism, for example, in the Bhagavad-Gita the god Krishna appears to the hero Arjuna in the form of his wagon driver (Vasudeva) and finally reveals to him his divine role as creator and destroyer of the world with the words: "Know that I am Time, which causes the world to perish when the time is ripe for it." The ancient Aryans of India honored Varuna as their chief divinity, a dark figure often identified with Yama, the god of death, the guardian of the *rta*, the fundamental order of the universe.[48] Subsequently displaced by Rudra and Brahman, Varuna's link to time nevertheless persists, for "time 'cooks' all things, truly it is the great Self." "He who knows in what time is cooked, he is an expert on the Vedas." [49] The god Shiva also bore the title of Maha-Kāla ("great time") or of Kāla Rudra ("all-consuming time"). As Heinrich Zimmer remarks, he symbolized the energy of the universe, the forms in which he revealed himself eternally creating, pre-

47. See Jean Piaget, "Psychologie et épistemologie de la notion du temps," *Verhandlungen der schweizerischen Naturforschenden Gesellschaft*, CXLV (1965), 25 ff.: "Our time concept seems not to correspond to a mere intuition, but seems to express a relationship of (1) its (time's) content, i.e., what happens in it (traveled space, achieved work, etc.) with (2) the speed of its flow in the form of speed-motion, being either a speed-frequency (e.g., of a rhythm . . .) or a power (force and speed), etc."

48. See S. G. F. Brandon, *History, Time and Deity* (New York, 1965), *passim*.

49. *Ibid.*, p. 34.

serving, and destroying.[50] The personification of Shiva as time was later incorporated into another image, the goddess Kāli (a word signifying the feminine form of *kāla*, "time"),[51] who represented his activating energy (*shakti*). With good reason Hermann Güntert equates the word *kāla* with the Greek *kairos* etymologically, and associates the latter with *kairóo* which means "to attach the threads of a web together."[52] In this sense *kairos* signifies the "right order" in time. The association of *kairos* with goddesses weaving time alludes once again, we must mention in passing, to the idea of a "field" in which "meaningful connections" are interwoven like threads of a fabric.

One of the oldest original gods of ancient Iran was Zurvan, a deity who later split up into two divinities, Ormuzd and Ahriman, or "Zurvan eternity" (*akarana*) and "Zurvan who for a long time followed his own laws" (*dureghō-ehrodhāta*).[53] Later on, in Mithraism, his second form was frequently equated with the evil principle, Ahriman.[54] He signifies time as the ruler of fate, bringing old age, sickness, and death in its train. "Zurvan eternity," on the other hand, signifies the final, eternal substance of reality lying behind all things. Subsequently, in Mithraism, we come across the god Aion, who is presumably descended from this ancient Persian Zurvan.[55] He was frequently depicted with a lion's head and a snake wrapped around him, the signs of the zodiac surrounding him (sometimes they were engraved instead on his body). Like his derivative, the god Phanes in Orphic mysticism, he represented the eternity of the world-creating principle.[56] Aion's essential quality is identity, that of the

---

50. H. Zimmer, *Myths and Symbols of Indian Art*, quoted in Brandon, *History*, pp. 45 ff.

51. Brandon, *History*, pp. 36, 37.

52. *Der arische Weltkönig und Heiland* (Halle a. S., 1923), pp. 232–33.

53. Ahriman might also be the eldest god of all. See Brandon, *History*, p. 38.

54. *Ibid.*, p. 44.

55. *Ibid.*, pp. 39–43.

56. *Ibid.*, p. 47.

The Mithraic god Aion [Photograph by William Bandieri; reproduced by permission of the Museum of Modena.]

cosmos is order, and that of time transformation. To a similar triad the ancient philosopher Pherecydes alluded when he said: "Zeus always existed, and Chronus, and Chthonia; from his seed Chronus created fire and wind and water. *He is time.*"

Another god who personified the same creative time principle in late antiquity was the Gnostic daemon Ialdabaôth, who was depicted with a serpent's body and a lion's head.

Mayan time-space of thirty-six hundred years [Source: W. Cordan, *Das Buch des Rates* (Jena, 1962), p. 227, reproduced by permission of Eugen Diederichs Verlag.]

He was the Demiurge who created a defective, perishable (because temporal) world.[57] A cult of Cronus (who was later viewed as identical with Chronus, the god of time), closely associated with Serapis, was also widespread in Egyptian syncretism. Cronus was a three-headed god, whose middle head consisted of a lion symbolizing the present, while his left head was in the form of a wolf representing the all-devouring past, and his right head was a "cajoling dog" signifying the future.[58] According to Plutarch, this late Egyptian form of Cronus was also identified with the underworld jackal god Anubis.[59] In Rome, on the other hand, Aion was equated with the two-headed forms of Janus,[60] and in the gnosis of the *Corpus hermeticum* this same god was finally defined as the cosmic Demiurge, who himself created the universe, time (*Chronos*), and becoming (*Genēsis*).[61] Among the ancient Mayans also, time was often portrayed as being "carried" by a god: for instance, one inscription depicts the number god Nine carrying a

57. See *ibid.*, pp. 50–51.
58. According to Macrobius, *Saturnalia* I.20.13.
59. See Brandon, *History*, p. 59.
60. *Ibid.*, p. 60.
61. *Corpus hermeticum* XI.2, ed. Nock-Festugière (Paris, 1960), I, 147.

vulture, *cuch,* on his back. By a play of words this *cuch* signifies a cycle of four hundred years and the entirety, therefore, a burden of thirty-six hundred years.[62]

These mythological associations mentioned in passing should suffice to demonstrate that the archetypal image of a god in his world-creating energy lies behind most personifications of time. Psychologically speaking, this god personifies *psychic energy in its multivalent, instinctual, image-generating, spiritual-creative power which embraces all psychic processes.*[63] Insofar as this psychic energy appears to be isomorphic with physical energy in terms of numerical rhythms, it is intimately related to number, and herein lies the isomorphism of the number field with the order of the collective unconscious. The idea that time consists of dy-

I

Chinese incense seal clock [Source: J. T. Fraser, ed., *The Voices of Time: A Cooperative Survey of Man's Views of Time as Expressed by the Sciences and by the Humanities* (New York: Braziller, 1966), p. 383, reproduced by permission of J. T. Fraser.]

namics and rhythmically structured patterns can be illustrated by the symbol of the old Chinese fire clock. This type of clock was constructed by spreading a combustible powder over a labyrinth and igniting it at one end, so that its burning head crept slowly forward like a fuse. Time was

62. See W. Cordan, *Das Buch des Rates: Mythos und Geschichte der Maya* (Jena, 1962), p. 164.

63. See Jung, *Symbols of Transformation, CW,* Vol. V, esp. ¶¶ 198–99. Concerning theriomorphic manifestations of energy see particularly ¶ 261. See also *Corpus hermeticum* XI.2.

marked off according to the progress of the fire. The labyrinths were usually mandala-shaped (see illustration). Such clocks depicted the pattern of a relatively closed system.[64] When a specific energic process had elapsed within this pattern, a time interval was also completed. In such instruments "time" is represented by an energic process moving within a pattern. The gap in the rim (I) shows where the system is open to human contact.

Practically speaking, this "hole" in the mandala of the fire clock signifies the spot at which man relates himself to time,[65] and at which he, along with the sum total of possible unknown conditions in which he finds himself, can exert an influence on time. For unconscious influences can easily cause one to wind a watch wrongly, or not at all. Time has a "hole" at this spot, where it begins and ends. This hole in the time-space continuum figures as an archetypal motif in other contexts. The *fenestra aeternitatis* ("window into eternity") plays an important role in Western alchemy. In the Middle Ages the Virgin Mary was extolled as the "window of enlightenment" or "window of escape" (from the world),[66] and in alchemy these attributes were transferred to the philosophers' stone.[67] The *mysterium fenestrae* also has a place in the cabala, where it signifies the light connecting the *sephiroth*, from the "crown" to "wisdom" and "intelligence," in order to unite the three upper *sephiroth* with the divine original light.[68]

64. It was frequently associated with symbolic subjects (written characters). Stylized phrases such as "long life," "double good fortune," and so on were often placed in the center. See Needham, *Science and Civilization*, III, 331.

65. It corresponds to the winder in our watches. In automatic watches, too, the wearer's movements keep the watch going, illustrating the same principle.

66. Ps. (?) Albertus Magnus, *Biblia mariana*, in *Opera* (ed. Borgnet), 37.385.

67. See Marie-Louise von Franz, *Aurora consurgens*, trans. R. F. C. Hull and A. S. B. Glover (New York, 1966), p. 379.

68. See Knorr von Rosenroth, *Kabbala denudata* (Sulzbach, 1677), II 281–82.

Paracelsus' pupil, Gerhard Dorn, in whose philosophy the "window onto eternity" or *spiraculum aeternitatis* ("airhole into eternity") figures prominently, was certainly influenced by these ideas.[69] He recommended a kind of alchemistic exercise in meditation, in which the instinctual aspect of the body was first to be subdued, by separating soul and spirit from it. Then soul and spirit were to be fused into a *unio mentalis* in order to be reunited subsequently with the purified body. Psychologically this *unio mentalis* corresponds to the building up of a spiritual attitude. In this manner, according to Dorn, the spirit operates on the soul like a *spiraculum vitae aeternae* ("airhole to eternal life"). It is a "window open to eternity," i.e., to the potential world of the *unus mundus* in God's mind. In truth, as Jung realized and pointed out, an experience of the Self opens such a window into eternity for the individual, because it enables him to escape from the stifling clutches of a one-sided view of life. Through this "window" man touches the eternal in himself, and at the same time the eternal can reach into his time-bound world in the form of synchronistic events.

In the picture the spiritual pilgrim leaves ordinary space-time behind and gazes through the "window of eternity" into the world of timeless order, the collective unconscious. The double wheel, representing here Ezekiel's vision, should be noted.

This double wheel confronts us with one of the most difficult problems posed by the motif of the double (timeless and temporal) mandalas: Are the two systems in any way "interlocked"? In other words, is there a possibility that synchronistic events may be *regular* manifestations? Certainly all the models of the timeless as well as the time-bound mandalas possess an internally ordered structure, but the manner in which they contact each other remains ob-

69. *Philosophia meditativa, Theatrum chemicum,* ed. Zetzner (Strasbourg, 1659), I, 400.

The hole open to eternity: the spiritual pilgrim discovering another world [Source: Nineteenth-century (?) woodcut, reproduced in C. G. Jung, "Flying Saucers: A Modern Myth," *Civilization in Transition, CW*, Vol. X, plate VII.]

scure. (We notice this too in the double wheel of the illustration.) When they consist of wheels, for instance, they do not work in unison but *are contiguous at the center,* which is a technical impossibility. *The two systems are incommensurable.* From this we can only conclude that the moments of contact occur when a spontaneous action emanates from their common center. This conclusion agrees with the empirical evidence that synchronistic events occur, as far as we can see, only sporadically and irregularly.

When a person plays with a divinatory mandala, *his* unconscious actions then induce the contact. These actions ultimately constitute an unknown and irregular factor. To be sure, something resembling a regular order does exist, but whether it is manifest in a synchronistic happening or not remains unpredictable. Only the *quality* of *possible* events can be foretold.

The mysterious point of contact between the two systems appears to be the center or a sort of pivot where psyche and matter meet. When an individual enters into relation with the forces of the pivot, he finds himself close to the sphere of "miracles" which seemingly could not occur without a corresponding attitude on his own part. Therefore the Chinese philosopher Mo Dsi said:

> It is not only he who is possessed of the most complete sincerity . . . who can give full development to his own nature . . . by this means he can do the same to . . . other men . . . and to the natures of animals and things. . . . He can assist the transforming and nourishing powers of Heaven and Earth. . . . It is characteristic of the most entire sincerity to be able to foreknow. . . . Both these [virtue and knowledge] are virtues belonging to nature, and *this is* the way by which a union is effected of the external and internal. . . . The way of Heaven and Earth may be . . . declared in one sentence. . . . *They are without any doubleness, and so they produce things in a manner that is unfathomable.*[70]

When such a constellation exists and eternity breaks through momentarily into our temporal system, the primal unity actively manifests itself and temporarily unites the double structures into one, so to speak. This is how the *unus mundus* becomes revealed in the phenomenon of synchronicity. But immediately afterward the flow of events resumes its course on the track of the ordinary temporal pattern, and the timeless order falls back into a latent condition once more. This is why it is possible to describe "quali-

70. *The Four Books: The Doctrine of the Mean*, trans. J. Legge (New York, 1966), pp. 398–99, 401, 403, 405.

tative fields" underlying synchronistic events,[71] but not the "just-so" occurrences themselves. The latter originate in the spontaneous manifestations of the unconscious objective psyche, which Jung calls the *spiritual* aspect of the unconscious.

71. The situations of the I Ching hexagrams or the zodiac signs and planets of the horoscope all represent examples of their systematic presentation.

CHAPTER FOURTEEN

The *Unus Mundus* as the World of the Spirit and "Spirits"

Insofar as, in accordance with Jung's hypothesis discussed earlier in chapter twelve, we do not experience the spirit as personally pertaining to us, it remains in its original condition, a "breathlike presence," like a ghost. Therefore it is frequently personified by primitive peoples and equated with the spirits of the dead. The question as to whether the appearance of so-called "spirits of the dead" really refers to personifications of unconscious contents in the living or to real apparitions of the dead themselves is a matter which has so far not been clarified. I have nothing to add on this score. In the following exposition only the relation of number to those contents which appear as "spirits" in dreams and waking hallucinations will be taken into account.

Since number appears to represent a particularly primitive expression in man of the "spirit," it seems natural to look for a historical connection between the two phenomena. Actually, an interesting combination of the realm of the dead and the number oracle is to be found in certain intuitive philosophical and religious conceptions among the natives of the West African coast. In contradistinction to European and Islamic geomancy which employ their techniques solely for magical purposes and do not encompass a profound philosophy like the I Ching oracle, African geomancy (introduced probably from the Islamic North) has undergone a penetrating intellectual and mystical interpretation among the Fon, the Mina of Togo, and the Yoruba tribes. West African medicine men have even developed an interpretation of geomancy which reveals an archetypal model of the *unus mundus*. I am taking the following facts from Bernard Maupoil's book, *La Géomancie à l'ancienne Côte des Esclaves*,[1] which deals with divinatory practices that remain extant today, but are on the point of declining. They were mostly investigated in Abomey and Porto-Novo.

According to the Fon, geomancy is based on the effect of a divinity called Fa (Ifa by the Yoruba, and Afa by the Togoland Mina) who is no voodoo, ordinary god, or demon, since he causes no possessions or trances and only performs philanthropic magic, eschewing the black variety. He enjoys no collective cult, preferring to reveal the truth "individually to individuals." According to legend Fa came from a mystical land called Ifé that lies in the direction of the sunrise, *to which the dead retire*. There they find the truth and Fa, the god of truth, "for only when one dies does one uncover the secret of life."[2] In Ifé this god also taught geomancy to the first diviners by causing an oil palm with sixteen branches to grow; around its trunk lay sixteen holes into which sixteen dates fell, corresponding to the sixteen signs of geomancy.[3] The dates of this curious tree possess six eyes (calling to mind the six lines of the I Ching hexagram). Even today the geomantic oracle is cast with dates (instead of dots), which are counted out. In Ifé the god Fa healed all sicknesses: "for when God created the world he created good and evil, concealing evil behind the good; it

---

1. (Paris, 1943). See also William Buscom, *Ifa Divination: Communication between Gods and Men in West Africa* (Bloomington, Ind., 1969).

2. See Maupoil, *La Géomancie*, pp. 23-24, 34.

3. See *ibid.*, p. 42.

does not come from man, but from God who willed that it should exist." [4]

Every living person possesses an invisible soul (*ye*), *but he does not understand its meaning;* "therefore whoever seeks the mystery of his life must for this reason approach Fa. He is called Fa and is the only principle (*ye*) which can reveal the truth about the greater life." [5] The root of the name "Fa" signifies the freshness of water, air, and also *refrigerium* in the sense of finding inward peace.[6] Fa is the "king of earthly life," the king of the oil palm, and the messenger of God. His pronouncements are wholly impartial and he never deceives man; he perceives all things, even man's most secret thoughts. Every difficulty, no matter how serious ("hot"), is assuaged through contact with Fa; it becomes "easy" and "cooled." Fa illuminates all men and, disguising nothing, "he stretches forth his open hands." A wise old medicine man said of Fa: "All the magicians try to describe Fa pompously, but I, although I am a *bokono* [magician], would not presume to define Fa. Only wonder-working nature itself, which has created Fa, can knowingly speak of him." [7] Fa imparts purely individual information to every person, ignoring the laws and judgments of mankind; only he who obtains information from him in the oracle can really understand to what it relates. He is *not* a force of nature, but rather portrays God's solicitude for his creation. He does not possess the blind passions of a voodoo. Neither is he human. Sometimes he may be glimpsed in a dream, where he usually appears as a soft, boneless, red or black humanlike figure with four eyes, two in front and two behind, two hands, and two feet, but he can hardly move his limbs. His epithets include the following: "Hard as a stone," "Search and see," "He who reveals what each

4. *Ibid.*
5. *Ibid.*, p. 325.
6. Certain experts derive the word *fa* from Buddha, and postulate Indian influence (*ibid.*, p. 17). This has not been proved however.
7. *Ibid.*, p. 12.

one contains in his heart," "Lord of life," "He who transmits the tidings of the dead," "The sun rises and the wall becomes red" (meaning that Fa dispenses enlightenment like the rising sun), or "The hole which calls us over to the Beyond" (*fenestra aeternitatis!*). In a prayer to Fa the birds and wild animals "which march past in the night and speak in man's language" are invoked. "They are the ones who receive the *number* of those who will die, and give the *number* of those who will (soon) be born." [8] It is by means of number that these "doctor animals" of Fa possess their power over the living.

These few indications suffice to show that psychologically Fa represents a symbol of the Self and of "absolute knowledge"; he stands above the voodoo spirits and is actually more friendly to man than God himself, who created evil. In this he resembles the European concept of the Sapientia Dei (Wisdom) similarly described in the Apocrypha of the Old Testament as being especially φιλάνθρωπος. This figure of Sapientia sometimes also endeavors to mitigate God's wrath against humanity.[9] Fa thus represents an aspect of the God-image in the unconscious psyche, compelling man to seek higher consciousness, and consequently he also refers to an aspect of the Self activating and sustaining the development of higher consciousness in the individual. It is this creative aspect of the unconscious to which numerical divination is linked, because number is the means par excellence whereby the spiritual aspect of the unconscious can produce order and meaningful realizations in our consciousness.

This facet of the Self archetype does not, however, embrace the *entirety* of the collective unconscious, which is certainly also the source of drives, chaos, and destructive passions. For this reason, in the opinion of the West Africans, there exists a still mightier, darker divinity, Gba'adu, beyond Fa's reach, who is also sometimes described as the

8. *Ibid.*, p. 364.
9. See C. G. Jung, "Answer to Job," *Psychology and Religion: West and East, CW*, Vol. XI, *passim.*

"wife of Fa" or "voodoo of Fa." [10] Gba'adu means "the calabash of existence" and was depicted as two calabashes, one lying on top of the other, symbolizing the original condition of the world in those days when the primal god and goddess still lay close on top of each other. Gba'adu is greedy for blood; he dispenses life and takes it back. He represents the most powerful magic, and "the highest possible degree of self-knowledge a man can attain." [11] Maupoil says: "Gba'adu is the most dreaded voodoo, for he possesses the most profound knowledge of Fa." [12] To some extent he portrays a still more comprehensive symbol of the *unus mundus* than Fa, since he embraces all of existence, including its dark, deadly, and chaotic forces. Fa—a spirit of truth— stands more for the "philanthropic" side of the Self symbol. Gba'adu represents the ultimate mystery lying beyond Fa. Whereas Fa can be described as that aspect of the Self turned toward human life, Gba'adu, as the mystery beyond earthly existence, cannot be experienced in this life, but is only revealed in death.

Gba'adu corresponds to the alchemical Mercurius, who was considered to personify the *unus mundus*, the "original, non-differentiated unity of existence . . . the primordial unconsciousness." [13] Among the Yoruba, moreover, the word for "one," *okan*, also means "spirit." [14] This "spirit" unites the opposites in itself in a *hieros gamos*, in the same

10. Maupoil, *Géomancie*, p. 87.
11. *Ibid.*, p. 89. He is that which prior to initiation a man calls *mavou*, "life."
12. *Ibid.*, p. 89. See also p. 90: "Considering the decay of the cult of Gba'adu and the mystery in which this cult has been shrouded until the present time, it would be imprudent to define him (Gba'adu) more precisely than by the words: 'Gba'adu, feared voodoo, symbol of heaven and earth in their fertile union, highest owner of the knowledge of Fa, having the goal of confirming an esoteric feeling of universal symbiosis.' Gba'adu is also related to a decayed cult of the four elements and the four cardinal points [of the compass]."
13. See *Mysterium Coniunctionis, CW*, Vol. XIV, ¶ 660.
14. See E. Fettweis, *Das Rechnen der Naturvölker* (Leipzig, 1927), p. 59.

way that the symbol of the two calabashes of existence representing Gba'adu's mystery does. In the mysteries of Mediterranean antiquity as well, there was a realization of the identity of marriage and death, an identity of birth and the eternal resurgence of life out of death.[15] According to certain ideas of the alchemists, the individuated human being who has become unified must join himself to this mercurial spirit,[16] "not with the world of multiplicity . . . but with a potential world, the eternal foundation of all empirical existence, just as the Self is the foundation and origin of the individual personality, past, present, and future."[17] This corresponds to the Eastern idea of an identity between the personal and impersonal *atman.*[18]

In the experience of death the alchemists likewise hoped to discover such an exalted and final step in the achievement of oneness, a holy marriage of opposites. This experience is particularly beautifully extolled in an ancient alchemical text which can be traced back to the Egyptian liturgy of the dead. In this text the *unus mundus* is pictured as a transcendental experience of wholeness attainable only in the resurrection mystery after death. "Then," as it says, "the soul calls to the body: 'Awaken out of Hades, rise up out of the grave, and keep awake out of the darkness. Clothe yourself in spirituality and godliness.'" Pneuma, soul, and body then become "the One in which the mystery is concealed." This One is a statue which was born of fire; it unites spirit, soul, and body and contains the four elements within itself.

> Thus arises *one* nature which pursues and conquers all natures, and this is the One which conquers every nature, that of fire and that of moisture, and transmutes all their natures. And behold, I also declare unto you that which will ensue when it is accomplished: then it will become

15. See *Mysterium,* ¶ 658.
16. *Ibid.,* ¶ 761.
17. *Ibid.,* ¶ 760.
18. See *ibid.,* ¶¶ 762–63.

a deathly *pharmakon* which speeds around in the body. As it has now gone into its individual body, so it murderously penetrates the other bodies. In putrefaction and in warmth arises that *pharmakon* which penetrates unhindered through every body.[19]

This death-bringing aspect of the Self symbol emerges, if I understand the text correctly, when the One (the Self) acquires its new, adequate, perfect body, namely, the supernatural resurrection body; then it destroys its former body and permeates all other bodies. Translated into modern psychological language this would mean: when the Self, in a state of "becoming" within earthly man, fully attains its "body," i.e., its goal—the mandala of the *unus mundus*—it exerts an annihilating effect on man's earthly existence, because it has attained a state of being as the all-permeating one-continuum which is opposed to all individual manifestations. Then death becomes "right"; it is connected with the achievement of the goal. In this alchemical text, too, the *unus mundus* is identical with the realm of the dead, the spirit land.

The death mystery described in the alchemical treatise of Komarios is, as I have pointed out, derived historically from the Egyptian rituals for the dead. In ancient Egypt the sky divinity (Nut) was represented by a feminine being, a woman or cow, and the earth divinity (Geb) by a man. In accordance with this reversal of the usual order, the Egyptians portrayed much of the realm we today consider symbolic and spiritual by material concrete objects and actions. For example, they chemically preserved dead bodies to represent an individual's attainment of immortality. This mummification process really signified an alchemical metamorphosis of the deceased into the universal god or the spirit of the *unus mundus*. In an old papyrus preserved in Cairo we can read the workshop directions for treating a

19. "Komarios to Kleopatra," in M. Berthelot, *Collection des anciens alchimistes grecs* (Paris, 1887-88), I, 297-98.

corpse, which demonstrate clearly how every step in the chemical treatment (such as leaching in a natron bath, anointing, perfuming, and swathing the corpse in linen bandages) signified such a deification process. In the text the corpse is even directly addressed as "this god." At the anointing of the head, for instance, the priest intones: "O Osiris NN to you the oil from the land of Punt which enhances your aroma with the fragrance of the gods. To you the emanation that proceeds from Ra. . . . Your soul mounts upon your body to the land of the gods; Horus, who comes forth as myrrh-oil from Osiris, be with you." Or witness these directions for anointing the body: "Receive the perfume in order that you may join yourself to the great Sun God." At the immersion of the spine in oil: "Take the emanation, which proceeded from Ra, the secretion which flowed out of Geb . . . to you the garment comes which came forth out of the Eye of Horus . . . it guides your way in Nu and so adorns your limbs that you become like unto he, when he rises up and descends, and you cease not in all eternity." At the immersion of the body in the natron bath it is intoned:

> O Osiris NN, the Nile, the Great One of the gods, comes to you; he gives you the waters . . . Nu which issues forth out of the Cave, the whirlpool which issues forth out of the cool flood. You drink from him and are satisfied through him. Your body is filled with fresh water, your coffin is filled with the flood, your throat is inundated —*you are Nu the Elder, the father of the gods.*[20]

The word "natron" comes from the Egyptian word *neter*, "god," so that the natron bath of the corpse undoubtedly denotes the deification of the deceased through immersion in a "god-substance." [21] As a result of "becoming

20. The entire text, insofar as it is preserved, is published in G. Roeder, *Urkunden zur Religion des alten Ägypten* (Jena, 1923), pp. 297 ff.

21. See O. Steuer, *Über das wohlriechende Natron im Alten Ägypten* (Leiden, 1937). Also G. Thausing, *Der Auferstehungsgedanke in ägyptischen religiösen Texten* (Leipzig, 1943), p. 122.

God," [22] the deceased actually rises above all preexistent "gods" and *is able to permeate the whole cosmos.*[23] Thus in one text the dead man says of himself: "I am Osiris, the Lord of the Heads, with the powerful phallus. I am Orion who draws near to his land, he who circles the heavenly orbits, the body of his mother Nut." [24] For this reason too the papyri contain numerous recipes for "the stepping forth into day," which are all designed to assist the deceased in attaining all-permeating spiritual power. In the Book of the Dead the deceased describes himself as follows: "I open up all paths that exist in Heaven, on Earth, and in that Duat ['underworld']. It is I whom he [Osiris] loves. I come as a mummy, as one transfigured." [25] Or:

> I enter as a falcon and leave as a phoenix. . . . His soul shall reside with men and the gods, and he shall not be repulsed by them, he shall step forth in the daytime taking on all the forms he desires. He shall enter and leave through the secret gates. . . . He shall know his forms in the light . . . his power shall be greater than that of the gods.[26]

Indeed, the body of the deceased does contain all the other gods, for he says of himself: "My hair is Nu, my countenance is Ra, my eyes are natron, my ears are Wepwawet . . . my teeth are Khopri, my neck is Isis . . . my throat is Neith . . . my back is Seth, my phallus is Osiris." The conclusion of the embalming papyrus runs:

> To you Osiris NN the incense comes which proceeded from Horus, the myrrh which proceeded from Ra, the natron proceeding from Nekhebit . . . the resin which issued from the mighty gods, the gum that issued forth from the blessed Wennofer [Osiris]. . . . You tread upon an earth of silver and a floor of gold, you cleanse yourself upon a stone of silver and a floor of gold, you shall

22. See Roeder, *Urkunden zur Religion*, p. 269: "He shall be a god in Eternity," etc.

23. See *ibid.*, p. 264.   24. *Ibid.*, p. 262.

25. *Ibid.*, p. 209.   26. *Ibid.*, p. 234.

be buried in a hollow of malachite . . . you perceive your name in all the names, your soul in the Heavens, your body in the Duat, you dwell in eternity and remain forever young. . . .[27]

The deceased thereby becomes one with *all* the gods and with the totality of an otherworldly land *which is simultaneously matter in its various aspects* (natron, oil, water, gold). In this form he attains the sun god's orbit, rotating eternally in a cyclical vortex, similar to the cyclical whirling movement of matter described in the Komarios text.

During this mysterious transformation into the universal cosmic spirit, the deceased first sojourns in the realm of the god Aker, whose acquaintanceship we have already made as the double lion, guardian of the threshold to the Beyond and keeper of the two horizons.[28] In the form of Aker he "guards his own image";[29] sometimes he also becomes the sun god in the egg, or the double lion sitting beside the primeval waters, between the mountains of the East and the West.[30] As we have already shown, psychologically the lion personifies the psychic energy which has vanished into the collective unconscious and its "forms," the obscure archetypal structures which now become contained within him.

But after the deceased voyages as a star across the ocean of the heavens, he is feared by the spirits in Nu (the primeval waters), and the "enlightened simply abide in him." In Kurt Sethe's view the ordinary dead, who are not yet enlightened, simply abide, like the unborn, in the primeval waters of Nu which shelter all creative potency and the potencies of future "becoming." Only the enlightened dead, who have become circumpolar stars that never set,

27. *Ibid.*, p. 256.
28. See above, chapter five.
29. See Constant de Wit, *Le Rôle et le sens du lion dans l'Egypte ancienne* (Leiden, 1951), p. 95. Aker is he "whose forms are mysterious" (p. 97). He guards the secrets of the underworld (p. 98).
30. *Ibid.*, pp. 103, 101.

thereby retaining their identity, develop the capacity to "proceed in and out in all forms." [31] In other words, only the enlightened dead acquire the freedom to move about the entire universe.

Ancient Chinese culture also provides us with evidence of a connection between the *unus mundus* concept and the dwelling place of the dead. In his book *Tod, Auferstehung, Weltordnung*, Carl Hentze has taken pains to show that in China antique bronze vessels often bore a sign which can be interpreted as two hands holding a lozenge-shaped figure. [32]

Left, the character for *lung,* "to play, gamble"; *right,* the radical character of *suan shu,* "to calculate" [Source: *left,* Carl Hentze, *Tod, Auferstehung, Weltordnung* (Zurich, 1953), p. 17, reproduced by permission of Origo-Verlag (characters on p. 276 are also from this source); *right,* Joseph Needham, *Science and Civilization in China* (Cambridge, 1959), II, 4, reproduced by permission of Cambridge University Press.]

This character signifies *hiàng,* "sacrificial performance" (to the ancestral spirits) and also *lung,* "to play, gamble." The root character for "calculation," *suan shu,* is likewise connected with it. The lozenge-shaped object itself is explained as *yü,* "previous stone," [33] which in this context also has the meaning of "wholeness" and total world, signifying the highest value. The reason that jade possesses precisely these symbolic powers is given in an old Chinese text (chapter 9 of the Kuan Tzu, ca. 500 B.C.) in the following words:

> Jade is warm, agreeable, . . . this (may be called) its "benevolence." Its lines run back and forth near each other, communicating systematically, they (may be called) its

31. Thausing, *Auferstehungsgedanke,* p. 91, and K. Sethe.
32. (Zurich, 1953), pp. 15–19.   33. *Ibid.,* p. 18.

"wisdom." It is hard, but not over-compacted (*tsu*), this (may be called) its "righteousness." It is sharp but its angles are not hurtful, this (may be called) its "conduct." It is fresh and bright, but cannot get dirty, this (may be called) its "purity." It can be broken but not bent, this (may be called) its "courage." Its cracks and spots all appear on the exterior, this (may be called) its "refined quality" (i.e., it does not try to cover up its weak points). Its flourishing, shining, agreeable lights reflect each other but do not trespass upon one another, this (may be called) its "tolerance." Upon being struck it gives a clear, far-away and pure sound, not screaming, this (may be called) its "gentleness." These are the reasons why the rulers of men appreciate and value it for making auspicious seals.[34]

Considered from a psychological point of view, the precious stone jade clearly represents a symbol of the greatest *psychic* value, and is an image of the Self. In the pictographs described by Hentze, this precious jade stone, which signifies the totality of the world, is indicated by lozenges. The lozenges, according to Hentze's interpretation, are two

mirror-image houses or house urns facing each other.[35]

They are the urns of the houses in which the dead were believed to reside.[36] As Hentze says, they represent "the total world, the entirety of the world," "in that an upright and an inverse world together constitute the whole world, namely, that of the dead and that of the living." [37] This "entire world" also resembles the womb, a sort of place of origin for all creation (like the waters of Nu in Egypt!).[38]

34. Joseph Needham, *Science and Civilization in China* (Cambridge, 1959), II, 43.
35. See Hentze, *Tod*, p. 24.
36. *Ibid.*, p. 26.
37. *Ibid.*, pp. 31, 98, 29.
38. *Ibid.*, p. 98.

In some renderings this double house is again doubled, resulting in a mandala.[39] As a symbol of wholeness this double

house 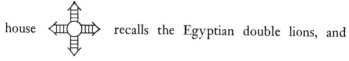 recalls the Egyptian double lions, and

even more the double mandalas discussed earlier, which were cited as symbols of the timeless and space-time–bound aspects of the universe. In the Chinese view their united action symbolizes the wholeness of existence, embracing both the world of the living and that of the "spirits" in their reciprocal penetration.

This unified action of two heterogeneous worlds as long as life endures in space and time was most impressively declared by the Zen master Ma; when he fell seriously ill and lay not more than twenty-four hours away from his death, the director of the monastery approached him and asked: "How has the Venerable One's state of health been recently?" The master replied: "Buddha with the sun visage, Buddha with the moon visage." As Wilhelm Gundert explains, this saying can be traced back to a passage in the third Sutra of the Name of Buddha, where in celebration of the twelfth month[40] it reads:

> Thereafter I saw a Buddha with the name of Moon-Visage. The lifespan of this Buddha was only one day and one night. Beyond the Illustrious One with the moon visage I saw another Buddha: he bore the name Sun-Visage. The lifespan of this Buddha with the sun visage came to a full thousand and eight hundred years![41]

This might be taken as an allusion to the mandala consisting of two systems, the one temporally and spatially limited, the other of greater duration. But both are called "Buddha,"

39. *Ibid.*, pp. 163 ff.
40. Perhaps this is no coincidence either; just as the cycle of the year is completed in twelve months, Ma's life comes to a close at this particular moment.
41. *Bi-Yän-Lu: Niederschrift von der Smaragdenen Felswand*, ed. W. Gundert (Munich, 1960), p. 97.

both are facets of the great One,[42] of which the dying Ma became conscious.

If we reflect on these mythological assertions from the standpoint of the present day, we come up against a difficult problem, because they are not verifiable statements that can be scientifically evaluated. Nevertheless, I feel that some tentative conclusions can be formulated, which lie more in the direction of hypothetical ideas and questions than scientific statements.

According to the main argument of this book, it appears that matter and psyche form merely the inner and outer aspects of the same transcendental reality. We ventured this conclusion because the ultimate constituents of matter present themselves to our observing consciousness in forms similar to those forms representing the ultimate foundations of the inner factor, the collective unconscious. This transcendental unitary reality (*unus mundus*) calls forth the hypothesis of animate matter.[43] We know that at death the material part of man dissolves into inorganic material constituents, into something, therefore, which modern physics would define as an electromagnetic field, whose excited points represent particles. The old religious texts referred to, which aim, as it were, at an introspective perception of the same process, describe death as an ascension into the realm of the gods, i.e., into the archetypal field of the collective unconscious. When this happens it is as if the psychic experience of identity, attached during our lifetime to experiences of the body, were displaced by the world of elementary particles and "fields" and the depths of the collective unconscious. But then the crucial question becomes: Does

42. Gundert explains in the *Bi-Yän-Lu:* "In the Sutra quoted by the Patriarch many other Buddhas besides these two are mentioned by name and they, together with the unnumbered and unnamed, form only the facets of one and the same Body of Light."
43. See also G. Schramm, *Belebte Materie* (Pfullingen, 1965), and R. Linssen, *Spiritualité de la matière* (Paris, 1966). Except for the hypothesis of animated matter, however, I do not identify with these authors' views.

this signify the dispersion and dissolution of an individual's experience of identity and a consequent resurgence of complete unconsciousness? Or does a contraction of consciousness into the "small world-system" mandala occur, which enables our individual consciousness to survive? What would immortality mean, ultimately, if I myself were not conscious of it? In the texts we quoted the survival of the personality after death is regarded as dependent on "self-knowledge" or "enlightenment." According to Egyptian belief only those who have established relations with their Ba-souls and the "never-setting stars" are capable of post-mortal consciousness. Similarly the West Africans maintain that only those who, with the help of the god Fa, have made their *ye* (life principle) conscious can enter the timeless world *with* their ego consciousness and by this means retain their ego identity as they "proceed in and out in various forms."

The Chinese concept of life after death, as described by Richard Wilhelm, seems to me to throw interesting light on this problem.[44] The Chinese distinguish between a bodily and a psychic aspect of man, which both disperse at death into an animated universal substance. But a psychic element survives as a third factor capable of consciousness; it consists of a tendency to consciousness, so to speak, which must, however, be concentrated during the course of one's lifetime so as to survive death. During one's lifetime this tendency to consciousness must construct a subtle body round itself,

> a body of a spiritual kind which now in death supports it when it has to detach itself from the physical body which was previously its helper, because it can no longer reside there. To begin with, this psychic something is very delicate and only in the greatest sages does it possess the inherent stability to endure after death.

44. R. Wilhelm, *Weisheit des Ostens* (Düsseldorf, Cologne, and The Hague, 1951), pp. 28 ff.

For the remainder of mankind the possibility of preserving one's conscious identity rests on the concerted efforts the living must make to remember them.[45]

By building up the spiritual body through meditation exercises, the Chinese attempted in this life to disengage the energies attached to one's ordinary body and thus to endow the seminal power, the entelechy—or, translated into our modern terms, the self—with a new body. This process involves a retrograde movement of life energy (as we also saw indicated in the "heavenly orders"). In this way a field of force forms around one's psychic core, a force to which Richard Wilhelm attributes a definite rhythm, or calls it a "small world-system." This ego with its subtle body is no longer bound to the physical body. It forms a kind of universal ego into which the previously dominant ego has been transposed. After this spiritual body has been built up, an individual lives simultaneously on this side of life and in the Beyond. "This beyond is, however, neither temporally nor spatially divided from this side; rather it is Tao, the Meaning which uniformly permeates all existence and becoming."[46] The psychic kernel of the soul, which has become conscious, and its surrounding field of energy thus also seem in some way able to retain an individual identity after death within the psychophysical *unus mundus*.[47]

Speaking psychologically, this would mean that the Self, as a psychophysical monad or ultimate nucleus of the personality, does not merely engender the ego consciousness emanating from it at birth and during the growth of the individual's personality. At death it also draws the ego back into itself and contracts, just as the sap in a tree produces

45. In Chinese Taoism, on the other hand, little value was attached to the survival of individual consciousness, since the latter was in any case regarded as being irksome. Instead, the Taoists strove for the detachment of the ego from the body and its enlargement, in order for it to become identical with all the contents of the archetypal field and the cosmic aspect of the Self (*ibid.*, p. 33).

46. *Ibid.*, p. 59.

47. This view persisted especially among the Confucians.

budding leaves in the spring and then sinks back into the trunk in the autumn, while the leaves produced by it are cast off and wither away.

If one observes bubbles floating on a liquid it can often be noticed that a larger and a smaller one become reciprocally drawn to each other. The smaller, as if simultaneously attracted and repelled, circles around the larger one. Then it suddenly rushes toward the larger one and unites with it into one. In the same way the ego complex at the center of our consciousness seems to revolve in a half-attracted, half-timorous and fearful state around the Self's greater inner center. The moment of death forms the decisive shock, and the longed-for *coniunctio* experience of both worlds, as the ego plunges into the inner monad and unites with it. When an individual consciously participates in the individuation process, and thereby prepares himself for this moment by exerting himself to experience it as consciously as he can, he will succeed in experiencing the ego's transposition into the Self knowingly. But when he remains, as it were, hemmed in by floating psychic contents which are autonomous and unintegrated, consciousness becomes deflected and slips into a state of unconsciousness, which the ancient texts symbolized as being imprisoned by underworld demons. Then after death the deceased must set out on the long journey to the Self before he can attain peace and eternal life.

If we accept the idea that the psychic and physical realms are two identical facets of the primal unity, then not only the ego, *that constant personification of the Self* (as Jung also calls it), must possess a material background (the body), but also the Self must possess one. Mythological texts attempt to describe this body belonging to the Self as the philosophers' stone or the mandala. This principle holds good not only for the ego and the Self, but for all remaining unintegrated single complexes. In the analysis of a woman whose brother had "disintegrated" into incurable schizophrenia, I was actually able to observe how partial souls belonging to her brother had activated parapsychological semimaterial haunting incidents in the patient's neighborhood. When I related this story to Jung, he told me that he had often witnessed such phenomena and considered it possible that partial complexes were capable of "haunting" a living person.[48]

If further observations prove this hypothesis to be empirically correct, it will throw new light onto one of parapsychology's biggest problems, namely, the question as to why "spirits" and "haunting" phenomena so often appear in a foolish, half-intelligent, half-senseless guise. If they are only partial souls manifesting themselves, their behavior becomes understandable because we know that psychic complexes possess a certain inherent intelligence, but at the same time tend above all else to perpetrate senseless and annoying tricks within our psyche.

The much discussed question of whether the "manifestations" in séances represent unconscious complexes belonging to the participants or are "real spirits" becomes, from this point of view, irrelevant; they simply represent autonomous complexes that can belong either to the living or to the dead. But in this connection even the word "belong" is really imprecise, since "autonomous" means that such complexes are largely unattached and free-floating. This view has already been advanced by Pascual Jordan.[49]

Whenever, as a result of great effort, a strong personality succeeds in making such a free-floating complex conscious, he frees, as it were, not only himself but the universal psyche

48. See also Jung's dissertation, "On the Psychology and Pathology of So-Called Occult Phenomena," *Psychiatric Studies, CW*, Vol. I.

49. *Verdrängung und Komplementarität* (Hamburg, 1947), pp. 79–80. Following F. Moser he advances the view that in a séance "an unconsciousness can become operative which can then no longer be attributed to the individual members of the circle—the facts of the experience seem to favor the idea that here complexes (or . . . fragments of the personality) can appear which can no longer be associated with the individual unconscious of one particular member of the sitting. . . ." These complexes are only fragmentarily developed.

from this "spook." A Chinese story serves to illustrate this point clearly. It involves the ancient Chinese folk belief that the souls of people who commit suicide are condemned to wander about carrying a rope, trying to coerce others to commit suicide as well. The tale runs as follows: One day a soldier who is quartered in a strange town looks through a window and sees a distraught young woman sitting inside her house. Above her head an evil spirit dangles a rope to induce her to kill herself. The soldier wages a ferocious battle against the wicked ghost and finally defeats it, but as a sign of his nocturnal fight with the suicide devil he subsequently bears a ring of red flesh around his arm. It consists of the rope, which became a part of his flesh and can perform no more mischief. Here the evil concatenation exerted by the autonomous suicide complex is literally "integrated" by the soldier. It becomes a living part of him, which "distinguishes" but does not injure him.

Such an integration of a complex which appears to be initially autonomous can never be accomplished solely by means of the ego. It must be achieved *deo concedente*, so that the greater powers of the Self assist the ego and act in harmony with it.[50] This means that it is only when the ego plays a properly coordinated role in the rhythmic play of Tao, the Self, that it can bring about such an integration.

As we have seen from the material presented, the "numerical play" of collective unconscious contents is a symbol for the *unconscious creative urge toward higher consciousness*. It proceeds from the symbol of the Self as the end-image of the individuation process. In such an advanced state of consciousness resides the freedom (proceeding in and out in all forms) to traverse the whole field of the unconscious, unlike an identification with partial complexes that signifies imprisonment by underworld demons. The Fon magicians of West Africa convey the essence of this

---

50. In the Chinese story this is indicated by the figure of the soldier, a man who serves higher powers.

freedom beautifully when they say that it consists of "the highest possible degree of self-knowledge a man can attain."

Not only unintegrated partial complexes can "haunt" the living. According to the mythological documents of mankind, the "enlightened" dead can also manifest themselves as "breathlike presences" in the realm of the living. But, in contrast to the trivial, somewhat meaningless ghost phenomena we have already discussed, they appear to wish to create meaningful order. Because of this, young shamans among the circumpolar peoples sleep by the graves of great shamans, in order to receive their teachings. This phenomenon also accounts for the fact that incubation was practiced at the graves of heroes in antiquity, and later at those of martyrs and saints, so that one might receive their help. It is also the reason why even today one of the requisites for canonization in the Catholic church is the performance of post-mortem miracles by the deceased. But since the manifestations of *these* souls of the dead proceed along the same lines as the general tendency of the collective unconscious to achieve consciousness, they are and must remain identical with the purposes of the Self in its role as suprapersonal *atman* (or Tao)—they can manifest themselves in a numerical oracle as well as in Tao itself. The I Ching oracle and many other divinatory techniques already mentioned, therefore, represent mankind's efforts to make contact simultaneously with these spirits and spiritual tendencies of the unknown, because the language of number offers a form of communicating with them which, as we have shown, belongs to the rhythm patterns of the collective unconscious and the *unus mundus* itself.

From time immemorial number has been used most frequently to bridge the two realms because it represents the general structure of psychic and physical energy motions in nature and therefore appears, as it were, to provide the key to the mysterious language of unitary existence, particularly in its aspect of meaning (Tao).

CHAPTER FIFTEEN

Synchronicity and the *Coniunctio*

WHEN THE BUDDHA desired to marry, his future father-in-law, Gopa, required him to compete with other suitors in various contests demonstrating his mental capacities. One of these contests dealt with calculating sums, and he won it by calculating a number of more than fifty digits in the shortest time, thereby securing his bride.[1] This incident may have been a coincidence, but it encourages us to take special notice of the fact that Bhaskara, the most famous of all Hindu mathematicians, entitled his work *Lilavati*, a woman's name, belonging to his beloved only daughter. The story goes that she devoted so much of her time to the study of mathematics and other learned subjects (instead of enjoying herself with other young people) that her father became worried that she would never marry. Translated into modern psychological terms, she clearly developed a terrific father complex. Bhaskara consulted well-known astrologers and with their help discovered that there was only a single precise hour in which his daughter would be able to marry.

---

1. Transmitted in the text called *Lalitavistera*. See E. Kramer, *The Main Stream of Mathematics* (New York, 1951), pp. 5–6.

Accordingly he arranged for her wedding, to the son of a couple with whom they were acquainted, to take place at this exact time. In a festive mood the company gathered around the water clock to await the arrival of the hour— but in vain; The glass did not empty, and with despairing exclamations those present discovered, too late, what had gone wrong. As she bent over the glass a pearl of the bride's necklace had broken off and fallen in, stopping up the vessel.[2] Lilavati therefore remained with her father, and to console her, he dedicated his work, which ranks among the most famous early treatises on number theory, to her. Do these constitute the playful origins of all the human arts, or has number an ultimate connection with the problem of Eros? We have long known that numbers did not always possess the dry-as-dust, abstract quality that characterizes them today; formerly they were not only something "god-like" but possessed—curiously enough—an all-embracing significance. They did not divide but united two worlds.

As we pointed out before, the ancient Mayans developed a divinatory technique comparable to that of the I Ching. Instead of yarrow stalks they counted off two kinds of grain: Indian corn and so-called *tzité* beans, which come from a pod-bearing bush. The oracle was called *tzité* after them. The grains of corn stood for the feminine element (corresponding to the Chinese Yin line), the *tzité* beans for the masculine (Yang) also expressed by a vulgar sexual term.[3] The *coniunctio* significance of this oracle can be traced back to the Mayan creation myth on the makings of man, preserved in the Quiche Mayan Book of Counsel. The myth begins with the creation of the world:

2. *Ibid.*, pp. 4 ff.
3. For this and the following see W. Cordan, *Das Buch des Rates: Mythos und Geschichte der Maya* (Jena, 1962), p. 170. All translations in the text are my own. Concerning a possible connection between the Mayan culture and China, see F. Roeck, "Kalenderkreise und Kalenderschichten im alten Mexico und Mittelamerika," *Festschrift für Pater W. Schmidt*, ed. W. Koppers (Vienna, 1928), pp. 621 ff. The Mayans also possessed the Lo-shu magic square.

These are the tidings. There was the latent universe. No breath. No sound. The World, inanimate and silent. And the expanse of Heaven was empty. . . . The surface of the Earth had not yet appeared. Only the calm Sea lay there and the wide space of Heaven. *Nothing was yet connected.* Nothing sounded, nothing stirred, nothing vibrated, nothing broke the silence of Heaven. Motionless and mute was the Night, the darkness. But in the water, surrounded with light, lay these: Tzakól the Creator; Bitól the giver of form; Tepëu the Conqueror and the green-feathered serpent Cucumáz; also Alóm, and Catalóm, the progenitors. . . . In darkness and night Tepëu and Cucumáz came together and spoke with each other. . . . And they perceived that with the light, man must appear. In this fashion they agreed upon Creation.

By their magic Tepëu and Cucumáz then completed the work of creation, forming the worlds, the plants, and the animals. They commanded the animals to honor them, but the animals remained mute. Then the two gods formed men out of clay, but they were too weak and sank down. Then the gods Tzakól and Bitól took council with two diviners, Xpiyacoc, the "daylight ancestor," and Xmucané, the "twilight ancestress," and summoning moreover a great assembly of spirits, they called out: "Cast the lot with grains of corn and the *tzité:* do this that we may know whether we should carve a mouth and eyes out of wood." Thus they spoke to the diviners.

The foretelling took place and the lot was cast with corn and *tzité.* "Fate," "Creation," the Old Ones called out in their place. . . . Beginning the foretelling they said [to Tepëu the Conqueror and Cucumáz the green-plumed serpent]: "Lie one upon the other! Speak, that we may hear. Decree whether wood should be collected, that the Creator and the Giver of form may fashion it. Whether that which issues forth from it shall sustain and nourish us when light comes, when dawn arises.
  "Thou corn! Thou *tzité!* Thou lot! Thou Creation! Thou womb of fire! Thou towering member!" Thus did

they address the corn, *tzité*, the lot, and Creation. "Look modestly away, Heart of Heaven, so that Tepëu and Cucumáz take no offence."—Then the lots spoke and prophesied: "Your figures of wood will prosper. . . ."

Nevertheless, this creation of man did not succeed and another creation was required to produce man as we know him today.

The sexual union of the two divinities, Tepëu and Cucumáz, clearly takes place at the same time that the *tzité* oracle is performed, as though they represent two aspects of the same primeval event. Together with the two types of grain, the "lot" and "Creation" are also invoked, as if to indicate that they signify another parallel. In this contest the "lot" refers more to the feminine matrix of existence and Creation to the world-energy materializing in it—an archetypal parallel to the feminine Sapientia Dei as the cosmic mathematical plan and her partner, Yahweh, who dynamically embodies its structure. In the Mayan oracle, through the lot two aspects of the number archetype are realized, so to speak: its orderedness represents the feminine and the archetype's dynamism represents the masculine element.

We can substantiate the fact that we are dealing here with an archetypal idea by reviewing West Nigerian geomancy. The same primeval figure stands behind Fa, the god of truth, who created the oracle in order to communicate his messages to man. This background divinity is called Gba'adu, and he represents a fearsome, unapproachable mystery. Gba'adu is also called "the calabash of existence," and his fetish consists of two calabashes lying on top of each other in an allusion to the Nigerian story of the world's origins; in the beginning the first father and mother of the cosmos were said to lie like two calabashes pressed close together in eternal cohabitation. As Maupoil stresses, the cult of Gba'adu conveys "an esoteric feeling of cosmic symbiosis, i.e., a oneness with the totality of the universe, which was represented by the symbol of the union of heaven and earth." [4] The Nigerians nevertheless fear this god and his symbols, because he stands for a "deathly" mystery, the primeval motif of the death nuptials, so to speak.

In ancient Egypt the same motif, along with a whole process of psychic maturation today termed the "individuation process," was projected onto post-mortem burial mysteries. The deceased's voyage through the universe was also pictured as a divine marriage. In the Lamentations for Osiris, for instance, the hired mourner, who personifies Isis, calls out: "Hail to you, I greet you my Lord, approach that I may glorify you as my Lord, and that I may behold you, I the beloved whom you adore." And in the twelfth hour she cries: "Hail to you Osiris, first of the Western Ones, raise yourself up, Lord. How good indeed these women are to your *ka* . . . you the Living One, your companions [i.e., Isis and Nephthys] embrace you." [5]

The wedding motif is also mentioned in the alchemical treatise of Komarios, which says in describing the resurrection mystery: "Behold, in the heart of the mountains, beneath the Masculine, there lies his companion with whom he unites and in whom he rejoices, and nature rejoices in nature, uniting with nothing that lies outside itself." [6] This idea of the *coniunctio* unifying the totality of existence was carried on by Arabic alchemists and transmitted back to the West where it reappears in descriptions of the body's resurrection.[7] The medieval alchemist Petrus Bonus, for instance,

4. See Bernard Maupoil, *La Géomancie à l'ancienne Côte des Esclaves* (Paris, 1943), p. 89.

5. See T. Hopfner, *Plutarch: Über Isis and Osiris* (Darmstadt, 1967), I, 63–64, II, 147–48. See also G. Thausing, *Der Auferstehungsgedanke in ägyptischen religiösen Texten* (Leipzig, 1943), p. 62. In other representations the deceased, having become the god of the Nile and appearing between two mountain caves, fructifies the earth as a woman.

6. M. Berthelot, *Collection des anciens alchimistes grecs* (Paris, 1887–88), I, 294 ff., and Marie-Louise von Franz, *Aurora consurgens*, trans. R. F. C. Hull and A. S. Glover (New York, 1966), pp. 275 ff.

7. See von Franz, *Aurora consurgens*, pp. 366–67.

portrays the resurrection of the dead as a *coniunctio* of this kind:

> Because our soul was generated *on the horizon of eternity,* before it united with the body . . . in the resurrection *coniunctio* the body will become wholly spiritual, as will the soul itself; and they will become one, just as when water blends with water and will thenceforth never more separate in eternity.[8]

Figures and pictures indicating the similar motif of a posthumous journey which culminates in a nuptial union and deification are also to be found in Chinese tombs dating back to the Han period.[9] After death an individual first disintegrates into two partial souls, one of which is called *p'o,* and belongs to the dark feminine Yin principle sinking down to earth, while the other, a light one, *hun,* belongs to the Yang principle mounting up to heaven. Both souls then embark on a journey, one traveling to the feminine divinity of the West and the other to the "dark city" of the East, the "dark mountain of death," or the "yellow springs." They traverse the twelve signs of the zodiac which (like representations of the decanates in the Egyptian posthumous journey to heaven) were illustrated in the tombs.[10] The *p'o* soul unites with the immortal divinity of the West and the *hun* soul with the lord of the East. Then, in the form of these two divinities, they celebrate the mystical resurrection marriage (*hsüan-t'ung,* "the mysterious alliance"). Through this union a new being is created, "weightless and invisible, and time and space are no longer any hindrance to its movement which, like the sun, can soar and sail with the clouds."[11]

This liberated, reborn spiritual being, which has the pow-

8. *Ibid.*
9. See A. Bulling, "Die Kunst der Totenspiele in der östlichen Han-Zeit," *Oriens extremus,* no. 3, ed. Benl, Franke, and Fuchs (Hamburg, 1956), pp. 28 ff.
10. *Ibid.,* pp. 48, 50.
11. *Ibid.,* p. 51.

ers of the cosmos at its disposal, is thereafter honored in the ancestor cult, while the impure souls of the dead that have not undergone this metamorphosis are accorded only dread. As in Egypt, the goal to which these liberated spirits move is the Great Bear in the North and the region of the circumpolar stars that never set.

These Chinese, Egyptian, and alchemical texts all assert that the dead person's existence expands into a form which on the one hand is identical with inorganic matter (natron, gold, and so on) and on the other with the collective unconscious (world of the gods and the stars). This means it enlarges into the primordial substance of the cosmos, in an animated form. At the same time, those realms of psyche and matter experienced in the course of one's life time as separate realities unite in a *coniunctio*. This development conveys the impression that the two realms owe their polarized condition to the life processes prevailing before death. With the cessation of earthly life, however, they become liberated from time and space and can join together in order to receive eternal life in the timeless depths of the *unus mundus*.

In China the same primordial image of a divine marriage was not only projected onto life after death, as in the West, but was also celebrated in the ancient annual ritual of communal marriage. This union denoted the harmonious coming together of the cosmic rhythms, Yin and Yang. Men and women grouped themselves in two rows facing each other and competed in stimulating antiphonies analogous to the way in which "light and shade mutually complement each other." The conclusion of the festival constituted a communal marriage, a hierogamy for which the rainbow served as a symbol. The festivities were seen to be mirrored in this symbol because it consists of a synthesis of contrasting light and dark colors belonging to Yin and Yang arranged in a rhythmical harmony (motif of stripes!).[12]

12. Cf. Marcel Granet, *La Pensée chinoise* (Paris, 1968), pp. 119–24.

In the ancient Chinese planchette oracle the fluctuations of Yin and Yang were represented in the two number fields mentioned above, and an exchange of attributes took place during their hierogamy. In other words, the transformative phases belonging to Yin received the numerical value of twenty-one, as uneven and therefore "masculine" numbers were coordinated with them, while conversely the numerical value of fourteen, an even and therefore "feminine" number, was assigned to the masculine Yang principle. In this manner heaven and earth exchanged their attributes through the divine marriage.[13]

In this oracle, as in the Mayan *tzité* oracle, a *coniunctio* of two cosmic principles accordingly takes place, and, insofar as number plays the decisive role, it is the factor most closely connected with the *coniunctio* motif. In an old commentary to the I Ching it is also stated that "the thoughts of men and of spirits blend together" in the oracle, uniting the worlds of the living and of the dead.[14]

When we attempt to transpose this mythologem or mythological motif into modern psychological terms, it means *that in a synchronistic event a coniunctio of two cosmic principles, namely, of psyche and matter, takes place,* and in the process a real "exchange of attributes" occurs as well. In such situations the psyche behaves as if it were material and matter behaves as if it belonged to the psyche. Number makes its appearance in this context as the *vinculum amoris,* the bond of love which unites the two principles by jointly ordering them.

In its profoundest sense number thus possesses the significance of an all-uniting Eros, although it connotes something different from the usual sense of the words love and Eros. By "love" we understand, for the most part, a warm human relationship normally of great importance to us. But Jung emphasizes that such a relationship always contains projec-

13. *Ibid.,* pp. 165–66.
14. R. Wilhelm, trans., *I Ching or Book of Changes,* English trans. C. F. Baynes (London, 1960), II, 327.

tions which we must withdraw in order to achieve objectivity and arrive at ourselves.

> Emotional relationships are relationships of desire, tainted by coercion and constraint; something is expected of the other person, and that makes him and oneself unfree. Objective cognition lies hidden behind the attraction of the emotional relationship; *it seems to be the central secret. Only through objective cognition is the real coniunctio possible.*[15]

This passage implies that a preconscious spiritual order lies at the base of all love relationships. Because there seems to exist such a spiritual "objective" order at the base of Eros, it is expressed in the seemingly abstract, feelingless, impersonal order of numbers, as a clear, immutable factor free from illusions. From this point of view we can understand why the Nigerians define their *coniunctio* symbol, Gba'adu, as "the highest possible degree of self-knowledge a man can attain": this cosmic ordering of the Self constitutes the ultimate mystery behind all human desire and behavior, an unfathomable and fearsome mystery.

The dead, according to many peoples' beliefs, concern themselves with this inexorable objective order behind all existence. One widely disseminated archetypal mythologem pictures them literally "killing time" in the Beyond at number games.[16] In many an Egyptian burial chamber the deceased is portrayed playing a *halma*-type board game with his wife or some other partner.[17] This game not only provided the dead with entertainment but magically protected them on their journey through the Beyond. The single

15. *Memories, Dreams, Reflections* (London, 1963), pp. 276–77 (my italics).

16. See also the popular American story by Washington Irving, *Rip van Winkle*. Rip van Winkle was carried off one night by skittle-playing ancestral spirits and discovered on his return that he had been many years absent. I am indebted to Dr. H. Greer for this reference.

17. See H. Bonnet, *Reallexikon der ägyptischen Religionsgeschichte* (Berlin, 1952), under "Brettspiel" and the further literature given there.

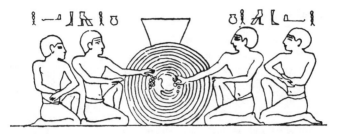

Egyptian snake game [Source: M. Pieper, "Das Brettspiel
der alten Ägypter," *Wissenschaftliche Beilage zum Jahresbericht des Königsstädtischen Realgymnasiums zu Berlin*
(1909).]

Serpent game board of limestone, from an early tomb near
Ballâs [Reproduced by permission of the Ashmolean Museum, Oxford.]

squares on the board represented the "houses" of individual
divinities and sacred symbols such as the Djed column[18] (the
"archetypal field" of the collective unconscious). Winning
the game also signified victory over the evil Mehen, serpent
of the underworld. For this reason the rules of play were
laid out in the deceased's tomb to assure a fortunate outcome
in this fateful game.[19] Besides this square game board they
possessed the so-called "snake game" as well, consisting of a
round board upon which the Mehen serpent wound his body
in a counterclockwise spiral that terminated at the center.
The game pieces were fashioned into spheres, and consisted
of dog and lion figures. Horus and Seth were said to have
competed in this snake game once against each other. The
details of the game have not yet been deciphered.[20] Ancient
Sumerian kings likewise appear to have known a board game
of this type, since similar boards have been discovered in

Egyptian chess game [Source: Pieper, "Das Brettspiel der
alten Ägypter."]

18. "Hall of the Thirty," "Blood of Isis," "House of Buto," etc.
19. See M. Pieper, "Das Brettspiel der alten Ägypter," *Wissenschaftliche Beilage zum Jahresbericht des Königsstädtischen Realgymnasiums zu Berlin* (1909).
20. See H. Ranke, "Das altägyptische Schlangenspiel," *Sitzungsberichte der Heidelberger Akademie der Wissenschaften, Philosophisch-
historische Klasse,* no. 4 (1920).

the tombs of Ur (2500 B.C.).[21] Similar ideas also seem to
have existed in China, for in tombs as early as the Han
period pictures or figures of the dead have been uncovered
which portray their occupation with various forms of board
games.

Chess, too, which comes from India, was known to the
early Chinese. Originally chess seems to have represented an
earthly mirror-image of "the stars' battles in Heaven," [22]
an outline of those battles from which man's destiny proceeded. Because of this chess also provided a divinatory
technique for the living. The victor's moves in this game
were noted, because they were taken to indicate harmony
with Tao.[23] This game was sometimes even used to map out
military operations, and also by means of it the soul of a
dead person could be called back and consulted.[24] For this
purpose the figures were *thrown* haphazardly onto the chess-
board to obtain divinatory information. This form of the
game was called "spirit chess." [25] Portrayals of a similar
game called *liu po* ("the six sages") are to be found as early
as the Han period. In them *liu po* is being played by winged
spirits of the dead.[26]

The board on which the *liu po* game was played is described in a poem from the third century B.C. entitled "The
Recalling of the Soul of Sun Yü." [27] It was played with
chessmen (*ch'hi*). In one picture an immortal holds up a
dice box while another holds some chessmen and two fur-

21. See R. C. Bell, *Board and Table Games* (London, Oxford, and
New York, 1969), Vol. II.
22. See Joseph Needham, *Science and Civilization in China* (Cambridge, 1959), III, 540 ff., 303 ff.; see also IV, pt. 1, 230, 265, 327 ff.
23. *Ibid.*, IV, pt. 1, 325, 315.
24. *Ibid.*, IV, pt. 1, 317, III, 305, 139-41. There was also a mathematical work (now lost) by the Japanese mathematician Fujiwara
Michinori (ca. A.D. 1157) called *Keishizan* which dealt with the mathematical permutation possibilities for combining I Ching hexagrams
(*ibid.*, p. 141), and many other works in this field, still unexplored.
25. *Ibid.*, IV, pt. 1, 326-27.
26. *Ibid.*, pp. 327-28.
27. *Ibid.*, III, 265.

Chinese spirits of the dead playing a board game [Source: Joseph Needham, *Science and Civilization in China* (Cambridge, 1959), Vol. IV, pt. 1, plate CXXIII, reproduced by permission of Cambridge University Press.]

ther figures look on. The TLV divinatory board (see below) resembles the board already described. Sundials of the Han period exhibit the same pattern, as do many later Buddhistic mandalas.

The precise connections of these patterned boards are disputed, but for our purposes the essential fact is that

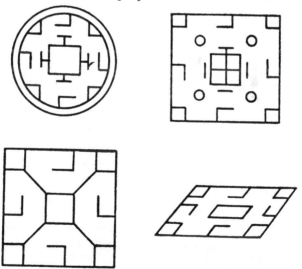

"TLV" patterns on mirrors and divination boards [Source: Needham, *Science and Civilization in China*, III, 304, reproduced by permission of Cambridge University Press.]

magician priests, gods, and especially the dead in their tombs all played games on this kind of board. As with most other cultures, it was not possible in Chinese culture to differentiate ritual, gambling, and divination at this level.[28]

Another game in China used for divining was called *tan-ch'hi* chess, which was played with twelve (later twenty-four) red and black pieces. The lower board was rectangular like the earth and the upper one round like heaven. By throwing pieces or shaking the board to alter their positions one could read a person's fate.[29] Allegedly the dead also enjoyed playing this game.[30]

According to these myths the dead occupied themselves with the primal ordering of existence, in which all things lie in their natural order beyond the realm of the wishes and desires haunting our ego and its temporal earthly existence. Only through the release from personal desire did the Chinese hope to obtain the ultimate knowledge of existence. Granet therefore says:

> The self-mastery and the knowledge of the inherent self and, resulting from it, of the world (for the cosmos forms a homogeneous whole), is achieved through the sacrifice of all appetites and desires. As a result a feeling of heightened power sets in, so that the "sage" feels himself to have gained a mastery which extends over the entire cosmos. This superiority and freedom is founded on rites wholeheartedly performed and on games which are wholeheartedly played by the player. . . . It is expected that a deeply serious and straightforward game will mediate clarity or

28. The ancient Etruscans, for instance, used the dice game for gambling and divination. See Z. Mayani, *The Etruscans Begin to Speak* (New York, 1962). pp. 68–69. A general survey of board games and their predominant mandala structures is provided by Bell's outstanding work, *Board and Table Games*. It also offers a hypothetical explanation of the Egyptian serpent game.

29. Sometimes individuals on earth played *liu po* against the gods and were even said on occasion to have won.

30. Needham, *Science and Civilization*, IV, pt. 1, 349. Cf. also W. B. Crow, *The Symbolism of Chess and Cards* (London, 1944), and the literature there cited.

> wisdom and bring about a liberation that frees man from
> all things. . . . The rites call for uprightness, the games
> require fixed rules or at least the prototypes of rules.[31]

The Chinese emphasize the fact that all concepts, even those
of number and of fate, contain a degree of concrete meaning and of uncertainty, thus preserving *room for play*.[32] A
rule for the Chinese is simply a prototype, for their concept
of order excludes the idea of a law. In this way the objective
order of existence can be revealed. The philosopher Hsü
Heng (A.D. 1209–81) cites an unknown speaker who says
in this connection:

> If we fully apprehend the patterns [*li*] of the things of the
> world, will it not be found that everything must have a
> reason why it is as it is? And also a rule (of co-existence
> with all other things) to which it cannot but conform. Is
> not this just what is meant by Pattern [*li*]?[33]

This order consists, as Joseph Needham points out, in the
fact that the forms of nature are all meaningfully and spontaneously ordered, like a fabric of myriad reciprocal strands
(*kuan thung*), in the great number matrix of the universe.
An esoteric branch of Chinese mathematics concerned itself
with this problem by conducting research into the permutations of I Ching hexagrams. Behind this work lies the operation of a cosmic Eros which corresponds to an individual's
urge to individuation and which, paradoxically, leads men in
the end to a state of universal relatedness with existence.

31. *Pensée chinoise*, pp. 316 ff.
32. *Ibid.*, p. 321.
33. Needham, *Science and Civilization*, III, 163.

SUMMARY AND OUTLOOK

T<small>HESE DISCUSSIONS</small> concerning the "spirit world" and the motif of the "cosmic marriage" may seem to have led us far afield from our initial reflections, and for the moment we must concede that these mythological motifs allude to far-reaching unknown relationships. Nevertheless several points strike me as salient. The concept of natural numbers rests on an archetypal foundation. It represents a preconscious pattern of thought common to all human psyches, and therefore constitutes the basis for transmitting knowledge to a greater degree than mythological images, which exhibit more ethnological variations.

Those aspects of the number archetype which present-day Western mathematics has made conscious in no way exhaust *all* its aspects. In particular, the relation of number to time remains largely unexplained. The ancient Chinese concept of number sheds light on some aspects of this relationship which would repay further study.

The preconscious aspect of natural numbers points to the idea of a numerical *field* in which individual numbers figure as energic phenomena or rhythmical configurations. This "field," which we take to represent the structural outlines of the collective unconscious, is organized around the central archetype of the Self. For this reason historical mandala structures deserve particular attention. In corresponding "cosmic models" and mathematical representations of God, the first four natural numbers predominate to an exceptional degree, just as they did in the systematic divinatory techniques of the past.

The assumptions underlying these techniques are based on the idea that time does not form an "empty" frame for the events taking place within it, but rather represents a sequence of qualitative, inescapable conditions for the events possible at any given moment. This orderly sequence is isomorphic with the natural number series. Whether the latter objectively corresponds to characteristics of the physical world remains an open question. Most certainly its pattern is applicable to the phenomena of the collective unconscious, the ultimate foundation of all human cognition. Since, generally speaking, contents of the collective unconscious which have not yet reached the threshold of consciousness tend to engender parapsychological syndromes, especially when they are constellated contents (in an "excited state," as physicists would say), these contents appear in conjunction with the preconscious aspects of the number archetype. On these foundations rests the concept of divination by means of numerical combinations.

These synchronistic and parapsychological aspects of number (when used for divination) can only be fathomed when we take into account the unconscious emotional setup and preconscious fantasies of the observer along with his conscious mental situation and outlook. The description of such phenomena will of course no longer produce universally valid theories, but rather transmittable realizations that can exert a mind-releasing, community-building effect, just as scientific advances did in the past. The common denominator in mankind's cognition processes thereby shifts from the level of doctrinaire intellectualism onto another plane. It centers instead on the realization of an a priori psychic structure common to all men. Depending on the epoch and an individual's creative abilities, the basic substratum becomes clothed in the most varied shapes and conscious formulations, progressively transforming "ancient, eternal truths" into more highly differentiated conscious patterns of realization.

As the ultimate verification of these processes stands the objective psyche and its synchronistic manifestations, which contain the mystery of the sporadic conjunction of psychic and physical events, revealing a common "meaning." This phenomenon seems to hint at the existence of the *unus mundus*, the transcendental unity of existence. In the past men tried to determine the meaning common to these two classes of events by using the rhythms of natural numbers. They worked on the assumption that these numbers illustrated some of the most primitive and basic forms of the spirit. When we take into account the individual characteristics of natural numbers, we can actually demonstrate that they produce the same ordering effects in the physical and psychic realms; they therefore appear to constitute the most basic constants of nature expressing unitary psychophysical reality. Because of this I would conjecture that the task of future mathematicians will be to collect their characteristics and analyze, when possible, every number in its logical relationship to all others.[1] This research should be undertaken in collaboration with physicists, musicians, and psychologists who are conversant with the empirical facts about the structural characteristics of numbers in different mediums.

Since the concept of the *unus mundus* transcends consciousness, it is represented in mankind's historical *Weltanschauungen* by *symbols*, which most frequently consist of a double mandala portraying both the timeless and time-bound order of existence. While the timeless order seems to relate to the general concept of acausal orderedness in the physical and psychic realms, the time-bound order refers more to

1. I have only gone so far as to enumerate certain characteristics of the first four numbers in juxtaposition. But it is very likely that they can be brought together in a single logical mathematical relationship. I lack the prerequisites for this task, because it may well lead to extremely complicated mathematical considerations, and possibly even to new discoveries.

peripheral phenomena, such as synchronistic happenings, that are creative acts in time. The timeless acausal orderedness lies at the base of all transmittable information and cognition processes operating in man, and the time-bound synchronistic phenomena underlie those individually experienced messages of the unconscious which can only be adequately interpreted by the individual. The two systems are incommensurable, and because of this they form a fitting symbol for the ultimate unity of existence as a *coincidentia oppositorum*. In their mirrored images, as one reality reflects off the other, lies the mystery of their experienceability by the individual.

BIBLIOGRAPHY

A. Books

Aitken, A. C. *Determinants and Matrices.* Edinburgh and London, 1944.

Allendy, R. *Le Symbolisme des nombres.* Paris, 1948.

Anrich, E. *Moderne Physik und Tiefenpsychologie.* Stuttgart, 1963.

Bäumker, C. *Das Problem der Materie in der griechischen Philosophie.* Reprint ed. Frankfurt a.M., 1963.

Bavink, B. *Weltschöpfung in Mythos und Religion, Philosophie und Naturwissenschaft.* Basel, 1951.

Baynes, C. A., ed. *A Gnostic Coptic Treatise.* Cambridge, 1933.

Beadle, G. and M. *The Language of Life.* New York, 1966.

Beauregard, Olivier Costa de. *Le Second Principe de la science du temps.* Paris, 1963.

Beit, H. von. *Symbolik des Märchens.* 2d ed. Bern, 1960.

Bell, R. C. *Board and Table Games.* 2 vols. London, Oxford, and New York, 1969.

Berthelot, M. *Collection des anciens alchimistes grecs.* 2 vols. Paris, 1887–88.

Bindel, Ernst. *Die geistigen Grundlagen der Zahlen.* Stuttgart, 1958.

———. *Die Zahlengrundlagen der Musik.* Stuttgart, 1950.

———. *Die ägyptischen Pyramiden.* Stuttgart, 1966.

Bi-Yän-Lu: Niederschrift von der smaragdenen Felswand. Edited by W. Gundert. Munich, 1960.

Böhm, W. *Die metaphysischen Grundlagen der Naturwissenschaft und Mathematik.* Vienna, Fribourg, and Basel, 1966.

Bohr, Niels. *Atomphysik und menschliche Erkenntnis,* Brunswick, 1958. English translation, *Atomic Physics and Human Knowledge.* New York, 1958.

Bonnet, H. *Reallexikon der ägyptischen Religionsgeschichte.* Berlin, 1952.

Borg, S. F. *Matrix-Tensor Methods in Continuum-Mechanics.* Princeton, N.J., 1963.

Botsch, W. *Morsealphabet des Lebens.* Stuttgart, 1965.

Brandon, S. G. F. *History, Time and Deity.* New York, 1965.

Bresch, C., and Hausmann, R. *Klassische und molekulare Genetik.* 2d ed. Berlin, 1970.

Brillouin, L. *Scientific Uncertainty and Information.* New York and London, 1964.

Carnap, R. *Physikalische Begriffsbildung.* Darmstadt, 1966.

Conrad-Martius, H. *Die Zeit.* Munich, 1954.

Cordan, W. *Das Buch des Rates: Mythos und Geschichte der Maya.* Jena, 1962. An incomplete English edition is *Popol Vnh: The Sacred Book of the Ancient Quiché Maya.* Edited by D. Goek and A. Recinos. London, 1951.

Corpus hermeticum. Edited by A. D. Nock and A. J. Festugière. 4 vols. 2d ed. Paris, 1960.

Crow, W. B. *The Symbolism of Chess and Cards.* London, 1944.

Danckert, Werner. *Tonreich und Symbolzahl.* Bonn, 1966.

Dantzig, Tobias. *Number: The Language of Science.* New York, 1954.

Daqué, E. *Der Schöpfungsmythus neu erzählt.* Leipzig, 1940.

Davis, Philip J. *The Lore of Large Numbers.* New York, 1961.

Dedekind, R. *Was sind und was sollen die Zahlen.* Brunswick, 1888.

Deichgräber, K. *Rhythmische Elemente im Logos des He-*

raklit. Akademie der Wissenschaften und Literatur in Mainz, No. 9. Wiesbaden, 1962.

Dorn, Gerhard. *Philosophia meditativa. Theatrum chemicum,* Vol. I. Edited by L. Zetzner. Strasbourg, 1659.

Dunne, J. W. *An Experiment with Time.* London, 1927; reprint ed., 1964.

Eckhartshausen, Ludwig von. *Zahlenlehre der Natur.* Leipzig, 1794.

Eddington, Sir Arthur. *The Philosophy of Physical Science.* Cambridge, 1939.

Fettweis, E. *Das Rechnen der Naturvölker.* Leipzig and Berlin, 1927.

Franz, Marie-Louise von. *Aurora consurgens.* Companion work to Jung, C. G., *Mysterium Coniunctionis,* Vol. III. Translated by R. F. C. Hull and A. S. B. Glover. New York and London, 1966.

Fraser, J. T., ed. *The Voices of Time: A Cooperative Survey of Man's Views of Time as Expressed by the Sciences and by the Humanities.* New York, 1966.

Fritsch, V. *Links und Rechts in Wissenschaft und Leben.* Stuttgart, 1964.

Gentzen, G. *Die gegenwärtige Lage in der mathematischen Grundlagenforschung.* Darmstadt, 1969.

Ghyka, M. *Philosophie et mystique du nombre.* Paris, 1971.

Gilson, E., ed. *René Descartes' "Discours de la méthode."* Paris, 1947.

Gmelin, P. "Über vollkommene und befreundete Zahlen." Dissertation, University of Halle a. S., 1917.

Gonseth, F. *La Géometrie et le problème de l'espace.* Neuchâtel, 1955.

———. *Les Fondements des mathématiques.* Paris, 1926.

Granet, Marcel. *La Pensée chinoise.* Paris, 1968.

Güntert, H. *Der arische Weltkönig und Heiland.* Halle a. S., 1923.

Hadamard, Jacques. *The Psychology of Invention in the Mathematical Field.* Princeton, N.J., 1945.

Hamilton, W. R. *Lectures on Quaternions.* Dublin, 1853.

Hartmann, F. *Geomancy.* London, 1913.

Heisenberg, Werner. *Physik und Philosophie.* Stuttgart, 1959. English translation, *Physics and Philosophy.* New York, 1958.

Hentze, Carl. *Tod, Auferstehung, Weltordnung.* 2 vols. Zurich, 1953.

Hopfner, T. *Plutarch: Über Isis und Osiris.* 2 vols. Darmstadt, 1967.

Hopper, V. F. *Medieval Number Symbolism.* New York, 1939.

Hurwitz, S. *Die Gestalt des sterbenden Messias.* Studien aus den C. G. Jung Institut, Vol. VIII. Zurich and Stuttgart, 1958.

Husserl, Edmund. *Über den Begriff der Zahl.* Halle a. S., 1887.

———. *Philosophie der Arithmetik.* Vol. I. Halle a. S., 1891.

I Ching. See Wilhelm, R.

Jaffé, A. *Aus Leben und Werkstatt von C. G. Jung.* Zurich, 1968.

———. *Der Mythus vom Sinn im Werk C. G. Jungs.* Zurich, 1967.

Jenny, Hans. *Kymatik.* Basel, 1967.

Jordan, Pascual. *Verdrängung und Komplementarität.* Hamburg, 1947.

Jung, C. G. *Collected Works.* Published for the Bollingen Foundation by Princeton University Press, Princeton, N.J., and by Routledge and Kegan Paul, London, 1953– . Seventeen volumes published to date. Cited throughout as *CW*.

———. *Aion. CW,* Vol. IX, pt. 2. 2d ed. 1968.

———. *Alchemical Studies. CW,* Vol. XIII. 1968.

———. *The Archetypes and the Collective Unconscious. CW,* Vol. IX, pt. 1. 2d ed. 1968.

———. "Flying Saucers: A Modern Myth." In *Civilization in Transition. CW,* Vol. X. 2d ed. 1970.

————. "Foreword to the I Ching." In *Psychology and Religion: West and East. CW*, Vol. XI. 2d ed. 1969.

————. *Memories, Dreams, Reflections*. Recorded and edited by A. Jaffé. Translated by R. and C. Winston. London, 1963. German edition, *Erinnerungen, Träume, Gedanken*. Zurich, 1962.

————. *Mysterium Coniunctionis. CW*, Vol. XIV. 2d ed. 1970.

————. "On the Nature of the Psyche." In *The Structure and Dynamics of the Psyche. CW*, Vol. VIII. 2d ed. 1969.

————. "On the Psychology and Pathology of So-Called Occult Phenomena." In *Psychiatric Studies. CW*, Vol. I. 2d ed. 1970.

————. "The Phenomenology of the Spirit in Fairytales." In *The Archetypes and the Collective Unconscious. CW*, Vol. IX, pt. 1. 2d ed. 1968.

————. "A Psychological Approach to the Trinity." In *Psychology and Religion: West and East. CW*, Vol. XI. 2d ed. 1969.

————. *Psychological Types. CW*, Vol. VI. 1971.

————. *Psychology and Alchemy. CW*, Vol. XII. 2d ed. 1968.

————. "Psychology and Religion." In *Psychology and Religion: West and East. CW*, Vol. XI. 2d ed. 1969.

————. *Seminar über Kinderträume*. Eidgenössische Technische Hochschule Lectures. Zurich, 1938–39.

————. *Symbols of Transformation. CW*, Vol. V. 2d ed. 1967.

————. "Synchronicity: An Acausal Connecting Principle." In *The Structure and Dynamics of the Psyche. CW*, Vol. VIII. 2d ed. 1969.

Kirfel, W. *Die dreiköpfige Gottheit*. Bonn, 1940.

Knorr von Rosenroth. *Kabbala denudata*. Edited by J. D. Zunner. Sulzbach, 1677.

Körner, St. *The Philosophy of Mathematics*. London, 1960.

Kramer, E. *The Main Stream of Mathematics*. New York, 1951.

Kretschmar, F. *Kerberos und Hundestammvater*. Stuttgart, 1938.

Kucharski, P. *Etude sur la doctrine pythagoricienne de la tétrade*. Paris, 1952.

Kükelhaus, H. *Urzahl und Gebärde*. Berlin, 1934.

Lautmann, Albert. *Symétrie et dissymétrie en mathématiques et physique*. Paris, 1946.

Leibniz, G. W. *Grundwahrheiten der Philosophie (Monadologie)*. Edited by J. C. Horn. Frankfurt a.M., 1962. English translation, *The Monadology and Other Philosophical Writings*. Translated by Robert Latta. New York, 1965.

———. *Dialogus de connexione inter res et verba*. Edited by W. W. Erdmann. Berlin, 1840. English translation, *Dialogue on the Connection between Things and Words*. In *Leibniz: Selections*. Edited by Philip P. Wiener. New York, 1951.

Leisegang, H. *Die Gnosis: Kröner Taschenausgabe*. Leipzig, 1924.

Linssen, R. *Spiritualité de la matière*. Paris, 1966.

Mahnke, D. *Unendliche Sphäre und Allmittelpunkt*. Halle a. S., 1937; reprint ed., Stuttgart, 1966.

Maritain, J. *Le Songe de Descartes*. Paris, 1932. English translation, *The Dream of Descartes*. New York, 1944.

Mathesius. *Weg zu Gott: Erlebnisse eines Mathematikers*. Zurich and Stuttgart, 1959.

Maupoil, Bernard. *La Géomancie à l'ancienne Côte des Esclaves*. Institut d'Ethnologie. Paris, 1943.

Mayani, Z. *The Etruscans Begin to Speak*. New York, 1962.

Meister, F. *Magische Quadrate*. Zurich, 1952.

Menninger, Karl. *Zahlwort und Ziffer: Eine Kulturgeschichte der Zahl*. Göttingen, 1958.

Merkel, R. F. *Leibniz und China*. Berlin, 1952.

Mikami, Y. *The Development of Mathematics in China and Japan*. Leipzig, 1913.

Milhaud, G. *Descartes savant*, Paris, 1921.

Mo Dsi. *The Four Books: The Doctrine of the Mean*. Translated by J. Legge. New York, 1966.

Needham, Joseph. *Science and Civilization in China*. Vols. II, III, and IV. Cambridge, 1959.

———. *Time and Eastern Man*. London, 1965.

Nielson, D. *Der dreieinige Gott*. Copenhagen and London, 1922.

Olsvanger, J. *Fu Shi: The Sage of Ancient China*. Jerusalem, 1948.

Ore, Oystein. *Number Theory and Its History*. New York, Toronto, and London, 1948.

Paneth, L. *Zahlensymbolik im Unbewusstsein*. Zurich, 1952.

Pierce, J. R. *Symbols, Signals and Noise: The Nature and Process of Communication*. New York, 1961.

Platzeck, E.-W. *Raimund Lull*. 2 vols. Düsseldorf, 1962.

Plenk, H. *Das Metaphysische in Mathematik, Physik und Biologie*. Vienna and Munich, 1959.

Poincaré, Henri. *Science et méthode*. Paris, 1927. English translation, *Science and Method*. New York, 1952.

Preger, W. *Geschichte der deutschen Mystik im Mittelalter*. 2 vols. Aalen, 1962.

Preyer, W. *Über den Ursprung des Zahlbegriffs aus dem Tonsinn und über das Wesen der Primzahlen*. Hamburg and Leipzig, 1891.

Raven, J. E. *Pythagoraeans and Eleatics*. Amsterdam, 1966.

Rickert, Heinrich. *Das Eine, die Einheit und die Eins*. 2d ed. Tübingen, 1924.

Riemschneider, M. *Von 0–1001: Das Geheimnis der numinosen Zahl*. Munich, 1966.

Roeder, G. *Urkunden zur Religion des alten Ägypten*. Jena, 1923.

Roscher, W. H. *Enneadische Studien*. Leipzig, 1907.

Rossi, P. *Clavis universalis: Arti mnemoniche e logica combinatoria da Lullo a Leibniz*. Milan and Naples, 1960.

Rothstein, J. *Communication, Organization and Science*. New York, 1958.

312   BIBLIOGRAPHY

Ruegg, H. *Imagination*. New York, Evanston, and London, 1963.

Rump, A. "Die Verwundung des Hellen als Aspekt des Bösen im I Ging." Dissertation, University of Zurich, 1967.

Russell, Bertrand. *Introduction to Mathematical Philosophy*. London, 1956. German edition, *Einführung in die mathematische Philosophie*. Darmstadt and Geneva, n.d.

Ruyer, M. *La Cybernétique et l'origine de l'information*. Paris, 1954.

Rzyttka, B. *Ars magna: Die grosse Kunst des Raimund Lull*. Vienna, n.d.

Scholem, G. *Von der mystischen Gestalt der Gottheit*. Zurich, 1962.

————. *Ursprünge und Anfänge der Kabbala*. Berlin, 1962.

Scholz, W. von. *Der Zufall und das Schicksal*. Berlin, 1924.

Schramm, G. *Belebte Materie*. Pfullingen, 1965.

Scotus Erigena, Joannes. *De divisione naturae*. Migne, Patrologia Latina. Vol. CXXII.

Sergescu, P. *Histoire du nombre*. Paris, 1949.

Smirnow, V. I. *Lehrgang der höheren Mathematik*. Vol. II. Berlin, 1964.

Sommerfeld, A. *Atombau und Spektrallinien*. Brunswick, 1919.

Speiser, A. *Die Theorie der Gruppen von endlicher Ordnung*. Basel, 1956.

Stenzel, J. *Zahl und Gestalt bei Plato und Aristoteles*. Homburg a. H., 1959.

Steuer, O. *Über das wohlriechende Natron im Alten Ägypten*. Leiden, 1937.

Strombach, W. *Natur und Ordnung*. Munich, 1968.

Thausing, G. *Der Auferstehungsgedanke in ägyptischen religiösen Texten*. Leipzig, 1943.

Theatrum Chemicum. Edited by L. Zetzner. 5 vols. Frankfurt, 1622.

Thompson, d'Arcy Wentworth. *On Growth and Form*. 2 vols. 2d ed. Cambridge, 1963.

Thorndike, L. *History of Magic and Experimental Science.* 6 vols. New York, 1923.

Vadis, Aegidius de. *Dialogus inter Naturam et filium philosophiae. Theatrum Chemicum.* Edited by L. Zetzner. Vol. II. Strasbourg, 1602.

Van der Leyen, Fr., ed. *Die Märchen der Weltliteratur,* Vol. VIII: *Russiche Märchen.* Jena, 1959.

Waerden, B. L. van der. *Einfall und Überlegung: Drei kleine Beiträge zur Psychologie des mathematischen Denkens.* Basel and Stuttgart, 1954.

Waller, M. D. *Chladni Figures: A Study in Symmetry.* London, 1961.

Weisskopf, Victor. *Knowledge and Wonder.* 2d ed. New York, 1966.

Weizsäcker, Carl Friedrich von. *Die Einheit der Natur.* Munich, 1971.

Weitzenböck, R. *Der vierdimensionale Raum.* Basel and Stuttgart, 1956.

Wenzl, Aloys. *Die philosophischen Grenzfragen der modernen Naturwissenschaft.* Urban Books 3. Stuttgart, 1960.

Weyl, H. *Philosophie der Mathematik und Naturwissenschaften.* Darmstadt, 1966. English translation by Olaf Helmer, *Philosophy of Mathematics and Natural Science.* Princeton, N.J., 1949.

———. *Raum, Zeit, Materie.* Darmstadt, 1961. English translation, *Space, Time, Matter.* New York, 1950.

Whitehead, A. N. *Introduction to Mathematics.* London, n.d. German edition, *Eine Einführung in die Mathematik.* Bern, 1958.

Whitrow, G. J. *The Natural Philosophy of Time.* London and Edinburgh, 1961.

Whyte, L. L. *Accent on Form: World Perspectives.* New York, 1954.

Wigge, H. *Der Zahlbegriff in der neueren Philosophie.* Langensalza, 1921.

Wilhelm, H. *Change: Eight Lectures on the I Ching.* London, 1960.

Wilhelm, R. (German translator). *I Ching or Book of Changes.* English translation by C. F. Baynes. 2 vols. London, 1960.

———. *Weisheit des Ostens.* Düsseldorf, Cologne, and The Hague, 1951.

Wit, Constant de. *Le Rôle et le sens du lion dans l'Egypte ancienne.* Leiden, 1951.

Yates, Frances. *Giordano Bruno and the Hermetic Tradition.* London, 1964.

Zitscher, F. *Philosophische Untersuchungen über die Zahl.* Bern and Leipzig, 1910.

B. ARTICLES

Beisswanger, P. "Die Phasen in Hermann Weyls Beurteilung der Mathematik." *Mathematisch-physikalische Semesterberichte* (Göttingen), Vol. XII, no. 2 (1965).

Bulling, A. "Die Kunst der Totenspiele in der östlichen Han-Zeit." *Oriens extremus,* no. 3. Edited by Benl, Franke, and Fuchs. Hamburg, 1956.

Chin-te-Cheng. "On the Mathematical Significance of the Chinese Ho-t'u and Lo-Shu." *American Mathematical Monthly,* Vol. XXXII, (1925).

Cohen, P. I. "The Independence of the Continuum Hypothesis." *Proceedings of the National Academy of Sciences* (New York), Vol. L and LI (1963–64).

Dehn, M. "Das Mathematische im Menschen." *Scientia* (Bologna), Vol. LII (1932).

Eliade, Mircea. "The Origin of Religion." *Hibbert Journal,* Vol. LVII (1959).

Engelhardt, Wolf von. "Sinn und Begriff der Symmetrie." *Studium generale* (Göttingen), Vol. VI, no. 9 (1953).

Fierz, M. "Zur physikalischen Erkenntnis." *Eranos Jahrbuch* (Zurich), Vol. XVI (1948).

Franz, Marie-Louise von. "Bei der schwarzen Frau." In *Studien zur analytischen Psychologie C. G. Jungs.* Edited by the C. G. Jung Institute. Vol. II. Zurich, 1955.

———. "Time and Synchronicity in Analytic Psychology."

In *The Voices of Time,* edited by J. T. Fraser. New York, 1966.

———. "The Idea of the Macro- and Microcosmos in the Light of Jungian Psychology." *Ambix. Journal of the Society for the Study of Alchemy and Early Chemistry,* Vol. XIII, no. 1 (February, 1965).

———. "The Dream of Descartes." In *Timeless Documents of the Soul,* by Helmuth Jacobsohn, Marie-Louise von Franz, and Siegmund Hurwitz. Evanston, Ill., 1968.

Friedrichs, K. "Über Koinzidenz oder Synchronizität." *Grenzgebiete der Wissenschaft,* Vol. XVI (1967).

Gilson, W. "Pourquoi St. Thomas a critiqué St. Augustin." *Archives d'histoire doctrinale et littéraire du Moyen Age,* Vol. I (1926–27).

Haase, R. "Eine unbekannte pythagoräische Tafel." *Antaios* (Stuttgart), Vol. XII, no. 4 (1970).

Hartner, W. "Zahlen und Zahlensysteme bei Primitiv- und Hochkulturvölkern." *Paideuma* (Leipzig), Vol. II, nos. 6–7 (1940–44).

Heisenberg, Werner. "Über den Formenreichtum in der mathematischen Naturwissenschaft." In *Transparente Welt: Festschrift für Jean Gebser.* Bern and Stuttgart, 1965.

———. "Wolfgang Paulis philosophische Auffassungen." *Zeitschrift für Parapsychologie und Grenzgebiete der Psychologie* (Bern and Munich), Vol. III, nos. 2–3 (1960).

Hilbert, D. "Über das Unendliche." *Mathematische Annalen,* Vol. XCV, no. 1 (1925).

Hofstätter, Peter. "Psychologie und Mathematik." *Studium generale* (Göttingen), Vol. VI, no. 11 (1953).

Höltker, P. G. "Zeit und Zahl in Nordwestafrika." In *Festschrift für Pater W. Schmidt.* Edited by W. Koppers. Vienna, 1928.

Holton, J. "Über die Hypothesen, welche der Naturwissenschaft zugrundeliegen." *Eranos Jahrbuch* (Zurich), Vol. XXXI (1962).

Holton, J. "The Roots of Complementarity." *Eranos Jahrbuch* (Zurich), Vol. XXXVII (1970).

Hornbostel, M. von. "Die Massnormen als kulturgeschichtliches Forschungsmittel." In *Festschrift für Pater W. Schmidt.* Edited by W. Koppers. Vienna, 1928.

Hund, F. "Denkschemata und Modelle in der Physik." *Studium generale* (Göttingen), Vol. XVIII, no. 3 (1965).

Hurwitz, S. "The God Image in the Cabbalah." *Spring* (New York), (1954).

Jammer, H. "Die Entwicklung des Modellbegriffs in den physikalischen Wissenschaften." *Studium generale* (Göttingen), Vol. XVIII, no. 3 (1965).

Jensen, J. H. D. "Zur Interpretation der ausgezeichneten Nukleonenzahlen im Bau der Atomkerne." *Die Naturwissenschaften* (Berlin and Göttingen), Vol. XXXV, no. 12 (1948), and Vol. XXXVI, no. 5 (1949).

Josten, C. "Robert Fludd's Theory of Geomancy and His Experiences at Avignon in the Winter 1601 to 1602." *Journal of the Warburg and Courtauld Institute* (Oxford), Vol. XXVII (1964).

Jung, C. G. "Ein astrologisches Experiment." *Zeitschrift für Parapsychologie und Grenzgebiete der Psychologie* (Bern and Munich), Vol. I, no. 213 (1957–58).

———. "Ein Brief zur Frage der Synchronizität." *Zeitschrift für Parapsychologie und Grenzgebiete der Psychologie* (Bern and Munich), Vol. V, no. 1 (1961).

———. "Nachruf auf Richard Wilhelm." In *Chinesischerdeutscher Almanach.* Frankfurt a. M., 1931.

Karger, F. "Paraphysik und Physik." *Zeitschrift für Parapsychologie und Grenzgebiete der Psychologie* (Bern and Munich), Vol. VIII, no. 3 (1965).

König, Marie E. P. "Die Symbolik des urgeschichtlichen Menschen." *Symbolon: Jahrbuch für Symbolforschung* (Basel and Stuttgart), Vol. V (1966).

Kling, L. C. "Archetypische Symbolik und Synchronizitäten im aktuellen Weltgeschehen." *Verborgene Welt,* no. 4 (1965–66).

Kreittner, John. "Man's Mathematical Mind." *Main Currents in Modern Thought*, Vol. XIV, no. 5 (May, 1958).

Lee, T. D. "Space Inversion, Time Reversal, Particle-Antiparticle Conjugation." *Physics Today*. Vol. XIX, no. 3 (March, 1966).

Leibniz, G. W. "Abhandlung über die chinesische Philosophie." *Antaios* (Stuttgart), Vol. VIII (1967).

Magnus, A. "Mathematik und ihre Anwendung in der Chemie." *Studium generale* (Göttingen), Vol. VI, no. 11 (1953).

Martin, Gottfried. "Methodische Probleme der Metaphysik der Zahl." *Studium generale* (Göttingen), Vol. VI, no. 10 (1953).

Meier, C. A. "Moderne Physik, Moderne Psychologie." In *Die kulturelle Bedeutung der komplexen Psychologie*. Edited by Psychologischer Club, Zurich. Berlin, 1935.

Müller, Gert. "Der Modellbegriff in der Mathematik." *Studium generale* (Göttingen), Vol. XVIII, no. 3 (1965).

Murphy, Gardener. "Pythagorean Number Theory and Its Implications for Psychology." *American Psychologist*, Vol. XX (June, 1967).

Neumann, E. "Die Psyche und die Wandlung der Wirklichkeitsebenen." *Eranos Jahrbuch* (Zurich), Vol. XXI (1952).

Niggli, P. "Symmetrieprinzip und Naturwissenschaften." *Studium generale* (Göttingen), Vol. II, nos. 4–5 (1949).

Nowacki, Werner. "Die Idee einer Struktur der Wirklichkeit." *Mitteilungen der Schweizerischen Naturforschenden Gesellschaft in Bern*. New series, Vol. XIV (1957).

O'Bryan, A. "The Story of Naqoilpi the Great Gambler." In *The Dîné-Origin Myths of the Navahos*. Smithsonian Institution, Bureau of American Ethnology, Bulletin no. 163, Washington, D.C., 1956.

Pauli, Wolfgang. "Naturwissenschaftliche und erkenntnistheoretische Aspekte der Ideen vom Unbewussten." In *Aufsätze und Vorträge über Physik und Erkenntnistheorie*. Edited by W. Westphal. Brunswick, 1961.

Pauli, Wolfgang. "Sommerfelds Beiträge zur Quantentheorie." *Die Naturwissenschaften* (Berlin and Göttingen), Vol. XXXV, no. 5 (1948).

―――. "Die Wissenschaft und das abendländische Denken." In *Internationaler Gelehrtenkongress: Europa—Erbe und Aufgabe, Mainz, 1955*. Wiesbaden, 1956.

Pauling, Linus. "Structural Significance of the Principal Quantum Number of Nucleonic Orbital Wave-Functions." *Physical Review Letters*, Vol. XV, no. 11 (September 13, 1965).

Piaget, Jean. "Psychologie et épistemologie de la notion du temps." In *Verhandlungen der schweizerischen naturforschenden Gesellschaft* (Bern and Geneva), Vol. CXLV (1965).

Pieper, M. "Das Brettspiel der alten Ägypter." *Wissenschaftliche Beilage zum Jahresbericht des Königsstädtischen Realgymnasiums zu Berlin* (1909).

Porkert, Manfred. "Wissenschaftliches Denken im alten China." *Antaios* (Stuttgart), Vol. II, no. 6 (1961).

Portmann, A. "Die Zeit im Leben der Organismen." *Eranos Jahrbuch* (Zurich), Vol. XX (1952).

Ranke, H. "Das altägyptische Schlangenspiel." *Sitzungsberichte der Heidelberger Akademie der Wissenschaften, Philosophisch-historische Klasse*, no. 4 (1920).

Rhally, M. "Varieties of Paranormal cognition." In *Spectrum Psychologiae: Festschrift für C. A. Meier*. Edited by C. T. Frey Wehrlin. Zurich, 1965.

Riemschneider, Margarete. "Glasberg und Mühlebrett." *Symbolon: Jahrbuch für Symbolforschung* (Basel and Stuttgart), Vol. VI (1968).

Rivier, D. "La Physique et le temps." *Verhandlungen der schweizerischen naturforschenden Gesellschaft* (Bern and Geneva), Vol. CXLV (1965).

Roeck, F. "Kalenderkreise und Kalenderschichten im alten Mexico und Mittelamerika," and "Über eine mögliche Beziehung der Maya-Kulturen mit China." In *Festschrift für Pater W. Schmidt*. Edited by W. Koppers. Vienna, 1928.

Sawyer, W. W. "Algebra." *Scientific American,* Vol. CCXI, no. 3 (September, 1964).

Schuyler, C. "Islamic and Indian Magic Squares." *Part I: History of Religions, International Journal for Comparative Historical Studies,* Vol. VIII, no. 3 (February, 1969).

Seidenberg, A. "The Ritual Origin of Counting." *Archive for History of Exact Sciences* (Berlin and Göttingen), Vol. II (1962–66).

Sergejew, J. "Psychologische Hintergründe grosser Entdeckungen." *Bild der Wissenschaft* (Stuttgart), no. 6 (1970).

Stegmüller, W. "Bemerkungen zum Wahrscheinlichkeitsproblem." *Studium generale* (Göttingen), Vol. VI, no. 10 (1953).

Urban, P. "Philosophische und empirische Aspekte der Synchronizitätstheorie." *Grenzgebiete der Wissenschaft* (Abensberg), Vol. XVII, no. 4 (1968).

Vonessen, F. "Reim und Zahl bei Leibniz." *Antaios* (Stuttgart), Vol. VIII (1967).

Weyl, H. "Über den Symbolismus in der Mathematik und mathematischen Physik." *Studium generale* (Göttingen), Vol. VI, no. 4 (1953).

Wilhelm, H. "Der Zeitbegriff im Buch der Wandlungen." *Eranos Jahrbuch* (Zurich), Vol. XX (1951).

Wolf, Karl Lothar. "Symmetrie und Polarität." *Studium generale* (Göttingen), Vol. II, nos. 4–5 (1949).

Yates, F. "Ramon Lull and John Scotus Erigena." *Journal of the Warburg and the Courtauld Institute* (Oxford), Vol. XXIII (1960).

INDEX

Absolute knowledge, 200, 201, 203 n., 206, 209, 210, 268
Acausality, 11, 37. *See also* Orderedness
Aegidius de Vadis, 142
Agni, 225
Agrippa von Nettesheim, 142
Aion, 256, 257, 258
Aitken, A. C., 26 n., 27
Aker, 92 ff., 274
Alchemy, alchemist(s), 179, 181, 185, 197, 260, 269, 270, 271, 289
Allah, 240
Allendy, R., 63 n., 104 n.
Amino acids, 105
Anrich, E., 16 n, 37 n., 46 n., 47 n. 48, 50 n., 72 n., 94 n., 116 n., 134
Archetype(s), archetypal, 4, 7, 11, 13, 14, 17, 20, 31, 32, 36 n., 37, 45, 50, 51, 53, 56, 65, 73–74, 77 n., 96 n., 126, 134, 142, 144, 153, 155, 187, 216, 217, 218, 223, 225, 227, 243, 246, 251, 254, 260, 293; contamination of, 65, 80; dynamic, 155, 288; luminosity of, 199; of number, 100, 206 (*see also* Number); of order, 45, 142, 203; realm of, 80, 142; of Self, 268; trans-gressive aspect of, 53; of wholeness, 124; as world-forming principle, 203
Archetypus mundus, 172
Archytas of Tarentum, 248 n.
Aristotle, 38, 84 n., 248
Arithmetic: binary, 90, 96 n., 99; Chinese, 24, 227–28; Western, 40, 76, 82, 143 n.
Ars magna (of Lüll), 204
Astrology, 179, 182
Atom(ic), 46, 50, 51, 90

Babylonians, 27
Backward. *See* Retrograde
Bavink, B., 90 n.
Baynes, C. A., 90 n.
Beadle, M., 106 n.
Beauregard, O. C. de, 17, 192, 193, 207, 208, 209, 221, 223 n.
Beisswanger, P., 29 n.
Beit, H. von, 104 n.
Bell, R. C., 296 n., 298 n.
Bernoulli theorem, 100
Berthelot, M., 179, 182 n., 196 n., 197 n., 271 n., 289 n.
Beyond, the, 92, 93, 162, 274, 280, 293
Bhagavad-Gita, 225, 255

321